HALKA CHRONIC

PAGES OF STONE

GEOLOGY OF WESTERN NATIONAL PARKS AND MONUMENTS

ROCKY MOUNTAINS AND WESTERN GREAT PLAINS

The Mountaineers • Seattle

THE MOUNTAINEERS: Organized 1906
"... to explore, study, and enjoy
the natural beauty of the outdoors."

Published by The Mountaineers
306 2nd Avenue West, Seattle, Washington 98119

Published simultaneously in Canada by Douglas & McIntyre, Ltd.
1615 Venables Street, Vancouver, British Columbia V5L 2H1

Cover design by Emily Silver

Cover photos by David Lucas and Halka Chronic.
Large photo: Longs Peak, Rocky Mountain National Park.
Top inset: Toadstool Rock, Badlands National Park.
Bottom inset: Grotto Geyser, Yellowstone National Park.

Other photos by author unless otherwise credited.
Manufactured in the United States of America.

Library of Congress Cataloging in Publication Data

Chronic, Halka.
Pages of stone.

Bibliography: v. 1, p.
Includes index.
Contents: v. 1. Rocky Mountains and Western Great Plains.
1. Geology—United States. 2. National parks and reserves—United States. 3. Natural monuments—United States. I. Title.
QE77.C57 557.3 82-422
ISBN 0-89886-095-4 (v. 1)

First Edition
1 2 3 4 5 6 7 8 9

To all who treasure the jewels
that crown our nation

Acknowledgments

Many people helped me with this book. A lot of them—too many to name individually—are members of the National Park Service (a wonderful breed!). There are others, colleagues and friends and relatives, who read over parts of my manuscript and offered suggestions, or who lent me their photographs or gave me permission to adapt their maps and diagrams. I thank them all most heartily. My daughters Emily Silver and Betsy Chronic did much of the art work. Unless otherwise indicated, the photographs are my own.

Contents

Dream Lake in Rocky Mountain National Park lies in a glacier-carved basin below the sharp prow of Hallett Peak. In the upper part of the glacial trough, piles of rocky rubble mark avalanche chutes and collapsed lateral moraines.

Introduction

Geology is a detective story. In it, detectives question today's world for clues to the mysteries of the past. They find their clues in weathering and erosion, from desert to jungle, from mountaintop to storm-swept sea. They find them in the way rock material is deposited by water and ice and wind, and in modern volcanoes that erupt dark clouds of ash and fiery flows of molten rock, as did their antecedents at the dawn of Planet Earth. They find them along earthquake zones, where age-old forces strain rock against rock. They find them in many kinds of laboratory experiments, such as those dealing with high temperatures and pressures that simulate the white-hot depths beneath the earth's crust. The detectives are geologists.

To couple their clues with events of the past, geologists hike the hills, rock hammer in hand, mapping and measuring changes in rock types. They collect specimens, photograph landforms, and ultimately restudy their data and photos and collections in the laboratory. They look carefully, of course, at the broad pictures, but they also examine small features within the rocks: diagnostic minerals, tiny fracture patterns, distinctive fossils. With modern tools like electron microscopes and X-ray cameras, and with modern procedures that include delicate chemical analyses, they discover features not available to geologists a century ago. By measuring the decay of radioactive minerals and the products of that decay, for instance, geologists can judge with a fair degree of accuracy the age of many of their rock specimens.

As they put their clues together and examine them in the light of clues collected by their predecessors and their field companions, geologists come up with geologic maps that show the kinds of rocks exposed at the surface, whether they are flat-lying or tilted, and the position of breaks or faults that disrupt expected patterns. Because the record of ancient animal life is also a rock record, some of their work and many of their clues converge with the work of other detectives—biologists. Together the two groups of scientists learn of the origins of modern animal and plant species and record the way that living things have coped with an ever-changing world. Fossils preserved in rock furnish undeniable proof of the theory of evolution: that the animal and plant species we take for granted today evolved from simpler and more primitive ancestors by a process of natural selection or "survival of the fittest."

And so geology is also history, or prehistory, a course without lectures, with The Earth for its textbook. In this textbook are mountains formed by the breaking and folding of hard rock or by the eruption of molten rock, valleys that sank as long slivers of the earth's crust, canyons carved by ice and running water. In its pages are the three main classes of rocks: sedimentary rocks, deposited as mud and sand on long-ago sea floors; igneous rocks, formed from hot, liquid magma that burst through to the surface or cooled slowly far underground; and metamorphic rocks, altered by the pressure and heat of deep burial and stresses caused by moving continents.

And in the book—a living part of it—are the parks and monuments that are our national heritage. There, of course, are the very best pages, the shining examples, the "gee whiz" geology of our gee whiz nation. There, the book is filled with superlatives, for how else can one describe these areas—their scenic beauty, their varied fauna and flora, their historic and prehistoric values, their often remarkable geology? Taken together, they illustrate gloriously almost every one of the principles of the geologic book, almost every one of the principles on which the geologic detective story is based. In seeing the national park areas, you will I hope come to understand not only these splendid pages of the textbook Earth, but the usually more prosaic pages between.

Think of geology as a logical science—no magic, no abracadabra. It deals with things that can be looked at, touched, and sometimes heard, smelled or even tasted. It interprets the past history of the earth in the light of the present, and it uses knowledge of the present to re-create the past. Today's streams and rivers wash rocks and sand and silt from today's mountains and deposit them on floodplains and deltas far from their source. So rivers of the past wore down mountains, slowly (*very* slowly by human standards) destroying them, depositing their debris in ancient floodplains and deltas. As sand, clay, and limy mud today come to rest in horizontal layers on sea floor and lake floor, so they did in the past, forming strata that, depending on their composition, have hardened into sandstone, shale, and limestone. As portions of the earth's crust rise and fall today, or break along great belts of faults, bit by bit, with each movement perceptibly or imperceptibly shaking the land, so mountains were raised again and again during the immensity of time since the earth formed. Within human lifespans, volcanoes have awakened overnight to belch fiery molten lava, to create new mountains, or to reshape old ones, just as they have done repeatedly during the history of the earth.

National park areas (and throughout this book I use that term to include national monuments) are crisscrossed with inviting trails. Accept their invitations, for the best way to learn about geology is with your feet on the ground. But whether you travel by trail or highway, let the rocks be your hosts. Allow yourself time to stop and visit, to get acquainted, to ask them questions. Look at landforms—mountains, plains, valleys—and ponder their origins. National park viewpoints may help you with explanatory displays. Guide leaflets will lead you on many trails and along some highways. At visitor centers you can find displays, topographic maps, and, for some parks, geologic maps prepared by the U.S. Geological Survey. Park interpreters lead excursions, give talks, show slides, and answer questions.

Collecting specimens of any kind, plant, animal, fossil, or just plain rock, is prohibited in national parks and monuments. Park rangers understandably frown on visitors who display the traditional geologic tools: rock hammers and collecting sacks. An observant eye, a wondering mind, perhaps a pair of binoculars and some sturdy boots, are all the tools you need. Collect knowledge and understanding. Look at the present, understand the past, and you will glimpse the future.

PART 1.
OUR GEOLOGIC LEGACY

I. Drifting Continents

The crust of the earth is thinner than the shell of a ping-pong ball, relative to its size, of course. On it, disordered humps and ridges of mountains and broad depressions of ocean basins make no more impression than little furrows and ridges inherent in the plastic ball. No mountains ride as high as the suture joining the two halves of the ball. No ocean basin is as deep as the dent that finally forces its retirement.

But the shell of our planet, the crust, seems to have a life of its own. Parts of it jostle and separate and shift about, seemingly independently, or sink or rise or slide over one another or spit out molten rock or crunch together in magnificent fender-benders. Fortunately for us, these crustal movements are slow almost beyond our comprehension. We are reminded of them, though, by events like earthquakes and volcanic eruptions, and we can see in the rocks that make up the earth's shell a long trail of evidence that

On August 18, 1959, sudden movement along a fault caused the Hebgen Lake earthquake. U.S. Highway 287 was severely damaged by fault movement, earthflow, and rapid changes in lake level.

J. R. Stacy photo courtesy of NOAA

The steep front of the Teton Range is set off from the level foreground by the Teton Fault. Fault movement that lowered the valley and raised the mountains exceeded 10,000 meters (30,000 feet).

points to equally spirited behavior in the past. In places, rocks are visibly folded, bent, and long broken. We have undeniable proof that in the past whole mountain ranges were lifted and then washed away, deep basins were filled with their debris and later turned into new mountains.

Deciphering the evidence in the rocks, on both local and continental scale, has told us a lot about the history of the earth's crust. The crust is the outermost shell of the earth, the hard part that lies above a white-hot, incandescent, semimolten layer called the mantle. Under the oceans, the crust is fairly thin and consists of heavy, black, iron-rich rock full of crystals of an olive green mineral called olivine. This makes it, in geologic parlance, olivine basalt.

Continental crust is formed of all the other kinds of rock: sandstone and shale, granite and limestone, and a whole host of others, some of which you'll learn to recognize in the national parks. There is hardly any olivine basalt. The continental crust is about ten times as thick as the oceanic crust, one reason why continents project higher than ocean basins.

For many decades geologists, although they could look at rocks and explain them on local scales, couldn't explain away the problems they found in the earth's crust as a whole. Some suspected, because of similarities in their coastlines, that South America, Africa, and the other continents had once been joined together. Some observed continuity of certain rock types between America and Europe. Some said the Red Sea was the site of crustal splitting. But no one could explain how the rocky crust, much more brittle and fragile than the shell of our ping-pong ball, could possibly divide and drift around on the semisolid mantle that underlies it.

Then came revolution — a 20th-Century revolution in geology as exciting and thought-provoking as the biological revolution of the 19th Century brought about by Charles Darwin and the concept of evolution. Suddenly (and this is the exhilarating thing about scientific revolution) foggy concepts and muddy ideas began to clarify. Because of some new thoughts propounded by just a few geologists, pieces of the puzzle — the spherical puzzle of the earth's crust — began to slip into place.

What was all the excitement about? What were the tenets of this new revolution? A new theory called the Theory of Plate Tectonics stated that continents do indeed drift, but *with* the underlying mantle

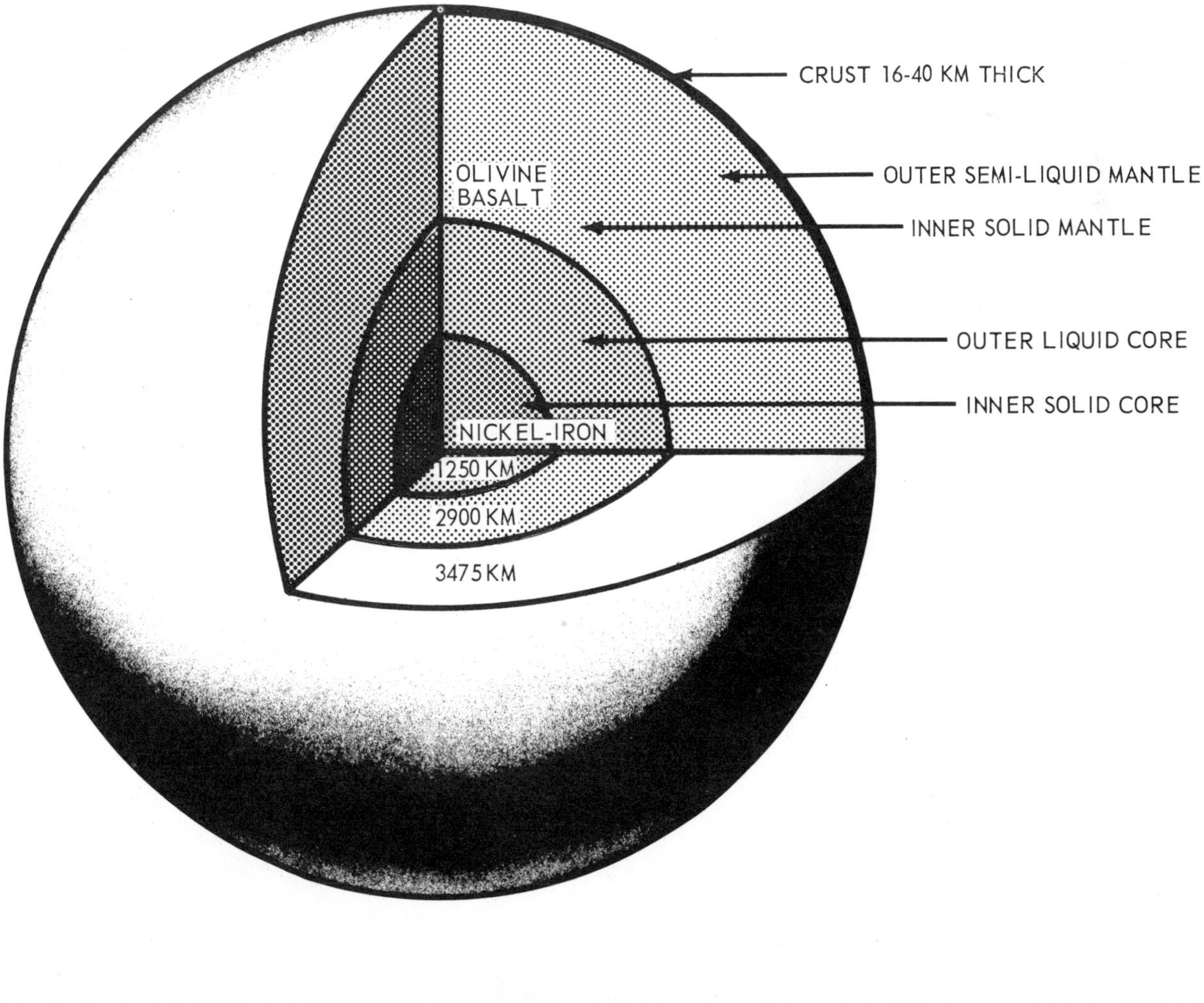

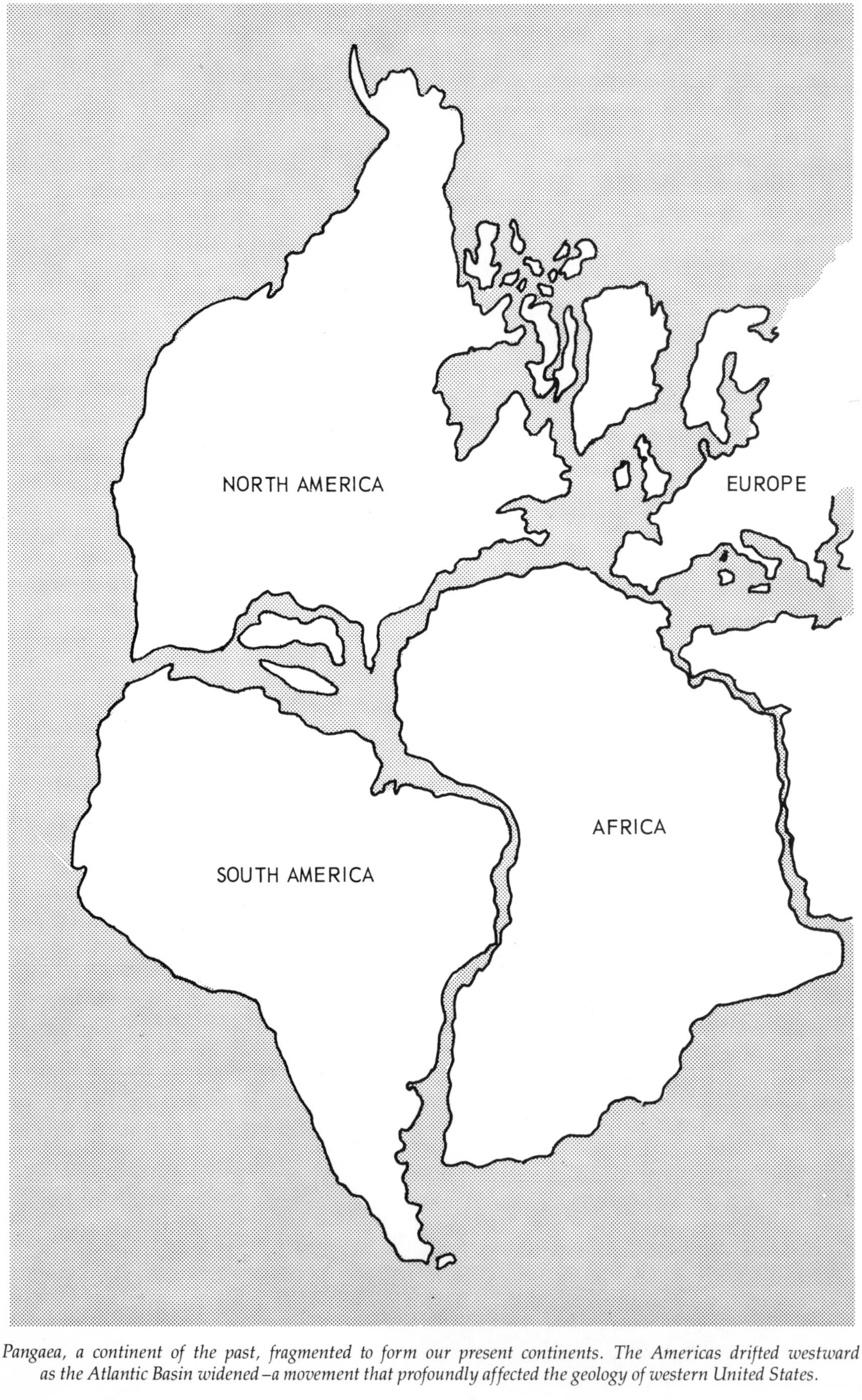

Pangaea, a continent of the past, fragmented to form our present continents. The Americas drifted westward as the Atlantic Basin widened—a movement that profoundly affected the geology of western United States.

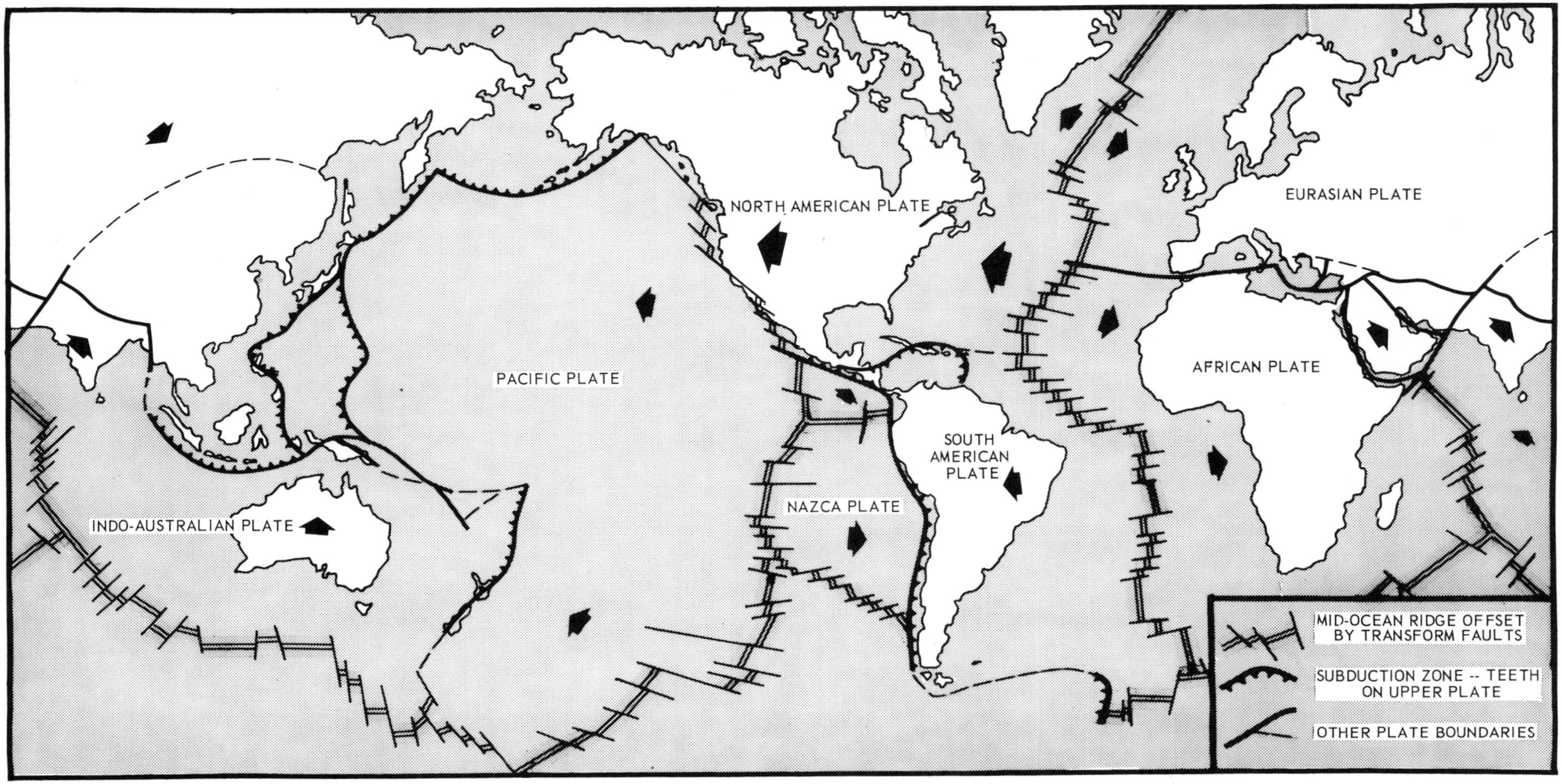

The earth's crust is divided into a mosaic of large and small plates bounded by mid-ocean ridges and zones where collision is taking place. Plate margins are sites of frequent earthquakes and volcanic activity. Magnetic soundings show that mid-ocean ridges are offset by numerous transform faults.

The design of the earth's crust is reflected in our national parks. In this diagram, the ocean is narrowed to a fraction of its real relative size.

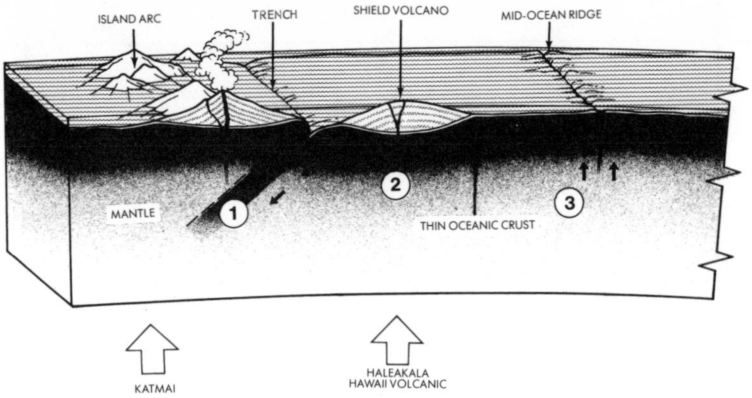

(1) *Carried along by convection currents in the mantle, oceanic crust is drawn under and melted in subduction zones, forming basalt magma which erupts along island arcs.*

(2) *Shield volcanoes form as plumes of basalt magma rise above isolated "hot spots" below the ocean floor.*

(3) *At mid-ocean ridges, basalt magma rises to form new oceanic crust.*

instead of across it. Floating like pats of butter on porridge, they are rafted passively by ponderous, slow-moving convection currents in the mantle, currents powered by the white-hot stove of the earth's interior. With a rolling motion like that of boiling water, huge hot plumes of the mantle rise, arch upward, and plunge again into the depths.

The new theory explains so much! It tells us why oceanic crust is made of basalt and why continental crust is not, why mountain ranges and plateaus exist, why some ranges are coastal and some are not, why we have earthquakes and why they are more frequent in some regions than in others, why there are deep ocean trenches, why there is a volcanic "ring of fire" around the Pacific, why during geologic time seas have flooded across continents, why ocean-laid sediments and shells of ancient sea animals can be found now on top of some of our highest peaks.

The theory tells us that the crust is composed of individual plates, seven large ones and about a dozen smaller ones. (Hence, plate tectonics. "Tectonic" comes from the Greek *tekton,* a carpenter or builder.) Like the plates of a turtle shell, crustal plates meet along sutures, submerged volcanic mountain chains extending for thousands of kilometers along the floors of major oceans, or deep-sea trenches like those near the Philippines or Puerto Rico or the California coast, or linear ranges of mountains like the Himalayas. New crust forms along some of the sutures—the mid-ocean ridges—as molten lava welling up from the mantle hardens into rock. The new crust, created in narrow bands, is then pushed apart by still newer lava. Continued activity makes of each sea floor two wide conveyor belts moving in opposite directions. And, as the sea floor spreads, the continents are rafted farther apart. Their rate of separation varies, averaging about 2 to 5 centimeters (1 to 2 inches) a year in the present Atlantic.

Sea-floor spreading is a vital part of the Theory of Plate Tectonics and has been proven beyond any doubt by methods I won't go into here. But as sea floors spread and continents move apart, something has to give. If new crust forms, old crust, somewhere, must be destroyed. There is only so much room on the face of the earth. Mid-ocean ridges, as we've seen, form some of the plate boundaries. What of the others? This is where the fender-benders come in. Plates collide and, in doing so, create mountains, deep ocean trenches, and lines of volcanoes. Collisions may occur between two continental plates, two oceanic plates, or an oceanic and a continental plate. (Since most plates are partly continental and partly oceanic, what is meant here is the oceanic and continental parts of plates.)

The only type of collision we need concern ourselves with in the western United States is the continental-oceanic one. The North American Plate, though oceanic in its eastern, Atlantic portion, is continental in its western half. The entire plate drifts westward because of sea-floor spreading along the Mid-Atlantic Ridge, and has been doing so for the last 100 to 150 million years. Long ago it crashed head-on into the Pacific oceanic plate. In doing so, it shoved up *over* the Pacific Plate and thereby created much of the

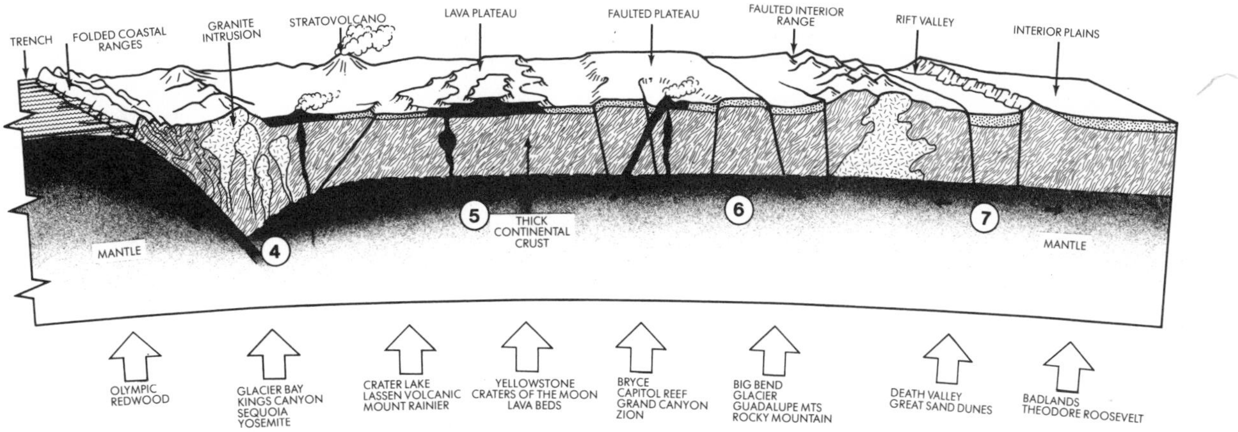

(4) *Melting of continental crust along a subduction zone creates granitic magma, which may cool slowly, below the surface, in batholiths that are later bared by erosion. Or the magma may erupt explosively to form stratovolcanoes.*

(5) *Flood basalts, exceptionally fluid in nature, rise above "hot spots" below continental crust.*

(6) *Interior ranges push upward in response to compression along the distant continental margin.*

(7) *Rift valleys are tensional features where the crust drops as neighboring areas are pulled apart.*

scenery in the western part of the continent.

The Pacific Plate of course resisted, for its mid-ocean ridge was creating new crust, too, and shoved back against the incursion of the North American Plate strongly enough to buckle the continental crust as far east as the Rockies. The continent broke and bent and broke again, even shoved eastward over itself in places. But by and large the margin of the heavy Pacific Plate was pushed downward by the lighter continental plate, and pulled downward by gravity and the rolling convection currents of the earth's interior. Eventually it remelted deep down within the mantle. The melting caused some more scenery, because where oceanic crust was melted (along with some slices of continental crust that also were drawn downward), plumes of molten rock bubbled upward again through the edge of the continent to create a volcanic landscape of lava plateaus and mountains.

Both the San Andreas fault and Mount St. Helens tell us these processes are still going on.

II. Rocks, Time, and Fossils

Rocks are what scenery is all about. Without exception, even when they are not the main attraction, rocks are important parts of the scenery of our western national parks and monuments. Streams, lakes, forests, and summer wildflowers are closely tied in with rocks and with soil formed from them.

Geologists recognize three main classes of rocks:

• Igneous rocks originate from molten rock material, or magma, that rises from as much as 300 kilometers (200 miles) below the surface. Igneous rocks are further divided into two main groups: intrusive igneous rocks that cool and harden *below* the surface, and extrusive igneous rocks that cool and harden *at* the surface. Though the two types may be chemically similar, they look different because slow cooling below the surface gives large crystals time to grow. Most extrusive igneous rocks (also called by a more familiar name, volcanic rocks) are so fine textured as the result of rapid cooling that you can't even see individual crystals without a lens. Extrusive igneous rocks, as we've seen, can erupt under water as well as on land.

• Sedimentary rocks form from broken or dissolved pieces of other rocks. They are layered, or stratified, and so collectively are called strata. Layered volcanic rocks—lava flows and widespread sheets of volcanic ash—are often stratified too, especially when they are interlayered with sedimentary rocks.

• Metamorphic rocks come into existence when pre-existing rocks are altered by pressure and/or heat. Their grains may fuse together, as is the case with metasedimentary rocks, which still look like the sandstones and mudstones of which they were made, or they may be altered so much that the original materials have recrystallized into new minerals, so that it's next to impossible to deduce their original nature. Much-altered metamorphic rocks commonly

COMMON IGNEOUS ROCKS

INTRUSIVE (Coarse-grained)	QUARTZ CONTENT	COMPOSITION	DESCRIPTION	EXTRUSIVE (Fine-grained or glassy)
GRANITE	HIGH	ACIDIC	light-colored, with abundant quartz and feldspar, peppered with black mica (biotite) and/or hornblende	RHYOLITE (usually volcanic ash or tuff)
GRANODIORITE	FAIRLY HIGH	↑ INCREASINGLY ACID	light gray rock with a moderate amount of quartz, peppered with black mica and hornblende	RHYODACITE
QUARTZ DIORITE	MEDIUM		intermediate between grano-diorite and diorite	DACITE (viscous lava that forms volcanic domes)
DIORITE	MEDIUM		medium gray rock	ANDESITE (moderately viscous lava, ash)
GABBRO	LOW	BASIC	dark gray to black rock	BASALT (fluid, sometimes bubbly lava, pumice)

COMMON SEDIMENTARY ROCKS

ROCK	DESCRIPTION
MUDSTONE	grains of silt and clay cemented together
SILTSTONE	grains of silt cemented together
SHALE	siltstone or mudstone that splits into flat sheets parallel to bedding
SANDSTONE	grains of sand (usually quartz) cemented together
GRAYWACKE	grains of pre-existing fine-grained rock cemented together
CONGLOMERATE	pebbles, cobbles and sand deposited as gravel and then cemented together
LIMESTONE	Calcium carbonate (calcite) rock deposited as limy mud or fragments of shells

COMMON METAMORPHIC ROCKS

ROCK	DESCRIPTION	DEGREE OF ALTERATION
SLATE	altered mudstone or siltstone that fractures along planes that are not parallel to the original layers	SLIGHT
QUARTZITE	sandstone or siltstone so tightly cemented that it breaks through individual grains	SLIGHT
MARBLE	recrystallized limestone or dolomite	SLIGHT
GNEISS	banded or streaky crystalline rock formed by re-crystallization of older granite, sandstone or sandstone-shale layers	SEVERE
SCHIST	Medium-grained rock formed by alteration of mud-stone and siltstone, with aligned mica grains that cause it to split along parallel lines	SEVERE

grade into intrusive igneous rock, making it difficult to draw the line between them. Since intrusive igneous rocks and highly altered metamorphic rocks both show visible mineral crystals, it is sometimes handy to get around this problem by speaking of them collectively as crystalline rocks.

By identifying one or two common minerals in each kind of rock, geologists further refine the rock categories (for instance, when they speak of quartz dacite or biotite schist).

Rocks are made of minerals, natural substances that are known to have quite definite chemical makeups. They very often also have recognizable colors, typical hardnesses, and characteristic ways of crystallizing. There are literally hundreds of different minerals, some much more common than others. A few you probably know quite well already: quartz (a form of silica), mica, native gold, gemstone minerals like ruby and diamond and garnet, and a mineral called water in its liquid phase and ice or snow in its solid, or crystallized phase. Identifying most other minerals takes a hand lens or microscope and quite a bit of knowledge. Minerals are not stressed in this book; if you like them you may already own one of the guidebooks used by rockhounds.

That brings us to time. Geologists are fascinated with time and regard it in quite a different manner than other people. For them, time goes back 4.6 billion years, to the creation of the earth; or 3.8 billion years, when the oldest rocks now known (metamorphic rocks of central and eastern Canada) were formed. The oldest rocks in northwestern United States, now exposed in the Rocky Mountains, came into being 2.3 billon years ago.

Normal hours and days, weeks and years don't mean much in such immensities of time; anyway, geologists only very recently learned how to measure geologic time with a fair degree of accuracy by measuring the alteration of radioactive minerals in rocks, or by relating natural rock magnetism to the known history of reversals in the earth's magnetic field, when the North Pole and South Pole switched their positive and negative magnetic charges. Before these methods were discovered, geologists invented their own calendar, with special names for the months, weeks, and days of geologic time, names that are still used because to geologists they are as familiar as their own rock hammers.

The largest units, the geologic months, are called eras. Eras are divided into periods, just as months are divided into weeks; periods are split up into epochs, which we can liken to days. Because Nature is less precise than Man, and because great chunks of the record of the past are missing completely, eras and periods and epochs are not as regular in length as months and weeks. The longest era lasted about 4 billion years, the shortest only 65 million.

ERA	PERIOD	EPOCH	AGE IN YEARS
CENOZOIC Age of Mammals	QUATERNARY Q	HOLOCENE Q	10,000
		PLEISTOCENE Q	3 million
	TERTIARY T	PLIOCENE Tp	12 million
		MIOCENE Tm	26 million
		OLIGOCENE To	38 million
		EOCENE Te	54 million
		PALEOCENE Tp	65 million
MESOZOIC Age of Reptiles	CRETACEOUS	K	136 million
	JURASSIC	J	195 million
	TRIASSIC	TR	225 million
PALEOZOIC Age of Fishes	PERMIAN	Pm	280 million
	PENNSYLVANIAN	P	320 million
	MISSISSIPPIAN	M	345 million
	DEVONIAN	D	415 million
	SILURIAN	S	445 million
	ORDOVICIAN	O	515 million
	CAMBRIAN	Є	600 million
PRECAMBRIAN P-Є	ORIGIN OF LIFE		1-2 billion
	ORIGIN OF EARTH		4.6 billion

Names for the time units are shown on the chart on the opposite page, along with abbreviations commonly used on maps and diagrams. Approximate ages in years are given as well. Names of eras make sense in Greek: *paleo* means "old," and *zoic* refers to "life" (as in zoological zoos). Mesozoic means "middle life." Cenozoic means "new" or "recent life."

Paleozoic periods are given names that relate to places where rocks of those particular periods were first studied. Cambria was a Roman name for Wales, where the Ordovices fought with the Silures. Devon is just south of Wales. (You can see how geology got its start. These are the coal-mining, iron-mining, and tin-mining parts of Britain, where it paid to be interested in rocks.) The next two periods are American: Mississippian and Pennsylvanian. Europeans call the same time interval Carboniferous because rocks of that age contain lots of coal, both in Europe and in eastern United States. Permian comes from Perm, a province in the Ural Mountains of Russia.

Names for Mesozoic periods are less systematic. Triassic is so-called because in Germany, rocks of this age are made up of three distinct layers. Jurassic rocks occur in the Jura Mountains of Switzerland. Cretaceous means "chalky," which is where the white cliffs of Dover come in—solid chalk.

The two Cenozoic periods hark back to some old and disproven ideas that divided rocks into four groups by how hard they were. The groups called "Primary" and "Secondary" fell by the wayside, but Tertiary (for not very well consolidated rocks) and Quaternary (for distinctly unconsolidated rocks) stayed in the geologic vocabulary. With sedimentary rocks, it's true that the youngest layers are usually unconsolidated sand, clay, and gravel, whereas the older ones become compressed and cemented together with age. However, because many igneous and metamorphic rocks are well consolidated to begin with, hardness is not necessarily indicative of age. Tertiary and Quaternary rocks are near the surface and haven't had much opportunity to get squeezed, heated, or eroded away, so we know more about them than about older layers. Because of this, the Cenozoic epoch names are useful. Notice that they all end in "–cene."

Regardless of their age or origin, rocks as they occur in the landscape divide into recognizable natural units which geologists call formations. These units are distinguished by their composition, thickness, color, internal structure, mineral or fossil content, and appearance in outcrop. They are named after a locality at which they occur, usually a type locality which then becomes the standard for comparing other parts of the same formation. Let's look at a few examples from some of the parks in the Rocky Mountain region.

• The Brule Formation in Badlands National Park began its career as mud, sand, and volcanic ash, components that gradually hardened into mudstone and sandstone rich with clay minerals known to form

The Brule Formation, rich in volcanic ash, forms the White River Badlands of South Dakota and Nebraska.

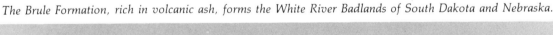

from decomposing volcanic ash. The formation is about 150 meters (460 feet) thick, and it characteristically weathers into the type of badland topography shown here. It is named for a small town on the South Platte River in Nebraska.

• In Glacier National Park the Grinnell Formation, named for Mount Grinnell, marks the slopes with horizontal layers of red and green quartzite and shale of Precambrian age. Billion-year-old ripple marks and mudcracks show up on some of the rocks, suggesting that they originated along the shore of an ancient sea, perhaps on a river delta. Surprisingly similar rock occurs as far south as Colorado.

• Longs Peak in Rocky Mountain National Park is made of Silver Plume Granite, a rock unit whose name comes from the town of Silver Plume, Colorado. The Precambrian granite, 1.5 billion years old, is so strong that where it has been carved by glacial erosion it stands in near-vertical cliffs.

• Cliffs of pink Weber Sandstone rise from the water's edge along the Yampa River in Dinosaur National Park. Wide-sweeping laminations show that it was originally a sea of sand dunes. Its name comes from Weber Canyon in Utah.

• The Green River Formation, largely a silty, buff-colored limestone that splits smoothly like shale, was

Precambrian sandstone and mudstone are metamorphosed to layered quartzite in Glacier National park.

Poorly cemented siltstones containing an abundance of volcanic ash form the Sentinel Butte Formation in Theodore Roosevelt National Park.

deposited in an ancient lake. Fossil fish are particularly common in this formation and are quarried commercially outside Fossil Butte National Monument.

• Rocks referred to as the Absaroka Volcanic Series occur in Yellowstone National Park. Formed by explosive eruptions, they consist of lava flows and volcanic tuff interlayered with fragments of lava cemented together with more tuff, as well as what appear to be ancient mud flows.

• The Spearfish Formation underlies Devils Tower and erodes to form the red "Racetrack" around the

The granite of Longs Peak, in Rocky Mountain National Park, is part of an igneous intrusion that cooled deep below the surface.

Weber Sandstone, product of an ancient desert, stands in cliffs above the Green River in Dinosaur National Monument.

Black Hills of South Dakota. It is a product of Triassic mud and sand deposited on Triassic stream and river floodplains.

• The Madison Limestone, gray, massive, cliff-forming, occurs in the Grand Teton Range, in northern Yellowstone, and as far east as its namesake, Madison, Wisconsin. Counterparts to the south are the Pahasapa Limestone of Wind Cave National Park, the Deseret Limestone of Timpanogos Cave, and the Redwall Limestone in Grand Canyon. The fine, even-grained rock is formed of the shells of countless minute, one-celled sea animals.

In Rocky Mountain National Park, schist and gneiss created from older sedimentary and volcanic layers have been intruded by granite sills.

The Green River Formation of Colorado, Utah, and Wyoming contains fossil fish that died in an ancient lake.

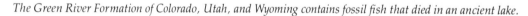

University of Wyoming photo

Sometimes geologists studying already established formations in greater detail find it logical and convenient to divide the former units, creating several new formations. In this case, the older unit is then termed a group. In this volume, group names are used frequently because the formations as first recognized are often easier to distinguish visually than are the new subdivisions.

Formations, which are *rock* units, may transgress *time* units such as periods and epochs. A formation made of beach sand, for instance, advances in time as well as place as the sea encroaches farther and farther across a sinking shore. Formations also may grade in composition from place to place, being, for example, pure marine limestone in one area but interlayered with silty shore deposits in another. Similarly, they may change in composition from bottom to top as their environment changes with time, as with a decrease in sand provided by rivers or an increase in stream pebbles and cobbles reflecting uplift of nearby mountains.

The curtain rose on the drama of life about 1.5 billion years ago, with a cast of players limited for a long, long time to minuscule noncellular and one-celled organisms that only gradually began to cluster together into multicellular plants and animals. About 600 million years ago, some of these organisms, both the one-celled and the multicellular ones, began to make themselves protective shells. Through eons of time, the shells of the organisms became part of the mud and ooze on the sea bottom. Found much later, they came to be called fossils (from the Latin *fodere*, to dig) as the early paleontologists who found them thought they had dug their way into the rock.

There are few fossils in Precambrian rocks, partly because those rocks have had such long histories of folding and breaking and metamorphism, and partly because living things had not yet begun to develop shells. But we are sure there *were* living organisms then, at least in the last part of Precambrian time, because we find seaweed-like incrustations and other strange markings in some Precambrian rocks. Some of the best relics of Precambrian life are in Glacier National Park, where strangely patterned metasedimentary rocks about a billion years old border a good many roads and trails. We also know these early organisms were quite diversified because suddenly in Paleozoic rocks, where fossils first become plentiful, almost all the major plant and animal groups that we know today appear. During the Paleozoic Era, sometimes called the "Age of Fishes," there were shellfish of many kinds, including relatives of clams and snails, crabs and lobsters, worms and corals, and even jellyfish that left circular impressions on muddy, wave-washed shores. After the middle of the era, there were increasing numbers of ungainly but rapidly modernizing fishes. These fishes were the first animals to have jointed vertebral columns, which turned out to be quite the best improvement yet, allowing excellent anchorage for muscles involved in swimming. There were plants too, and after the middle of the era some of the plants and then some of the animals left the sea and took up life partly or wholly on land. So fossils also come about in nonmarine deposits as plants and animals are buried by river muds or volcanic ash, or as animals leave their footprints in the sands of time.

The Mesozoic Era saw rapid evolution of land-living animals, particularly the newly evolved reptiles, so it is called the "Age of Reptiles." Turtles, crocodiles, swimming reptiles called ichthyosaurs, flying reptiles known as pterosaurs, and the giants of the animal kingdom, dinosaurs, roamed around the world. During this era, two other groups of vertebrate animals appeared: birds and mammals.

We don't yet know how it happened, but the dinosaurs and pterosaurs and ichthyosaurs vanished quite suddenly at the end of the Mesozoic Era, along with about 50 percent of the animal and plant species that then existed—a mass extinction. In a world without the "Big Brother is watching you" dinosaurs, the mammals rapidly diversified in their turn. So the Cenozoic Era became the "Age of Mammals" as they spread over the land to fill all the vacated ecologic niches. Some returned to the sea as the forerunners of dolphins and whales. Some moved into the air as bats. And somewhere along the line, not so very long ago, a group of mammals began to stand up on their hind legs, used their forepaws to grasp and grab, and developed large, very skillful, and extraordinarily inquisitive brains.

Have you noticed that in discussing the eras and periods and epochs and the history of life, I've always started at the bottom of the chart and worked up? That's the way the rocks read. By and large the oldest rocks—the sedimentary and volcanic ones, at any rate—are at the bottom; the youngest are at the top. And that arrangement is one of the most important precepts in geology. There are exceptions, especially among tightly folded strata or intrusive igneous rocks, but among stratified rocks *not* strongly folded or broken, the rule usually holds true. Geologists learn to read from the bottom up!

Another thing you may have observed is that in terms of years, eras and periods get shorter and shorter upward. This is because we know more about relatively recent events in geologic history than we do about long-ago ones dimmed by the mists of time. As mountains are built and glaciers grind them down and rivers wash them away and seas flood what was once dry land, as volcanoes spew lava and volcanic ash, as continents drift and collide with one another, parts of the earth's rock-recorded history are inevitably and irrevocably lost. Millions of years of the earth's story will never be told. Geologists, detectives that they are, build their case on the evidence that is left.

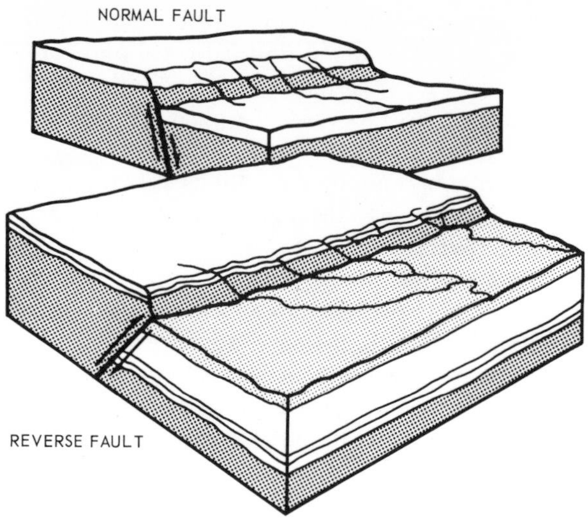

III. The Making of Mountains

Seen against the framework of plate tectonics, geologic processes classify into two groups: those that build and those that tear down. Let's look first at processes that build.

In the Rocky Mountain region, large-scale geologic structures—mountains and plateaus—can be classed by origin into three groups:

- Folded and faulted mountain ranges like the Northern and Southern Rocky Mountains.
- Fault-block ranges like the Tetons.
- Plateaus of flat-lying volcanic rocks like the Yellowstone Plateau.

As in the rest of the world, all these mountain structures can be laid, directly or indirectly, at the door of plate tectonics.

We've seen already how the North American Plate, drifting west as the Atlantic Ocean widens, pushes over the Pacific Plate, covering its eastern edge and even some of its former mid-ocean ridge. Stresses caused by westward movement and by collision between the plates bent, rent, and in places remelted the rocks of the western part of the continent, creating mountain ranges and intermontane basins and leading to the eruption of volcanoes. In some of the ranges, horizontal pressure dominated, and the crust was squeezed together and crumpled until it occupied less east-west space than it did before. Elsewhere, horizontal tension pulled the crust apart into separate blocks which tipped and tilted like so many jumbled dominoes. Over regions where oceanic crust was pulled downward as the continent slid over it, seafloor basalt and mud were scraped off the descending oceanic plate and piled on the western edge of the continental plate. Deep-melting magma made of seafloor or continental material collected in huge incandescent masses in magma chambers below the edge of the continental crust, cooling there or working its way to the surface to erupt as volcanoes.

Geologists have found it convenient to have precise terms to describe features caused by the bending and folding of rocks. An upward arch, on any scale, is an anticline; a downward bend is a syncline, as illustrated here. In eroded anticlines, the oldest rocks are near the center; in eroded synclines, the youngest are near the center—important relationships for those doing geologic mapping. Both anticlines and synclines may be tightly compressed, accordion pleated, though such tight folding is not common in the Rocky Mountains. Anticlines that are more or less equidimensional are called domes; large equidimensional synclines are basins.

Nearly all exposed rocks show signs of breakage, either in the form of cracks or joints along which there is no relative movement of the two sides, or in the form of faults along which there *is* relative movement. High-angle (near vertical) faults may be normal faults, with the upraised block not overhanging the downthrown block, or reverse faults, with the upraised block overhanging the downdropped block. In real life of course, erosion does away with the overhang. In low-angle (near horizontal) faults, usually called thrust faults, the upper block is thrust across the lower block, as the name implies. Faults of all kinds commonly occur not as single clean breaks, but as zones of disrupted rock. Because such zones

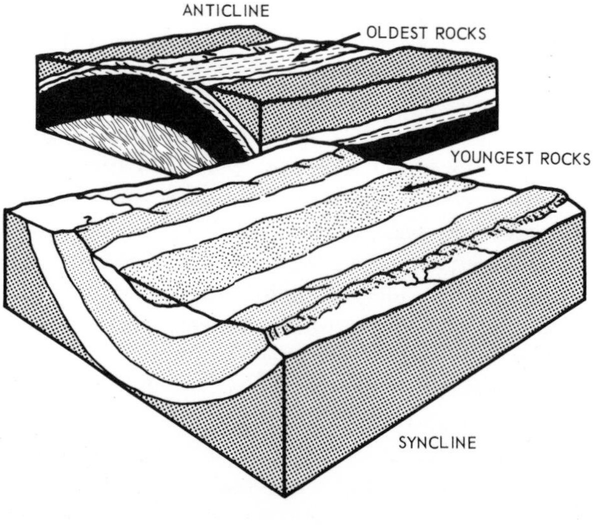

Several sets of parallel joints cleave granite exposed near Rocky Mountain National Park.

Hard layers of metasedimentary rock, exposed in Glacier National Park, are convincing evidence that rocks can bend and fold. When originally deposited, the layers were horizontal.

are lines of weakness, faults may show up as linear valleys or scarps, lines of springs, or lines of small volcanoes. Intrusions, metamorphism, and volcanism are commonly associated with them.

It seems strange that rock—"solid rock"—can bend and break. The necessary factors seem to be stress, pressure, temperature, and time, and the more of these factors the better. Stress comes, as we've seen, with the continent's westward drift and collision with the Pacific Plate. Pressure comes from deep burial under thousands of meters of overlying rock. Temperature, too, comes with depth. Time—there's all the time in the world.

Both volcanic plateaus and the cone- or dome-shaped hills and mountains commonly recognized as volcanoes develop around volcanic vents where molten rock (magma) reaches the surface through fissures or isolated, narrow, pipe-like conduits. Several types of volcanoes occur in Rocky Mountain parks:

- Plateau basalts occur where very fluid lava (magma that has reached the surface) flows quietly out over surrounding land, filling valleys and leveling topography, as it has done around Craters of the Moon National Monument and on the Yellowstone Plateau. Plateau-forming lavas are usually black basalt.
- Shield volcanoes develop when slightly less fluid lava flows from a central vent. These volcanoes range in size from small hills to the immense broad-based volcanoes of Hawaii. There are only a few shield volcanoes in the Rocky Mountain area.
- Cinder cones and spatter cones develop if the gas content of a fluid magma is very high. Bubbles rise to the top like froth on a glass of beer, splashing bubbly clots of magma around the vent. With greater force, the lava fragments shoot higher and fall to earth in a rain of cinder. Some of these small volcanoes occur at Craters of the Moon National Monument.
- Stratovolcanoes develop when moderately thick or viscous lava erupts repeatedly in violent bursts

Three kinds of volcanoes are present in the parks of the Rocky Mountain region.

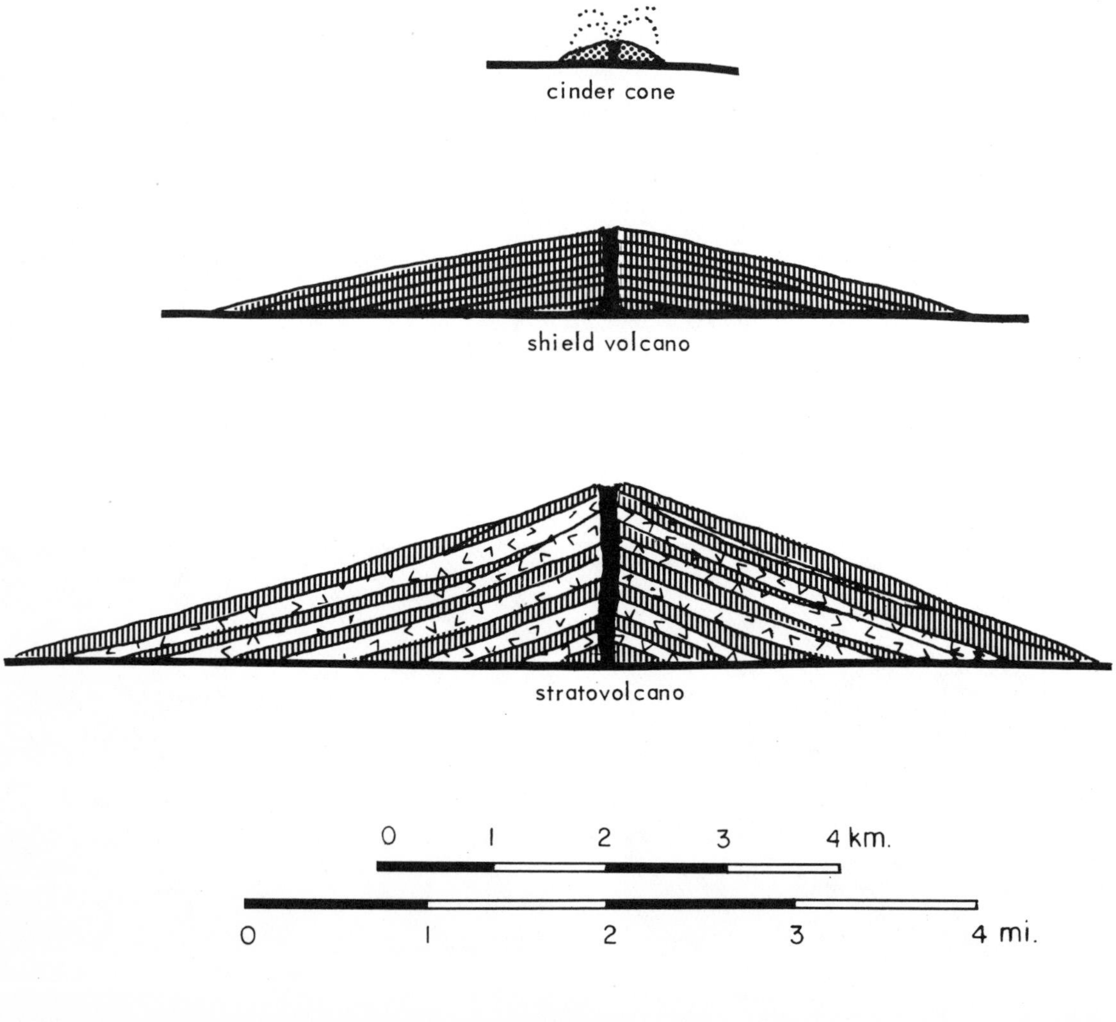

that shoot out fine, frothy pumice, blobs of molten rock and cinder, and chunks of solid rock, with other, quieter eruptions in which lava cascades down the volcano's flanks. Alternate layers of lava and pumice build up well defined and often very beautiful cone-shaped, crater-topped mountains. Many large stratovolcanoes once rose above the Yellowstone region.

Because their lava is thick and viscous, yet gaseous, stratovolcanoes are quite lethal. They are even capable of their own destruction, piecemeal or all at once. In historic time they have caused catastrophes around the world: the destruction of Minoan civilization in about 1470 B.C., of Pompeii and Herculaneum in 79 A.D., of the city of St. Pierre on Martinique in 1902, of Indonesian islands near Krakatoa in 1881. Mount St. Helens' eruptions are child's play by comparison, as these figures show:

Date	Volcanic site	Magma volume
May 1980	Mount St. Helens	1 km^3 (¼ mi^3)
1881	Krakatoa	70 km^3 (17 mi^3)
6,600 yrs ago	Mount Mazama	50 km^3 (13 mi^3)
600,000 yrs ago	Yellowstone caldera	1,000 km^3 (238 mi^3)

When stratovolcanoes blow off enormous quantities of foaming, explosive, gas-rich magma, the level of magma in the magma chambers lowers drastically, and the volcanoes not uncommonly collapse, leaving a circular depression called a caldera. Other signs of the volcano's passing remain as well—thick beds of volcanic ash, steaming fumaroles from which volcanic gases still rise, hot springs, and geysers. Yellowstone, scene of violent eruptions of the past, is thought by some to be a dying volcanic field.

IV. The Wearing Away

The rocks of the earth chronicle repeated periods of deposition when, on sea floors and lake floors and in continental basins, gravel and sand, silt, clay, and lime were deposited in horizontal layers to become, with time, sedimentary rocks. The rocks also chronicle uplift and mountain building and tell of the ceaseless cutting, carving, wearing, carrying, and ultimate depositing that bring rock materials from highland to lowland. Wherever land rises, it is worn away. And it is another adage of geology that uplift invites erosion. Streams gushing down steep slopes flow faster than sedate rivers of the valley, and the faster water is moving, the greater the burden it can carry.

Using processes that are operating around us today as keys to events in the geologic past, we find that the first step in the erosion process is weathering, the physical and chemical disintegration of rock. Water, ice, air, temperature changes, and plant and animal matter all play parts, in their special ways, to turn rock into soil.

Water in itself is not particularly corrosive. However rainfall and snowmelt, having absorbed carbon dioxide from the atmosphere, are weakly acidic. The dilute acid attacks particularly the calcium carbonate of limestone, a substance that also cements mineral grains of many sedimentary rocks, and the micas and feldspars of igneous rock. As minerals decompose, the rocks weaken and break down, sometimes grain by grain, into soil—a slow but relentless process. The presence of lichens and other types of plants and plant products speeds up the process. Air moist with mild acids attacks rock in the same way.

At suitable altitudes and high latitudes, water works also in its solid form, as ice or frost. Repeated growth and melting of ice crystals where water has seeped into rock pore spaces dislodges individual grains; development of frost in joints and other crevices wedges apart whole blocks of rock. For ice, unlike crystal forms of other minerals, occupies more space than its fluid counterpart, and in the process of crystallizing exerts a powerful pressure against its surroundings.

Temperature changes on exposed rock surfaces cause expansion and contraction of the rock itself. Especially in the outermost few inches, such expansion and contraction loosen individual mineral grains or thin flakes of rock. Mere unloading of long-buried rock as overlying material is washed away allows the rock to expand, a process that is accentuated in intrusive rocks that solidified at great depths under immense pressures. Such expansion creates joints concentric to the rock surface, separating large curving slabs of rock and allowing moisture to seep in. Coupled with frost action in the joints, this process (known as sheeting or exfoliation) rounds boulders and creates bare rock domes. Plant roots may grow into these and other joints, also forcing the rock apart, though whether the plant growth itself or the swaying in the wind exerts the necessary force is often hard to determine.

Once loosened or turned to soil, rock material is vulnerable to another process—transportation. Here again the present is our key to the past. Erosional processes we see around us today operated thousands, millions, and, with the exception of those incorporating plant and animal activity, even billions of years ago. They operate on every scale, from the transport of molecules in solution in water to the transport of great boulders by flooded streams. Again, we are looking at processes involving water,

Expanding from within, many types of rock develop curving joints concentric with their exposed surfaces.

ice, air, and temperature changes, as well as at two other forces: wind and gravity.

Through the ages, rivulets, streams, rivers, and the waters of seas and lakes have picked up where weathering left off, transporting broken-down rock material toward its ultimate resting place, the sea, in ways that are familiar to us all. Heavy rains, floods, and storms along coasts and in mountains are potent agents in these processes, for they move many millions of tons each year. But quieter streams and more leisurely rivers, acting through thousands of years, also move rock material, carrying minerals in solution, patiently rolling grains of sand, or repeatedly undermining cobbles and boulders until they roll a half turn or a quarter turn downstream. The heaviest floods are mudflows caused by sudden large quantities of water and rock material; in them, water is so thick with ground rock that it can almost float large boulders and cobbles in its cementlike mass. Acid-enriched water acts below the surface as well, etching and dissolving caverns in limestone and related rocks.

Rivers choked with flood debris may move tons of rock in a few hours.

Today, plant life lessens the effectiveness of water in erosion. The plants themselves shield the ground by intercepting falling raindrops. Their roots hold soil together. And when they die, their decomposing stems, trunks, and foliage mix with decomposed rock to form a spongy, water-absorbing humus layer. Along coasts, seaweeds slow erosion by lessening wave action. Before the advent of large marine algae and land plants, water must have been even more potent as a transporting agent than it is today.

With groaning weight and low-gear motion, ice, too, wears away the solidest rock. Glaciers form where winter snowfall exceeds summer melting. Snow compacts into the beady ice called névé (the skier's "corn snow"), then into a fused aggregate of beads, and finally into hard blue ice. When such ice becomes about 30 meters (100 feet) thick, it begins to flow—outward if it is on a flat surface, downhill if it is on a slope. The flow is rather like that of silly putty in that where movement is slow, plastic deformation takes place; where flow is rapid, the ice (or silly putty) may break. In mountainous areas, long tongues of ice creep down pre-existing stream valleys, breaking away rock loosened by weathering and using it to grind the more solid bedrock beneath. Grinding, scouring, and plucking, glaciers creep downhill to warmer elevations. Constantly replenished with new snow at the top, constantly melting at their lower ends, glaciers may appear to be static; in reality, they are in slow but constant motion. When mountain glaciers (also called alpine or valley glaciers) melt, they leave behind characteristic straightened valleys that are U-shaped in cross section, as well as scoop-shaped mountain cirques at their heads, and large piles of glacier-carried rock (called moraines) near their lower ends.

Many theories have been advanced to explain the changes that led in Pleistocene time (3 million to 10,000 years ago) to episodes of glaciation. The climate doubtless became wetter. Whether or not it initially was much colder is hard to say. Certainly each time that ice sheets covered large parts of America and Europe, air masses blowing across them would take on some of their frigidity.

Even without development of glaciers, ice helps in transporting rock material. On steep slopes, frost that forms under individual rocks lifts them slightly, nearly always at right angles to the slope. Then, as the frost thaws (at certain times of the year a daily event), the rock settles vertically. So, in a series of zigzag movements, rock and soil material move downhill—a slow process, but long enduring.

In the related process of soil creep, which may or may not involve frost, downslope transportation is also agonizingly slow. Many years may pass before there is visible change. But change there is, and it is widespread, for soil creep operates on most soil-covered hillsides, characteristically rounding them into the shape one sees on so many meadowed hills.

Though in desert regions it comes into its own, wind is not particularly significant in erosional processes in the Rocky Mountain region. Most certainly, however, it helps to clean away frost-loosened sand and small rock fragments from frost-sharpened peaks. Its effects can be seen in the sculpturing of semidesert areas such as Badlands and Theodore Roosevelt National Parks. Wind cleans away loosened material and, when it picks up sand-grain tools, functions in actively wearing down rock material. Sand-blasting of bare rock and soil may leave the surface deeply pitted. Wind, unlike water and ice, can move sand horizontally or swirl dust upward into the sky.

Gravity plays an obvious role in most processes of transportation, controlling the downhill movement of water, ice, and rock. It may act alone, tugging at cliffs until rocks tumble and fall. More frequently, it acts in consort with frost, which loosens the rocks; with snow, in avalanches that involve rock material and soil as well as snow; or with water, which lubricates landslides and adds to the weight and mobility of earthflows.

From sharpened peaks to terminal moraines, mountain glaciers leave signs of their passing; U-shaped valleys, cirques, moraines, and outwash gravels.

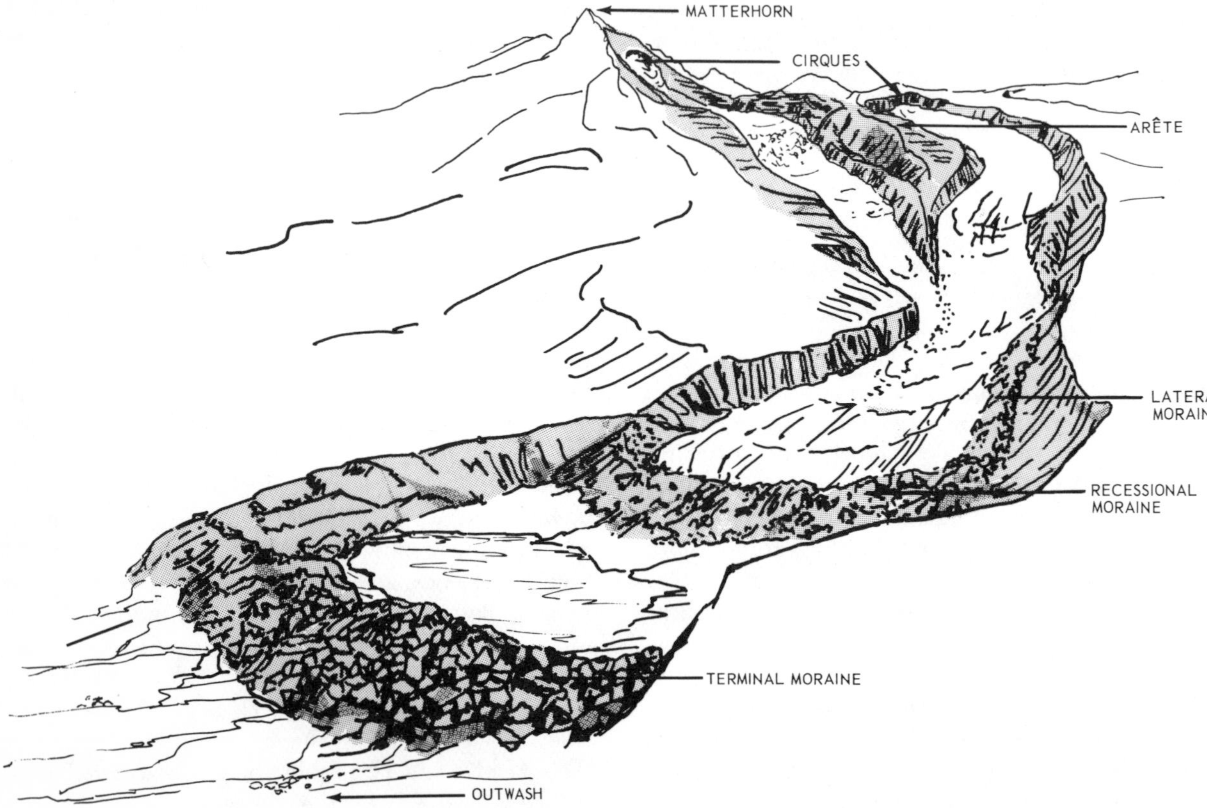

Rock fragmented by frost is moved downslope by oft-repeated freezing and thawing.

Trees bent by soil creep can be seen in many western parks.

U.S. Forest Service Photo

Landslides move tons of rock downward from steep mountainsides. This slide, west of Yellowstone National Park, was triggered by the Hebgen Lake earthquake of 1959. Smaller slides occurred in the park itself.

V. Understanding Maps and Diagrams

In addition to photographs, this book is illustrated with maps, diagrams, and sketches, most of them simplified in order to give a better understanding of the basic patterns of the geology in our national park areas. Both scenically and geologically, the parks and monuments are many-hued. Because they are different from one another—which adds to their attraction, of course—their geology cannot all be illustrated in the same way. This is of course true of other areas as well, all over the world. Some lend themselves to explanation through geologic maps, which show the types of rock (often the specific formations and their ages) that occur at the surface or just under whatever loose material like soil and rock debris is at the surface. Others are better illustrated with cross sections, which slice open the crust to give a picture of what geologists have deduced is below the surface. Still others are better illustrated by combining cross sections with maps, making block diagrams that show what a block of the crust would look like if it could be lifted out and away from its normal surroundings.

In this book I have tried, as a geologist would in illustrating a professional report, to use the types of illustrations most suitable to each park area, hoping that they will clarify the geology for you, the reader. Later, familiarity with maps and diagrams in this book may encourage you to delve into the professional literature as well.

Geologic maps are the prime product of most geologic research. They represent many hours and days and weeks of slow, patient, often drudging work by geologists or geologic teams who plot outcrop after outcrop, contact after contact, wherever rocks are exposed, to get a coherent picture of the geology of the area. The U.S. Geological Survey has at one time or another mapped most of the United States in considerable detail. Geologic maps of 7½- and 15-minute quadrangles, which cover areas of about 13 × 16 kilometers (7 × 9 miles) and 24 × 32 kilometers (14 × 18 miles), can be obtained from USGS map offices in Reston, Virginia; Denver, Colorado; and Menlo Park, California, as can maps of larger areas such as states and, in some cases, individual national parks. The park maps, when they exist, can usually be purchased at visitor centers.

Geologic maps show to the practiced eye not only the rock types but the attitude or position of sedimentary rock layers—whether they are horizontal or tilted, whether they have been folded or faulted, where their contacts lie. Interpretation of geologic maps is a skill well worth learning.

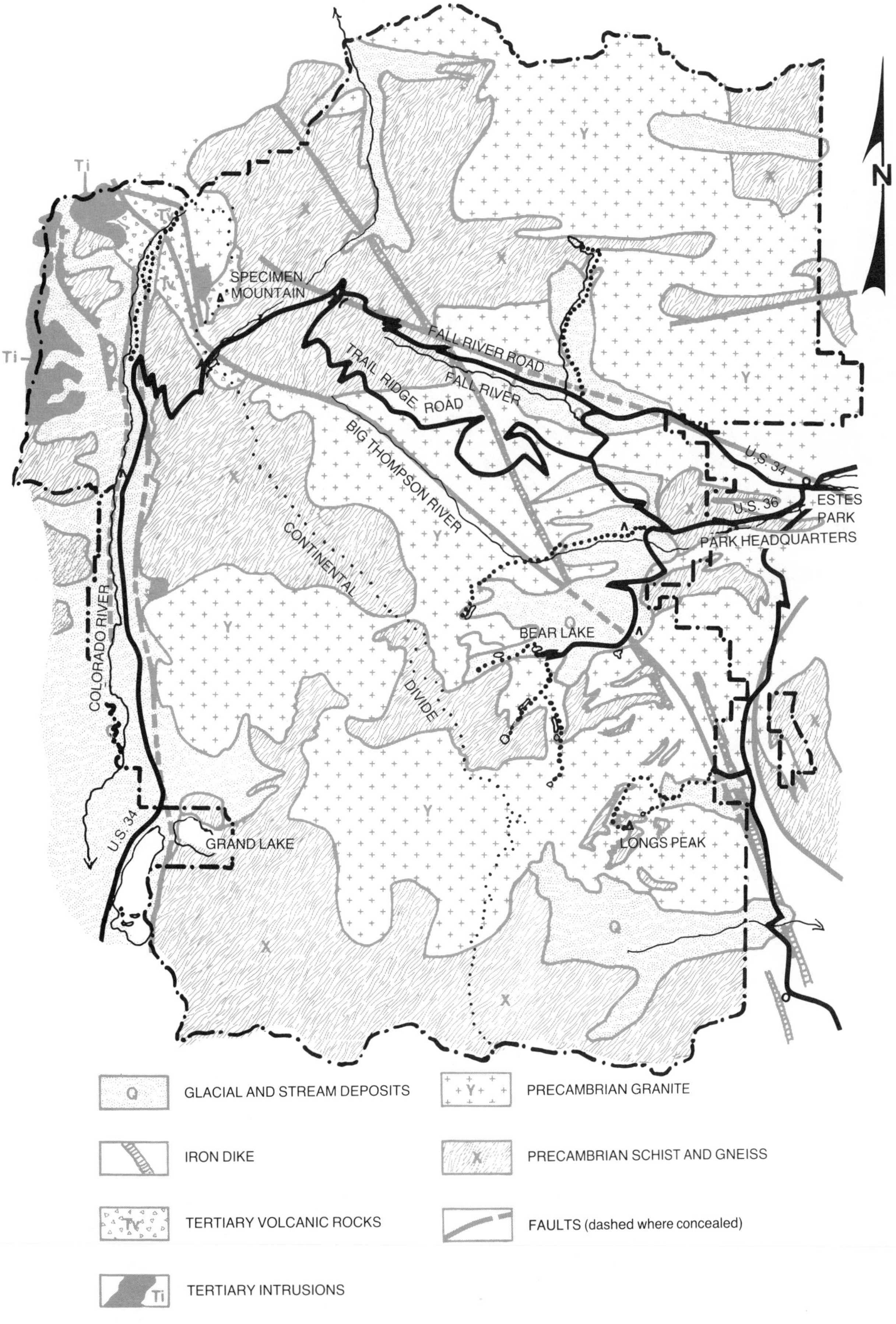

N
Ti
Tv
Ti
SPECIMEN MOUNTAIN
FALL RIVER ROAD
TRAIL RIDGE ROAD
FALL RIVER
BIG THOMPSON RIVER
U.S. 34
U.S. 36
ESTES PARK
PARK HEADQUARTERS
CONTINENTAL
DIVIDE
COLORADO RIVER
BEAR LAKE
U.S. 34
GRAND LAKE
LONGS PEAK
X
Y
Q
GLACIAL AND STREAM DEPOSITS
PRECAMBRIAN GRANITE
IRON DIKE
PRECAMBRIAN SCHIST AND GNEISS
TERTIARY VOLCANIC ROCKS
FAULTS (dashed where concealed)
TERTIARY INTRUSIONS

Cross sections are usually easier to understand and are a good way to show geology at a glance. They are made from maps or, where rock layers are well exposed, from the rocks themselves. Often the vertical dimension is exaggerated in cross sections in order to show the succession of rock layers more clearly. Unfortunately, vertical exaggeration also exaggerates folds, steepens faults, and lends unreal—sometimes really startling—ruggedness to the surface profile.

Combining cross sections with map information, block diagrams show the structure of the near-surface rocks as well as their surface expression. Like those explaining faults and folds in Chapter III, block diagrams are particularly good for illustrating the geologic and topographic changes that come with faulting, folding, uplift, and subsequent erosion of rocks.

Another type of illustration is the stratigraphic

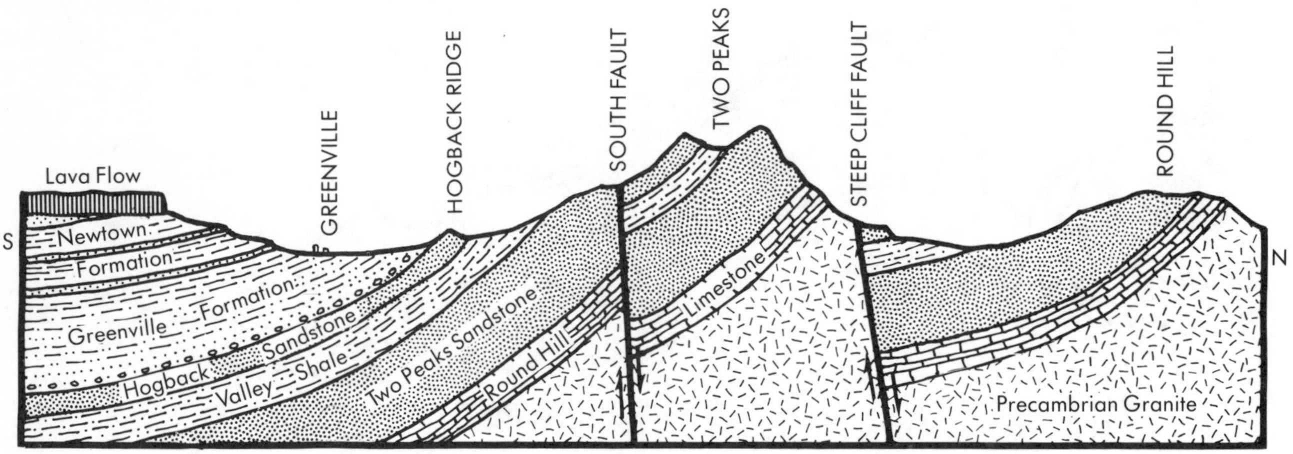

Sample Geological Cross-Section

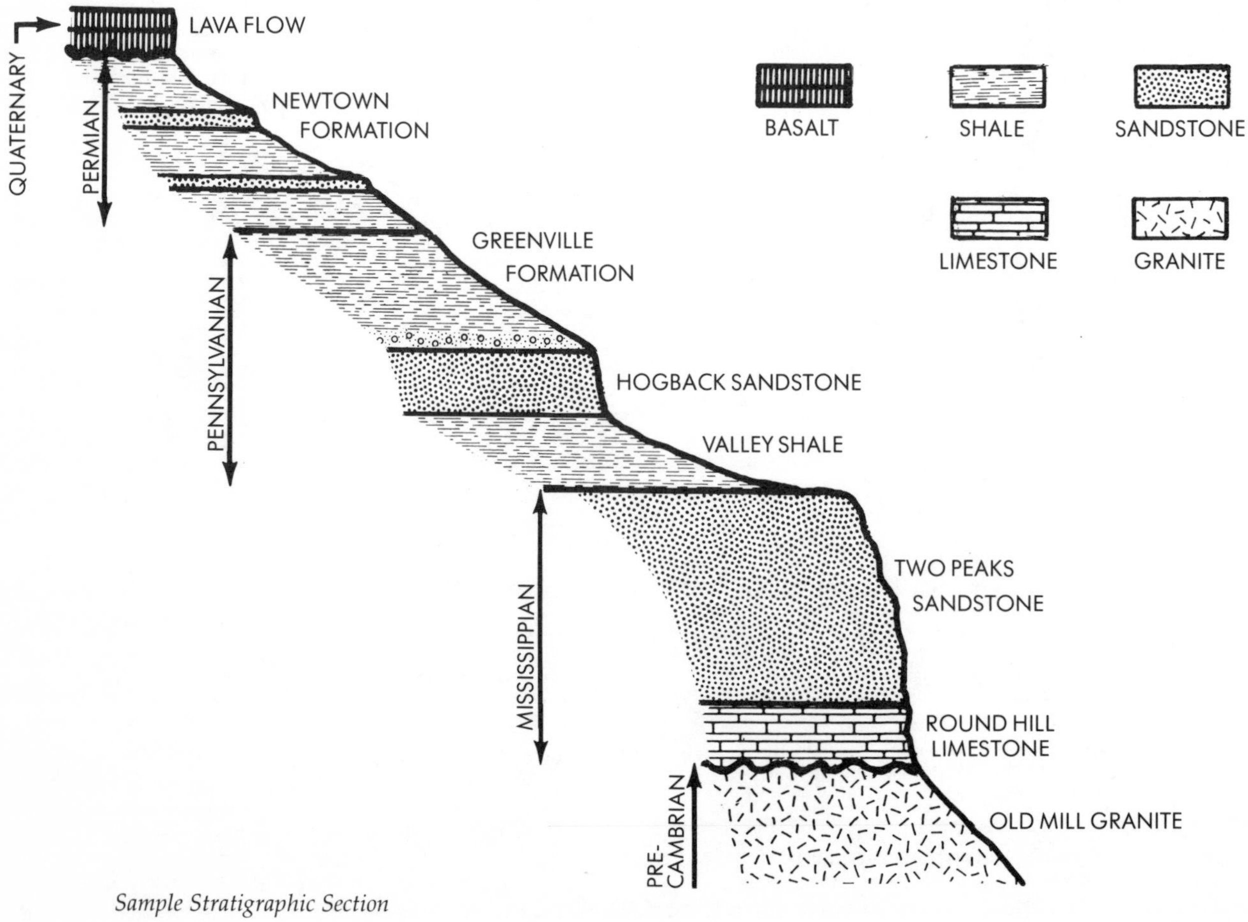

Sample Stratigraphic Section

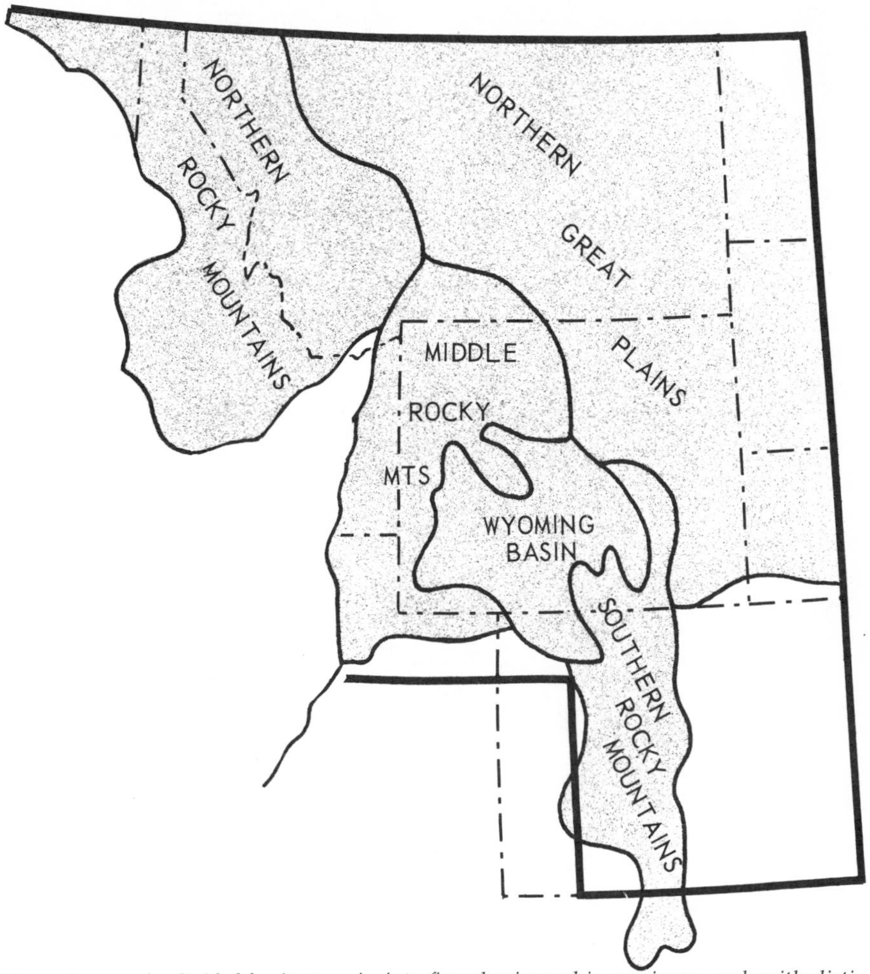

The Rocky Mountain region can be divided by its terrain into five physiographic provinces, each with distinctive geology and characteristic landforms.

diagram, suitable only for stratified rock. Some diagrams show idealized sequences of layered rocks put together by studying a number of related areas; they depict the strata as they would appear if piled on top of one another once more, in their original positions. Stratigraphic diagrams in this book also show how the successive rock layers weather—some as slopes, some as cliffs or ledges. Under natural conditions though, the rock layers may not always show these characteristics; thus one must make allowances in trying to match up scenery and stratigraphic diagram. Undermining by a stream, for instance, may create unexpected cliffs in a normally slope-forming layer. The diagrams indicate predominent or *average* rock types and *average* thicknesses and *average* weathering characteristics. In spite of all the variables, they are a useful way to demonstrate the nature of stratified rocks and the relationship between their appearances at different sites. In this book, small sketches of some of these sites appear next to some stratigraphic diagrams, and even smaller sketches show some of the fossils that occur in the successive layers.

Now let's get to the parks. Start anywhere. In this book they are discussed in alphabetical order. To find your way around, refer to the small maps distributed at entry gates by the National Park Service.

VI. Other Reading

In almost every national park and monument visitor center there are books and pamphlets for sale on the geology of that particular area. Some visitor centers have handout sheets describing local geology. The reverse side of a few park topographic maps (among them Grand Teton, Dinosaur, and Craters of the Moon) are printed with excellent discussions by U.S. Geological Survey geologists. Nature trail leaflets note geologic features, as do some road guides to park highways.

The books and articles listed below are of a more general nature. Some are college textbooks; others address the geology of whole states or regions, or geologic processes such as volcanism or glaciation. Many of these books are somewhat technical, but others are written for those who have little or no background in geology. All will in some way enrich your understanding of the geology of the parks and monuments.

Alt, David D., and Hyndman, Donald W. 1972. *Roadside Geology of the Northern Rockies.* Mountain Press, Missoula, Montana.

Bullard, F. M. 1962. *Volcanoes: In History, in Theory, in Eruption.* University of Texas Press, Austin, Texas.

Chronic, Halka. 1980. *Roadside Geology of Colorado.* Mountain Press, Missoula, Montana.

Chronic, John and Halka. 1972. *Prairie Peak and Plateau, a Guide to the Geology of Colorado.* Colorado Geological Survey Bulletin 32, Denver, Colorado.

Clark, Thomas H., and Stearn, Colin W. 1968. *Geological Evolution of North America.* Ronald Press, New York.

Colbert, E. H. 1955 (paperback 1961). *Evolution of the Vertebrates.* Wiley, New York.

Colbert, E. H. (editor). 1976. *Our Continent: a Natural History of North America.* National Geographic Society, Washington, D.C.

Cowen, R. 1975. *History of Life.* McGraw-Hill Book Co., New York.

Curtis, B. F. (editor). 1975. *Cenozoic History of the Southern Rocky Mountains.* Geological Society of America Memoir 144.

Decker, Robert and Barbara. 1981. *Volcanoes.* W. H. Freeman and Company, San Francisco.

Dott, R. G., and Batten, R. L. 1976. *Evolution of the Earth.* McGraw-Hill Book Co., New York.

Flint, R. F. 1971. *Glacial and Pleistocene Geology.* Wiley, New York.

——— 1973. *The Earth and its History.* W.W. Norton & Co., New York.

Garner, H. F. 1974. *The Origin of Landscapes.* Oxford University Press.

Gilluly, J.; Waters, S. C.; and Woodford, A. O. 1975. *Principles of Geology.* W. H. Freeman, San Francisco.

Hamblin, W. K. 1975. *The Earth's Dynamic Systems.* Burgess, Minneapolis, Minnesota.

Hamilton, Warren. 1978. *Plate Tectonics and Man.* Reprinted from U.S. Geological Survey Annual Report, Fiscal Year 1976, U.S. Government Printing Office, Washington, D.C.

Hintze, Lehi F. 1973 *Geologic History of Utah.* Brigham Young University Studies, 20, part 3.

Kay, M., and Colbert, E. H. 1965. *Stratigraphy and Life History.* Wiley, New York.

Kurten, B. 1972. *The Age of Mammals.* Columbia Press, New York.

Macdonald, G. A. 1972. *Volcanoes.* Prentice-Hall, Englewood Cliffs, New Jersey.

Marvin, U. B. 1973. *Continental Drift.* Smithsonian, Washington, D.C.

Match, C. L. 1976. *North America and the Great Ice Age.* McGraw-Hill Book Co., New York.

Matthews, W. W. III. 1960. *A Guide to the National Parks, their Landscape and Geology.* Natural History Press, New York.

Oakshott, G. B. 1975. *Volcanoes and Earthquakes: Geologic Violence.* McGraw-Hill Book Co., New York.

Post, Austin, and LaChapelle, E.R. 1971. *Glacier Ice.* The Mountaineers and University of Washington Press, Seattle.

Seyfert, Carl K., and Sirkin, Leslie A. 1973. *Earth History and Plate Tectonics, an Introduction to Historical Geology.* Harper & Row, New York.

Sharp, Robert P. 1960. *Glaciers.* University of Oregon, Eugene, Oregon.

Shelton, John H. 1966. *Geology Illustrated.* W. H. Freeman, San Francisco.

Stokes, William Lee. 1960. *Essentials of Earth History.* Prentice-Hall, Englewood Cliffs, New Jersey.

Stokes, W. L.; Judson, Sheldon; and Picard, M. D. 1978. *Introduction to Geology: Physical and Historical.* Prentice-Hall, Englewood Cliffs, New Jersey.

Sullivan, W. 1974. *Continents in Motion.* McGraw-Hill Book Co., New York.

Vine, F. J. 1970. *Sea-floor Spreading and Continental Drift.* Journal of Geological Education, vol. 18, no. 2.

Wilson, J. Tuzo, and others. 1972. "Continents Adrift." Readings from *Scientific American.* W. H. Freeman and Company, San Francisco.

Wyllie, P. J. 1971. *The Dynamic Earth.* Wiley, New York.

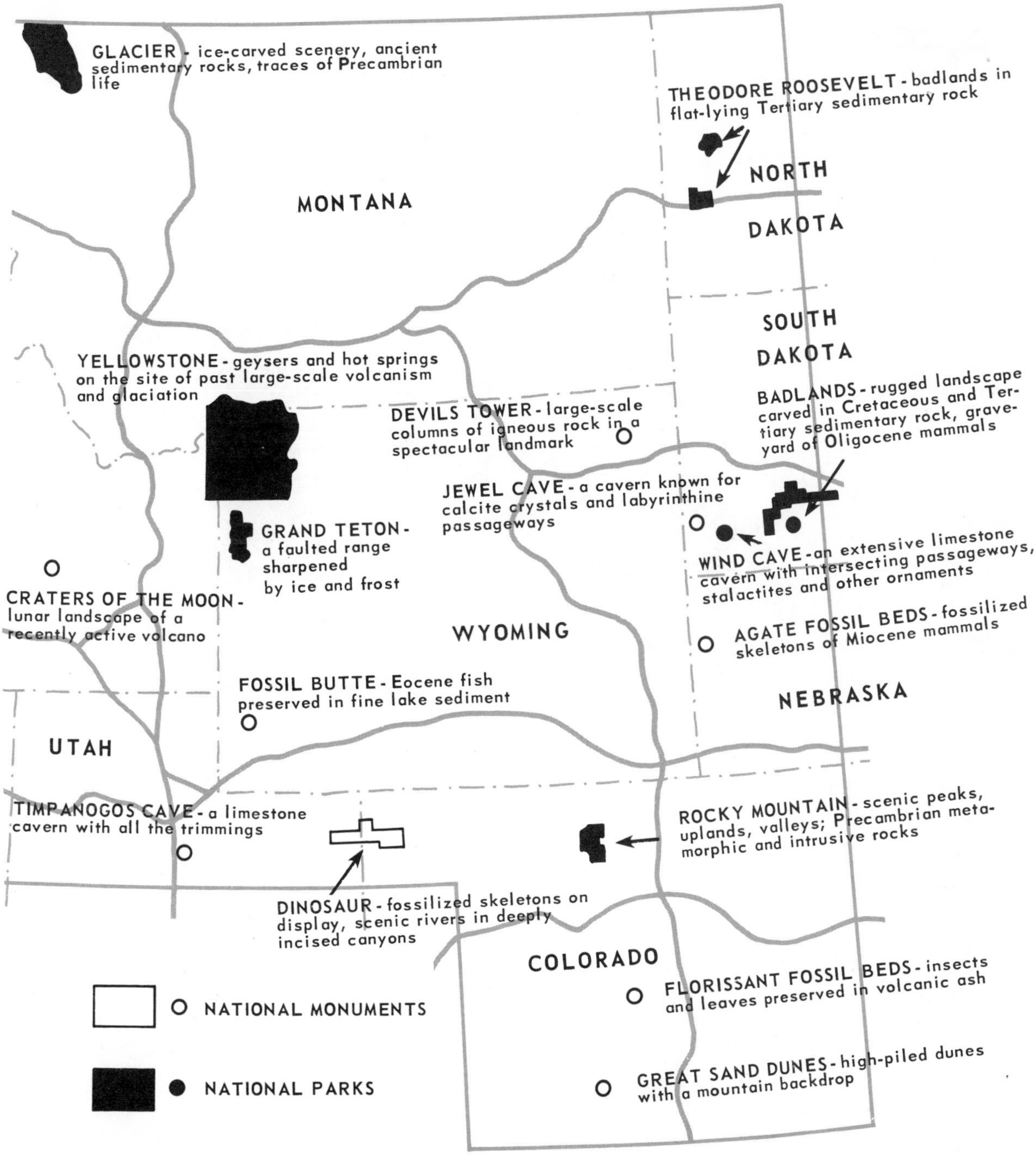
GLACIER - ice-carved scenery, ancient sedimentary rocks, traces of Precambrian life
THEODORE ROOSEVELT - badlands in flat-lying Tertiary sedimentary rock
MONTANA
NORTH DAKOTA
SOUTH DAKOTA
YELLOWSTONE - geysers and hot springs on the site of past large-scale volcanism and glaciation
DEVILS TOWER - large-scale columns of igneous rock in a spectacular landmark
BADLANDS - rugged landscape carved in Cretaceous and Tertiary sedimentary rock, graveyard of Oligocene mammals
JEWEL CAVE - a cavern known for calcite crystals and labyrinthine passageways
GRAND TETON - a faulted range sharpened by ice and frost
WIND CAVE - an extensive limestone cavern with intersecting passageways, stalactites and other ornaments
CRATERS OF THE MOON - lunar landscape of a recently active volcano
WYOMING
AGATE FOSSIL BEDS - fossilized skeletons of Miocene mammals
FOSSIL BUTTE - Eocene fish preserved in fine lake sediment
NEBRASKA
UTAH
TIMPANOGOS CAVE - a limestone cavern with all the trimmings
ROCKY MOUNTAIN - scenic peaks, uplands, valleys; Precambrian metamorphic and intrusive rocks
DINOSAUR - fossilized skeletons on display, scenic rivers in deeply incised canyons
COLORADO
NATIONAL MONUMENTS
FLORISSANT FOSSIL BEDS - insects and leaves preserved in volcanic ash
NATIONAL PARKS
GREAT SAND DUNES - high-piled dunes with a mountain backdrop

The national parks and monuments of the Rocky Mountain region illustrate many facets of earth science.

At Devils Tower, tall columns of igneous rock taper from 4 meters (12 to 15 feet) in diameter near their base to a mere 1.5 meters (4 to 5 feet) higher up. The massive base of the tower is formed, like the upper part, from intrusive igneous rock.

PART 2

THE NATIONAL PARKS AND MONUMENTS

Agate Fossil Beds National Monument

Established: 1965
Size: 12 square kilometers (5 square miles)
Elevation: 1,341 meters (4,400 feet) at visitor center
Address: Box 427, Gering, Nebraska 69341

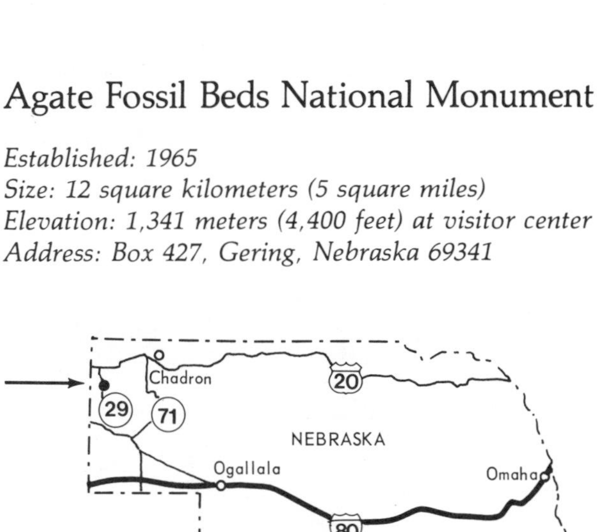

STAR FEATURES

• Twenty-million-year-old Miocene rocks in which abundant fossil mammal bones, all of extinct species, have been found.

• Unusual spiral fossil burrows known popularly as "Devil's Corkscrews," scientifically as *Daimonelix.* A few burrows contain bones of former beaverlike residents.

• Exhibits and displays, only partly completed and in temporary quarters at the time of this writing.

SETTING THE STAGE

In northwestern Nebraska, sedimentary rocks deposited 30 to 17 million years ago during the Tertiary Period are exposed in low bluffs and buttes along the Niobrara River (here hardly more than a stream) and its ephemeral tributaries. As early as 1892, geologists visited this region to collect spectacular "Devil's Corkscrews" or *Daimonelix,* now known to be filled-in and fossilized animal burrows. Later, fossil bones and skeletons of many Miocene mammals were discovered. By 1908 the Carnegie Museum of Pittsburg, the University of Nebraska, and other interested institutions were excavating here in search of these relics of mammalian evolution.

The best known fossil bone deposits occur in two isolated hills south of the river, where fossil-bearing layers are better exposed than they are farther north. In these buttes, which have come to be known as University Hill and Carnegie Hill, paleontologists (geologists who specialize in fossils) have found many skeletons of a small, two-horned rhinoceros which they named *Diceratherium,* of *Dinohyus* the monstrous pig, and of *Moropus,* a large, heavy-bodied animal that has been described as having a horse's head, a giraffe's neck, a tapir's torso, front legs like a rhinoceros, and hind legs like a bear. At another site some distance east of the present monument headquarters were found many skeletons of *Stenomylus,* a tiny, graceful camel hardly larger than a collie. Carnivores were not common, though some meat-eating animals resembling foxes and martens, and a true bear (one of the earliest known in North America) have been discovered. The bones of the beaverlike animal that dug the *Daimonelix* burrows, and a weasel that may have preyed upon it, were found in some of the corkscrew burrows. All of these animals belong to species now extinct.

Skeletons and reconstructions of animals from this locality are exhibited at the Carnegie Museum in Pittsburg, American Museum in New York, Denver Museum of Natural History, and other museums throughout the world. The Park Service plans new displays here, some of which will be in-place exhibits of the bone beds. Many more fossils must lie under just a few feet of overburden in the two fossil-bearing hills. The Park Service will remove some of

NPS photo

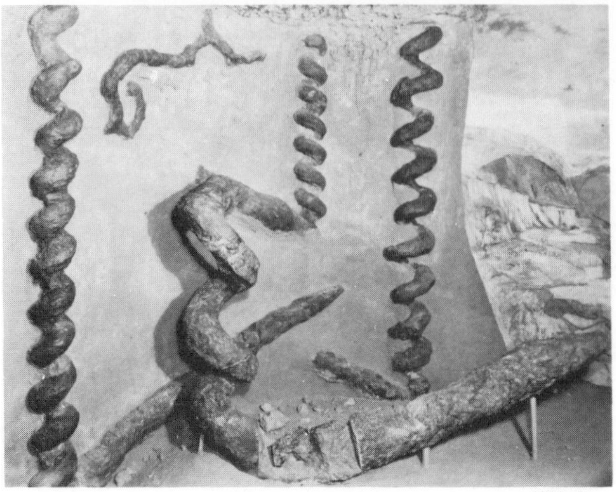

NPS photo

Left and above: *Tall siltstone spirals puzzled geologists for many years. Now we know that they are filled-in burrows of beaverlike animals that dwelt here 21 million years ago.*

the overburden, revealing these bone layers and enabling visitors to watch paleontologists at work on the deposits.

GEOLOGIC HISTORY

This part of North America saw its last flooding by the sea in Cretaceous time, toward the end of the Mesozoic Era, about 100 million or 90 million years ago. We will pick up its story in the Cenozoic Era, the "Age of Mammals," after the region was lifted above sea level.

In western Nebraska there is no record of the earliest part of the Cenozoic Era, but during the Oligocene Epoch, 38 to 26 million years ago, the region was coated gradually with layers of stream-washed sand and silt carried out across the plains from lofty mountains to the west and north. These layers are now called the White River Group, a unit made up of fine sandstone, siltstone, and volcanic ash, the same rock layers that form the eroded scenery of Badlands National Monument in South Dakota. In this part of Nebraska these strata lie beneath the surface, buried by similar but younger Miocene layers.

Almost all the rock layers you see at Agate Fossil Beds National Monument are Early Miocene nonmarine sedimentary rock. Many of them may be old soil layers. They form the tops and sides of the low hills north and south of the Niobrara River. A few Oligocene rocks are visible along tributary channels south of the Niobrara. The uppermost Miocene beds are fine, orange-red sandstone that caps high ridges in the northern half of the monument. Below this layer, and forming most of the slopes and hills visible from the visitor center, are gray, fine-grained sandstone and siltstone of the Harrison Formation, part of a widespread unit that surfaces much of the northern High Plains.

Masses of animal bones occur at the bases of channel deposits of sand, silt, and volcanic ash. Many are battered by stream action or gnawed by predators.

In Miocene time, volcanoes northwest of here (probably in the Yellowstone area) contributed quantities of volcanic ash to the sedimentary layers of this part of the country. Fine splinters of volcanic glass make up a large part of the rock. Fortunately for paleontologists studying the fossils here, volcanic ash can be dated by analyzing the radioactive minerals present in it and measuring the amount of radioactive decay. A light-colored ash bed known as the Agate Ash, near the top of the Harrison Formation and 10 meters (30 feet) below the bone deposits, has been dated as 21 million years old.

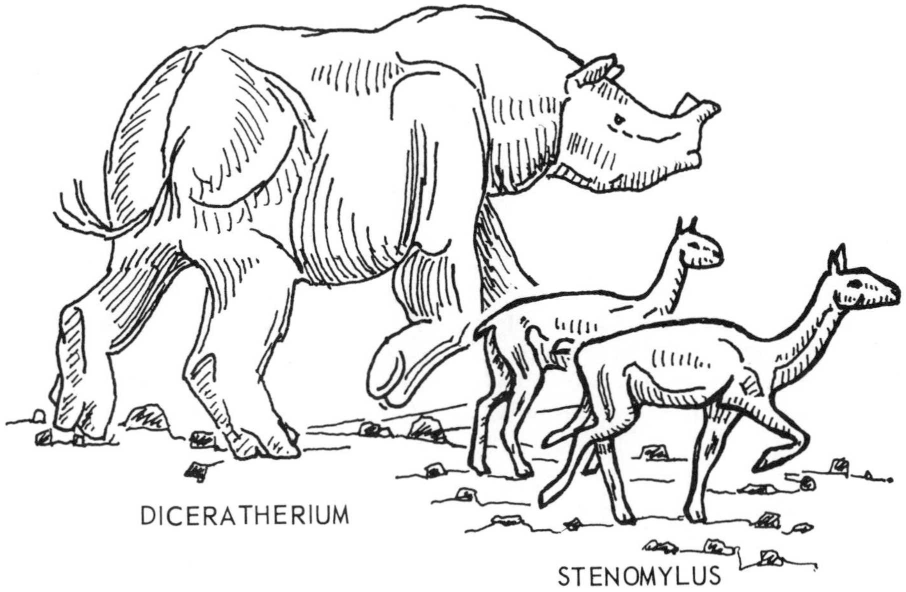

Some Miocene strata are coated with a hardpan upper surface cemented with silica minerals, particularly hard substances that tend to resist erosion. Groundwater dissolving silica from tiny fragments of volcanic glass redeposited it between grains of sand and gravel near the surface, probably as the groundwater was drawn to the surface and evaporated. Such hardpans still form today in arid regions where there is an abundance of fine, silica-rich volcanic material.

Sometime after deposition of the Agate Ash bed, probably about 20 million years ago, a large stream cut into a hardpan layer near the top of the Harrison Formation, at a level about 10 meters (30 feet) above the 21-million-year-old ashbed. As it broke through the hardpan, it eroded a valley several kilometers wide but probably less than 15 meters (50 feet) deep. There, in shifting channels, the stream deposited sand, silt, and fragments of broken-up hardpan. Particles of volcanic ash sifted down on the sediment, making up at least a third of the rock material. In shallow lakes within the valley, limestone was deposited.

At the time the valley existed, large numbers of mammals roamed the region, attracted maybe by streamside vegetation. They were occasionally swept up by flooding streams; their bodies collected in embayments and low spots in the channels and were quickly buried by sand and mud. Though their flesh soon decomposed, silica-laden water filtered into their bones, depositing silica and so preserving them. Only a fraction of the animal population was swept into the streams, of course, and only a fraction of those were preserved. Bone layers occur in a zone less than a meter thick, right at the base of some channel deposits.

Many of the bone deposits contain jumbled bones of several kinds of animals, suggesting that the skeletons were broken apart and separated as they were transported and deposited. Some individual bones are battered as if tumbled by rushing waters; some are gnawed by predators. Some seem to be aligned by flowing water. Yet many skeletons are complete. Those of the dainty, long-legged *Stenomylus* were found with their bones almost perfectly articulated but in awkward, unlikely positions, as if the tiny animals had been swept suddenly to their deaths by a churning river in flood.

What was western Nebraska like when these animals lived and died? The layered rocks tell us that it was a low, flat plain or savannah cut by broad, shallow watercourses. The climate was semiarid, as it is today, but temperatures were milder than today because the region was then at a much lower elevation. The surface, stable for a long time, weathered deeply. Severe monsoonlike storms occasionally turned the watercourses into raging floods.

Vegetation on the savannah and along the stream courses nourished herds of grazing and browsing animals. Their skeletal remains at times lay about on the surface, chewed by predators and scavengers, battered by wind. Possibly large amounts of volcanic ash contributed to the death of many animals by wearing down their teeth as they browsed on gritty, ash-covered vegetation, or by choking them at times of particularly heavy ash fall. Some may have starved as ash killed the food plants necessary to their survival. Others may have died in floods, dust storms, even quicksand. Bodies and bones of those that died near stream channels were, under just the right conditions, buried rapidly with mud, sand, and volcanic ash.

The little *Stenomylus* camels were found about a mile east of Carnegie and University Hills and come from a slightly older part of the Harrison Formation, below the Agate Ash and the hardpan and soil surface described above. They appear to have existed as a herd and to have perished together. Careful excavation and on-site studies of the positions of the skeletons may someday reveal the cause of their death and the exact conditions of their burial. *Daimonelix* burrows also come from these older rocks and can be found in the national monument almost anywhere that these rocks are exposed. Although the rodents that lived in them and presumably dug them are related to beavers, they seem to have lived on land and in group colonies somewhat like present-day prairie dog "towns."

Late in Miocene or early in Pliocene time, this region was elevated about 1,200 meters (4,000 feet) as part of a broad arch that extended from South Dakota to Arizona. Rock layers here were slightly bent in places to form gentle anticlines and synclines; in some places they were faulted. Streams were revitalized by Miocene–Pliocene uplift and, in Pleistocene time, by the increased rainfall that accompanied the Ice Ages, and they excavated new valleys down through the rock layers. By the end of Pleistocene time, the country was about as you see it now—a gently rolling plain with broad stream channels and occasional higher buttes and ridges.

OTHER READING

Hunt, R. M., Jr. 1978. "Depositional Setting of a Miocene Mammal Assemblage, Sioux County, Nebraska." Palaeogeography, Palaeoclimatology, Palaeoecology, vol. 24, pp. 1-52.

Skinner, M. F., and others. 1977. *Stratigraphy and Biostratigraphy of Late Cenozoic Deposits in Central Sioux County, Western Nebraska.* American Museum of Natural History Bulletin, vol. 158, pp. 263-370.

Badlands National Park

Established: 1929 as a national monument; 1978 as a national park
Size: 984 square kilometers (380 square miles)
Elevation: 745 to 990 meters (2,443 to 3,247 feet)
Address: P. O. Box 6, Interior, South Dakota 57750

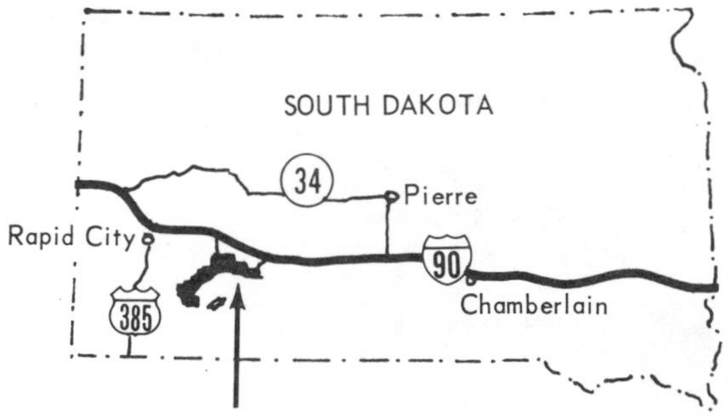

STAR FEATURES

• A close look at sculptured scenery produced by rain, wind, and frost in soft sedimentary rocks that edge the valley of the White River.

• Layered rocks of Cretaceous, Oligocene, and Miocene age, most of them river floodplain deposits and old soil horizons that contain a high proportion of volcanic ash and fossil bones of long-extinct mammals.

• Faults, fissures, and clastic dikes, well displayed by badland erosion.

• Visitor center exhibits, interpretive tours, self-guiding trails, and roadside exhibits explaining geologic highlights.

See color pages for additional photographs.

SETTING THE STAGE

Despite the complex-looking scenery here in Badlands National Park, the geologic picture is straightforward and simple. All the rocks are clearly exposed to view. All are sedimentary. All are in horizontal position. Most of them were deposited by sluggish but occasionally flooded streams that wound across marshy floodplains or a low, flat delta. Compared with those in many other national park areas, these rocks are very young (only 35 to 25 million years old) and not well hardened or indurated. They crumble and disintegrate easily. Grains of sand come loose in your fingers or under your feet, making climbing hazardous. Never having felt the pressures of deep

Islands of badlands jut from the lower prairie. Junipers (locally called cedars), cottonwood trees, and other greenery thrive in the moist soil of the Cliff Shelf.

Knife-edged ridges identify the Brule Formation. Horizontal ledges are layers of calcite-cemented nodules.

Bare moats at the bases of eroded walls and buttes show that the grassland is not regenerating where steep surfaces have eroded back.

burial, they are loose and porous, halfway between mud and mudstone, sand and sandstone. They waste away readily, washed by water or blown by wind.

The line of cliffs known as the Wall marks a dividing line across the park between the grassy expanse of the upper prairie to the north and the narrow band of grassland, the lower prairie, in the valley of the White River to the south. Along parts of the Wall, crested parapets rise well above the upper grassland. Crisp, pleated ridges separated by narrow ravines plunge sharply from crest to base, ending abruptly in barren moats that separate the Wall from flat-topped, sod-covered tables of the valley. Seen from above, the drainage pattern is dendritic, with tributaries that branch into finer and finer rills.

Why has erosion attacked with such ferocity here? For one thing, the prairie grasslands, first formed under more favorable climatic conditions, no longer regenerate themselves. For another, though total annual rainfall is only 38 centimeters (15 inches), rains when they come are often heavy, violent thunderstorms, bringing about what one might call a "cloudburst climate." And a third reason is that the rocks contain a high proportion of bentonite, a type of clay derived from volcanic ash. Bentonite swells when it gets wet and slakes as it dries, leaving a scruffy, dusty, gritty deposit that blows away in the wind or washes away in the next downpour. Hammered by raindrops, this loose material splashes into miniature craters; where there is a slope, most of the

Fine sedimentary rocks, rich in volcanic ash, absorb water and puff up when it rains. Dried, the puffy surface crumbles, to be swept away by the wind.

Lower parts of the Brule Formation are finely marked with small rills. A flat, white-floored moat surrounds each slope.

splash goes downhill. Raindrop impact, too, may reorient the clay particles, pounding them into a cover impervious to rain; thus runoff increases and its ability to cut gullies is strengthened. Certainly the balance of power is upset, with erosion gaining the upper hand. Accelerated erosion prevents plant growth, and lack of plant cover causes accelerated erosion, making the Badlands self-sustaining.

The White River initiated the erosion process. Fed partly from the Black Hills 50 miles west, it knifed deeply into soft sediments to carve its channel. Then, as its gradient lessened, it swung from side to side, widening its valley. Wind and rain for a million years and more attacked the barren valley walls, moving them little by little back from the river. Gradually the cliffs receded, at an average rate of perhaps a centimeter (about half an inch) a year. They still recede, though certainly not as rapidly now as during the rainy years of the Pleistocene Ice Age. Features photographed many decades ago now show visible changes: cliffs reshape, new gullies are born, slopes are cut more deeply by twisting rills and rivulets, spires wear away. Mudflows and small landslides plummet down gulches, speeding the erosional process. Narrow-stalked "toadstools" topple. Wind scours hollows around pebbles and cobbles, shrubs and surveyors' markers. Rain-fed rivulets are white with clay, bound for the White River.

A few ridges seem straighter and sharper than others. They mark clastic dikes where fine material, sometimes silt or clay but more often fine volcanic ash, filled deep vertical fissures. These clastic dikes are most apparent from above and can be seen from viewpoints along park roads. From the air, some can be traced across ridges and ravines for a mile or more as they interlace with others in a crisscross pattern. Necessary conditions for their formation are:

- deep cracking and fissuring caused by shrinkage of clay minerals or compaction of underlying rocks.
- rocks soft enough to break, yet hard enough to stand as vertical faces.
- a source of fine, loose silt and volcanic ash to fill the fissures before they widen or collapse.

Most of the clastic dikes are less than 30 centimeters (12 inches) thick.

The interesting moats at the bases of cliffs and pinnacles and the distinctive grass-covered sod "tables"

Two converging clastic dikes cut the Chadron and Brule Formations.

of the lower prairie are all too often ignored by visitors. Grass-bound sod protects the tables from downward erosion but not from undercutting at the sides. (In this woodless region, early settlers hewed rectangular blocks of sod for bricks; both they and their crude homes were known as "soddies.") Notice how the sod tables slope up toward the Wall, the source of the sediment of which they are made. Heavy rainfall churning down gullies and gulches of the Wall leave the tables as isolated remnants of a once-continuous prairie surface. As the Wall retreats or as isolated buttes and mesas wear away, bare, scoured moats widen around them, for climatic conditions are no longer favorable to development of new sod.

While driving through the park or walking along its trails, watch for other erosional and sedimentary features. The softest rock forms gentle slopes and rounded hills; harder rock sharpens and steepens the cliffs. Beds of resistant pebbly sandstone, formed along winding river channels, now project as ledges or cap "toadstools." Some rock layers contain hard, lumpy concretions that grew when calcium carbonate (the mineral calcite) coagulated around silt and clay particles and glued them firmly together. Such nodules seem commonly to form around decomposing animal or plant material; some of them contain fossil bones or shells.

At a few places the ground is closely covered with small, rounded pebbles, a type of surface geologists call desert pavement. It forms naturally as a result of wind erosion, for as wind blows away particles of silt, sand, and clay, it leaves the pebbles that were originally scattered both horizontally and vertically through the rock layers. Many of the pebbles come from hard, ledge-forming channel sandstone. In terms of rock types, they match up with rocks of the Black Hills, their probable source. In the Sheep Mountain Table area, the same process paves the surface with fragments of chalcedony from the many chalcedony veins.

Little rills that groove the sides of the Wall and its ridges commonly flow in deep cracks that develop as the clayey rock swells and shrinks with each good soaking. In places the channels are roofed over; eventually such roofed channels enlarge and their roofs collapse, here and there leaving short-lived natural arches. Such channels also develop on the valley floor where the surface is held together by grass roots. There, collapse may leave sod-covered bridges.

The White River Badlands have been described as the world's greatest graveyard. Fossil bones of mammals, birds, and reptiles occur at several levels in these rocks and, because erosion is rapid, new fossils are exposed every year. If you should see a bone, a bit of skull, or a tooth jutting from the surface, report

Color banding and nodular layers characterize the Brule Formation. Rain-fed rivulets travel underground here, emerging at the round cave opening.

your find to a park ranger. *Don't try to collect these fossils.* Unauthorized collecting is prohibited in national park areas, and nonprofessional collecting usually means fossils are lost to science. They will probably be lost to you as well, since special know-how is needed to remove the delicate bones intact and to prevent them from disintegrating.

Animals buried in the Badlands sediments may have died entrapped in soft, muddy marshes; possibly they drowned during floods. Some of them may have been killed or their food supply destroyed by heavy ashfalls from volcanic eruptions. Or perhaps, gathering around diminishing waterholes in times of drought, they perished in great numbers as animals do today on the plains of Africa. Then, somehow, they became covered. As their flesh decayed, groundwater deposited calcium carbonate and silica in the porous bones. Teeth, the hardest parts of animal skeletons, needed no added silica for preservation of their finest detail.

Fossils excavated from the Badlands by authorized scientists are now on display at the Museum of

Geology of the South Dakota School of Mines and Technology in Rapid City, the Denver Natural History Museum, the Field Museum in Chicago, the Smithsonian Institution in Washington, and the American Museum in New York City. Among large animals whose bones came to rest here are 50 kinds of plant-eaters (including ancestors of horses and camels), 14 kinds of carnivores (including saber-toothed cats), and an alligator. Small animals such as monkeys, turtles, mice and other rodents, moles, lizards, and a few birds have been found as well. Small rodent bones are hard to see in the Badlands rock layers but, along with little fossil hackberry seeds, they occur in nearly every anthill!

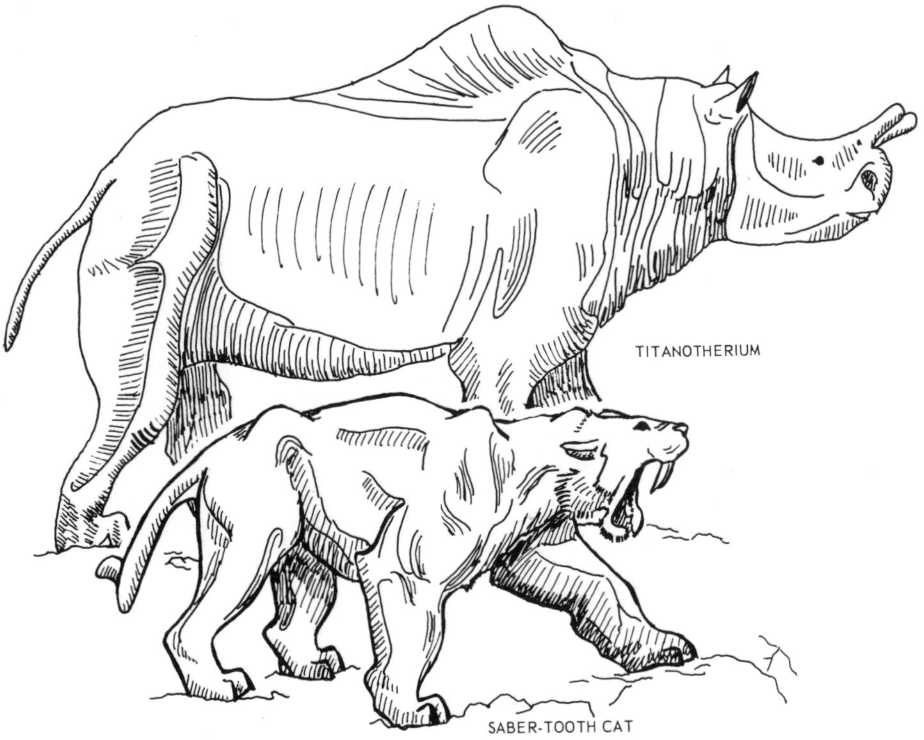

GEOLOGIC HISTORY

Mesozoic Era. About 75 million years ago, this area was part of the floor of a broad, shallow sea that extended across America from the Arctic to the Gulf of Mexico, the last great sea the interior of North America was to know. In it swam large aquatic reptiles, turtles, fishes, and strange octopuslike ammonites with beautiful coiled shells built in chambers like those of their modern relative, the chambered nautilus. Snails and clams dwelt on the sea bottom in soft, dark gray mud that later became compacted into the Pierre Shale.

By the end of the Cretaceous Period (and the end of the Mesozoic Era) the sea shallowed, leaving sandy beach and bar deposits. Then it withdrew completely, forced to retreat by rising land. Not far to the west, the earth's crust was in the first throes of the convulsion that would eventually create the Rocky Mountains, and with them the nearer bulge of the Black Hills.

Cenozoic Era. The land here rose slowly, remaining essentially horizontal. Horizontal color banding and layers of hard, ledge-forming rock are neatly offset by small faults that probably resulted from the uplift; most of them involve displacement of only a few feet. One is hard put to find evidence of folding here. During the first part of the Cenozoic Era, rivers and streams of the rising land stripped away some of the beach and bar deposits and exposed the upper Pierre shales to the elements. Through millions of years, in a valley closely parallel to the present valley of the White River, soils formed and plants grew, and no doubt many animals made their homes. The exposed surface of the Pierre Shale gradually became tinted with red and yellow-hued iron oxides, marking the zone now referred to as the Interior Soil Zone.

As the Rockies continued to rise, the Black Hills pushed sharply upward into an oblong dome 2,400 meters (8,000 feet) high. They were of course immediately attacked by erosion. The uplift gave new life to rivers once clear and placid, turning them into churning torrents heavy with silt and sand. Annual rainfall during the Oligocene Epoch is thought to have been about 130 centimeters (50 inches), with times of flood and times of famine, and long dry spells alternating with monsoon downpours. (Present rainfall averages 40 centimeters or 15.5 inches.) Seasonally flooded rivers filled the earlier valley with sand, gravel, and silt and spread out across the plain thus formed, depositing layers of clayey gray and pink mudstone known now as the Chadron Formation. In marshes bordering the rivers, in shallow lakes, and around seasonal waterholes, animals died and were buried. Some were fossilized.

Many of these animals have modern descendants: frogs, alligators, turtles, tiny three-toed horses, and humpless camels. Others are completely extinct: strange, lumbering titanotheres as large as elephants, and browsing, cud-chewing oreodonts as abundant as the herds of wildebeest that now roam the plains of Africa.

As time went on, volcanic ash began to drift into this region from volcanoes far to windward in the Yellowstone area. As the Brule Formation—more

The Brule Formation's angular ridges and sharp color banding show up especially well near Dillon Pass. Lower rounded ridges are the Chadron Formation. At the very base is the colorful Interior Soil Zone of the Pierre Shale.

mudstone and sandstone — was deposited, increasing amounts of fine ash were incorporated into the sediments. Composed of fine needles and tiny bubbly grains high in silica, the ash strengthened the silt and clay so that now the Brule Formation characteristically stands as steep slopes and sharp ridges. Thin limestone beds were deposited in shallow ponds and lakes, and conditions twice became suitable for the growth of limestone-cemented nodules or concretions. Animal life continued to be abundant. Presumably the climate was mild, plant life was lush, and food was at least seasonally plentiful. Large predators, a saber-toothed cat among them, lived off the plant-eaters and small rodents.

The record of sedimentation and animal life continues into the Miocene Epoch, but Miocene rocks are not widespread in the park area. Most of the known Miocene fossil localities, like Agate Fossil Beds National Monument, are farther south. White, cross-bedded Miocene channel sandstone does cap the highest ridges along the Wall, and blocks of it have tumbled onto the platform of the Cliff Shelf. Miocene rock forms most of the surface of Sheep Mountain Table and Hay Butte. Changes in animal species indicate that the climate was changing too, becoming cooler and drier, and that grassy plains were replacing forests in the western interior.

As broad regional uplift of Miocene–Pliocene time bodily lifted the Rockies 1,600 meters (5,000 feet) above their former position, the balance of power swung again, and erosion played an increased role in shaping the land. In Pleistocene time, the now-stabilized dunes of the upper prairie developed, as well as the sod prairie surfaces, testifying to climatic episodes both drier and wetter than at present.

BEHIND THE SCENES

Cedar Pass and Millard Ridge. "Passes" in the Badlands are roads or trails that ascend or descend the precipitous face of the Wall. Those of the present park road follow routes used by Indians, pioneers, and ranchers — and with good reason, for such routes sought out places where scaling the Wall was made easier by fault zones, landslides, or subtle changes in the rock itself. Here at Cedar Pass, the Wall stairsteps across a large landslide block known as Cliff Shelf.

Millard Ridge, on either side of Cedar Pass, is capped with pebbly channel sandstone and conglomerate of Miocene age, part of the Sharps Formation. This rock is harder and more durable than the rocks below, and probably more resistant than contemporary rocks now eroded off the High Plains surface to the north. A layer of blocky, white volcanic ash about 7 meters (20 feet) above the road marks the base of the formation. Below the blocky ash layer, mudstone of the Brule Formation extends all the way down to the grassy prairie of the valley.

West of Cedar Pass are many small faults fairly easily seen because they offset the horizontal color bands of the Brule Formation. In general, these faults trend northwest-southeast, parallel to the Wall. They may have been caused by shifting and settling of older rock layers beneath, or they may be surface expressions of much deeper crustal movement. Faulting occurred after early Miocene deposits were laid down and before deposition of Pleistocene gravel.

Junipers and other vegetation on the Cliff Shelf enjoy moisture caught and held by the backward-tilting block.

Cliff Shelf. The broken block of rocks that forms the Cliff Shelf was once as high as the main mass of Millard Ridge. Several hundred years ago it slid toward the lower prairie, to a small extent rotating backward as it slid. Movement continues from time to time; more than once the road has settled as the block dropped. Because sliding occurs on a curved faultlike surface, the top of the block now slopes back toward the cliff, forming a small catchment basin where a pond has become established. The basin overflows through several small sinkholes and tunneled channels eroded along fissures. Notice the many fine rills incised in the slope just back of Cliff Shelf. Such shoestring rills, no older than the landslide that bared the cliff, eventually enlarge into rivulets and then into typical badland gullies.

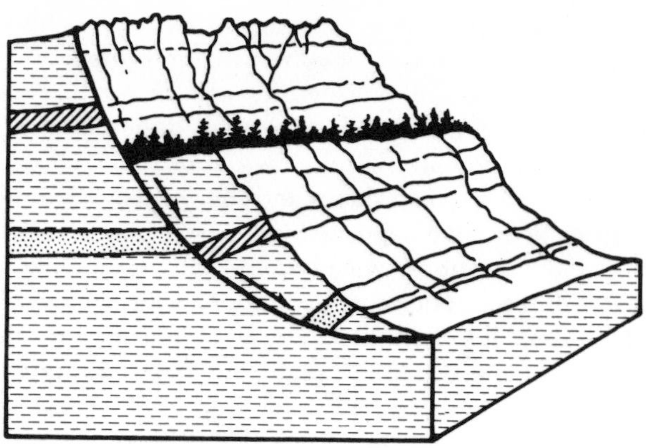

Several sharp peaks rise from the valley floor between Cliff Shelf and the visitor center. They show measurable changes in shape and contour since they were first photographed. Vampire Peak, for instance, lost its two-eared top to a thunderstorm in 1950. Cloudburst erosion is one of the main forces shaping the Badlands.

Scattered blocks of white Miocene sandstone, cross-bedded and pebbly, fell from the top of Millard Cliff and now lie on Cliff Shelf. Diagonal cross-bedding results from deposition by flowing water.

Pointed parapets of the Castle are carved in Miocene sandstone distinguished from underlying Oligocene rocks by its white color and finely divided spires.

Dillon Pass. The area around this pass is the only place in the park where all the pages of the Badlands sedimentary book can be seen at the same time. Formations here are shown on a roadside diagram. The Interior Soil Zone is especially prominent, its red and yellow mounds adding much in the way of color to the normally chalky tan Badlands scene.

Look for faults here; they show up well as offsets in the red and gray layers of the Brule Formation.

Fossil Exhibit. Oligocene turtles and other vertebrate animals that lived about 30 million years ago left their remains here in one of the nodular zones of the Brule Formation. Specimens are exhibited just as they were found, with only the upper surfaces cleaned off. Nearby exhibits describe the fossils and the geologic scene.

Norbeck Pass. At the base of the pass, well defined moats have developed below pleated ridges, and weathering of hard and soft layers has produced a number of "toadstools." Rocks on the highest ridge (flat-topped Norbeck Mesa) are Miocene. Several faults can be seen offsetting color bands of the Brule Formation.

Pinnacles. From Pinnacles Overlook a stormy sea of crisp pinnacles and flat-topped buttes rises above colorful rounded hills of the Chadron and Pierre Formations. Just south of here, Hay Butte is capped with erosion-resisting conglomerate (the same rock you are now standing on), formed along a river that swung across a wide floodplain. In places these deposits contain bones of three-toed horses and other Miocene animals.

Sage Creek. As the road drops into Sage Creek Valley, it crosses easily recognized red and yellow hills of the Interior Soil Zone. In places this ancient soil is 60 meters (200 feet) thick. Such deep weathering requires a humid climate and a long period of stability such as prevailed here in Eocene time. Below the soil zone are unaltered dark gray shales of the Pierre Formation.

Prominent layers of concretions cross the shaly slopes or jut from the high stream bank below the bridge. Plant or animal matter seems frequently to cause concretion growth, and most of these concretions contain fossil shells. Examine those that have fallen and broken, but remember that removing specimens is prohibited; leave what you find for others to enjoy. You may also see small golden pyrite crystals in the Pierre Formation here.

Sheep Mountain Table. Protected by a flat-topped cap of durable Miocene sandstone, this mesa offers superb views of the surrounding badlands, including those in the new southwestern part of the park. The corrugated mesa walls give a cross section of Miocene rock, with the blocky, white ash layer that marks its base. Below it are Oligocene mudstones of the Brule Formation.

Thin chalcedony veins lace these rocks in such abundance that some slopes are covered with a desert pavement composed exclusively of their gray-blue fragments. Chalcedony is a variety of silica deposited in cracks and fissures by groundwater traveling through rocks that contain soluble silica in the form of minute shards of volcanic ash.

The Wall. To many, the Wall *is* the Badlands. In places its plicated ridges rise 80 meters (250 feet) above the lower prairie, 50 meters (150 feet) above the upper prairie. In general, the Wall is composed of Oligocene and Miocene strata. Its intricate drainage pattern, with chevron-shaped ridges and steep, branching gulches, is typical of badland erosion.

Yellow Mounds. These unusual-looking hills are remnants of the thick soil zone developed on an eroded surface of the Pierre Formation, probably in Eocene time. The colors are chemically the same as yellow and red rust, the minerals limonite and hematite. They are produced by oxidation of iron-bearing minerals distributed through the original shale.

OTHER READING

Anonymous. *Badlands National Monument Road Guide.* Badlands Natural History Association Bulletin 4, Interior, South Dakota.

Baker, Charles L. 1951. "How the South Dakota Badland Formation was Made." Proceedings of the South Dakota Academy of Science, vol. 30.

Hauk, Joy Keve. 1969. *The Natural History of Badlands National Monument.* Badlands Natural History Association Bulletin 2, Interior, South Dakota.

Raymond, W. H., and King, R. U. 1976. *Geologic Map of the Badlands National Monument and Vicinity, West-central South Dakota.* U.S. Geological Survey Miscellaneous Investigations Map I-934.

Smith, Kenneth G. 1958. *Erosional Processes and Landforms in Badlands National Monument, South Dakota.* Geological Society of America Bulletin, vol. 69, pp. 975-1008.

Craters of the Moon National Monument

Established: 1924
Size: 216 square kilometers (84 square miles)
Elevation: 1,625 to 2,347 meters (5,330 to 7,699 feet)
Address: Box 29, Arco, Idaho 83213

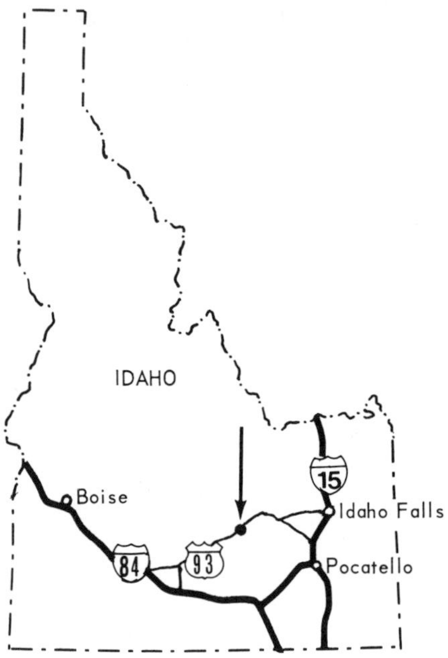

STAR FEATURES

• A world apart—a desolate, dramatic landscape of cinder cones, spatter cones, lava flows, and lava tunnels resulting from a late phase in the eruptions that built the Snake River plain.

• Many small but interesting volcanic features such as lapilli, bombs, and molds of trees that succumbed to volcanic flows.

• A loop road, guided and self-guided walks among varied surface volcanic features and lava tube tunnels, explanatory talks, and a small museum.

SETTING THE STAGE

The greatest flood of volcanic rocks in North America stretches from eastern Oregon and Washington into southern Idaho—the Columbia River and Snake River basalt plateaus, which together cover parts of three states. In the grim moonscape of Craters of the Moon National Monument at the northeast corner of these plateaus, there are vivid scars of quite recent volcanism, a record of the latest eruptions in the broad volcanic field. Smooth cinder cones and rough, uneven spatter cones ranging in age from 15,000 years to about 2,000 years rise above a sea of black lava flows whose ropy folds and jagged, blocky tops are so new that they are not yet mantled in vegetation.

Three kinds of small volcanoes and two kinds of lava flows are represented here, all with counterparts in Hawaii, Iceland, and other volcanic regions.

Cinder cones are steep-sided hills built of small, loose fragments of bubble-filled volcanic rock called scoria. Thrown into the air during early stages of eruption, when the molten rock (magma) is frothy and full of gas, scoria cinders fall on all sides of the volcanic vent. Most of them solidify before they reach the ground. As a cinder cone grows, loose cinders avalanche down both the outside and the inside of the crater, controlling the degree of slope at about 30 degrees. Strong prevailing winds often drive airborne material in one direction, so that the encircling ring of cinders becomes higher on one side than on the other. At times, cinder cones emit fiery fragments that do not solidify in the air but fall still molten to the ground to weld themselves in place. Late in cinder cone development, lava may flow from vents that open on the sides or at the base of the cone.

A double line of cinder cones stretches southeastward from the monument headquarters along two parallel fissures that cut the Snake River Plateau here in the national monument, and mark the so-called Great Rift. In parts of the monument some fissures are still partly open and visible as linear depressions in the lava surface. They show that the land here is still being pulled apart.

Interspersed among the cinder cones and helping to mark the two fissures are lines of spatter cones. Just as their name implies, these cones build up from dribbles and clots of lava that spatter out of volcanic openings and fall to the ground in still molten condition. Their sides are steeper than the slopes of cinder cones because the spatter adheres to itself and shows no tendency to slide. The spatter cones are smaller than most cinder cones, never over about 15 meters (50 feet) high.

NPS photo

A frozen river of lava shows the characteristic shiny surface and ropy texture of a pahoehoe flow. This one is surrounded by aa lava of an older flow.

The line of cinder cones and basalt flows extending south from Fissure Butte lies along the line of the Great Rift.

Shield volcanoes, broad, low lava cones, are less obvious than either cinder or spatter cones, but they occur here also. They are formed by very fluid lava that spills from vents onto an essentially flat surface and flows outward in all directions. Successive layers build a lava-covered surface with the highest points at the vents. Slopes may be only a few degrees, depending on the runniness of the lava. Since some of the lavas in this area were extremely fluid, the angles of slope are quite low.

Several of the small volcanoes here have broken, irregular craters. North Crater is an easily accessible example. As new vents opened up and lava welled forth, moving rivers of molten rock broke away huge pieces of crater wall and rafted them along in sluggish streams. The jagged crater fragments can be seen as craggy turrets projecting well above the rough sea of basalt.

Lava flows of two types were recognized and named by Hawaiian natives long before the advent of geologic studies here. The Hawaiian names—*aa* (pronounced "ah-ah") and *pahoehoe* (pronounced "pa-HO-ay-HO-ay")—have since been adopted as geologic terms. Both types occur here. Pahoehoe lava cools with an undulating, continuous surface that may be wrinkled or ropy. Lavas that form it are very hot; because their outside "skin" cools to plasticity even while the still-molten interior continues to flow, it commonly twists and folds with remarkable pliability. Pahoehoe lava moves rapidly, sometimes faster than a person can run. Often the outer skin thickens and becomes rigid enough to support itself, yet the interior goes on flowing, finally draining out from under the crust and leaving behind an empty lava tunnel. Several such tunnels at Craters of the Moon are ridged inside with high-water marks (actually high-lava marks), narrow benches that register the former positions of a succession of flow surfaces; tunnel ceilings are prickly with lava stalactites that vividly illustrate the fluid condition of the lava as it drained out of the tunnel.

Aa lava, on the other hand, has a rough, rubbly, quite obviously broken surface nearly impossible to walk across. It results from breakup of a thick, hard surface crust on a slow-moving, very thick and pasty lava flow. An aa flow advances at a crawl—only a few meters an hour. Coarse, broken blocks tumble from its steep advancing edge, to be followed by

Spatter cones form as molten lava is splashed from a volcanic vent. Big Cinder Butte, in the background, is an older cinder cone without a summit crater.

NPS photo

more broken blocks, so the flow seems to roll forward on itself like the tread of an armored tank.

The difference between the two types of lava seems to be a matter of temperature, silica content, and dissolved gases. Pahoehoe flows are hotter, less siliceous, and very gaseous; aa flows are cooler, more siliceous, and less gaseous. Both types contain small bubbles of volcanic gas that leave little rounded chambers as the flows solidify. These bubbles, called vesicles, may be pulled out and elongated by lava movement. They are in places so numerous that the rock looks like a sponge. Such rock, called scoria, is quite light in weight—a child can lift a man-sized block!

The blue sheen visible on many of the pahoehoe flows here, especially on Blue Dragon Flow along the Tree Molds Trail, is due to an unusual thin skin of volcanic glass, the very first cooling product formed when hot lava was exposed to air.

Often as cinder cones form the fire fountain throws out fragments larger than cinders, either solid blocks coated with lava or large blobs of thick, sticky lava. These fragments usually cool in the air before striking the ground. They are known as volcanic bombs, and many interesting ones have been found here. Some are shaped like footballs, with twisting ends that solidified as they whirled through the air. Others are long and ribbonlike and may have spun off the ends of the twisted ones. Breadcrust bombs appear to have hardened on the outside while gas bubbles inside were still expanding, so that their skins cracked like breadcrust in a hot oven.

Almost all the volcanic rocks in the national monument are made of basalt. Basalt magma originates 40 kilometers (25 miles) or more below the earth's surface, where heat from the earth's interior is passed upward toward the crust. By and large, the pressure exerted by overlying rocks is great enough to keep material below the crust in an almost solid state, even at temperatures of 1200°C (about 2200°F) or more. So it exists as a pasty, white-hot solid that can still flow just a little, like ice in a glacier or cement that has almost set. Stirred by convection, it circulates sluggishly, rising when heated from below, sinking when cooled from above.

At times some of the rising mantle material reaches a level where its excess heat is just great enough to overcome the effects of the great pressure, and it becomes truly fluid. In such cases it is buoyant, so it tries to rise through the crust. Magma always includes gases of various kinds, water vapor and smelly hydrogen sulphide among them. As it rises, its gases expand, making it even more buoyant. According to one theory, the magma forms a localized hot spot much like a slim but very large candle flame, and continues to rise through the entire thickness of the crust as a magma plume.

Such a plume, proponents of this theory say, exists under Craters of the Moon. Here, along linear fractures caused by the upward thrust of the plume itself, pressure is sometimes released, magma is mobilized, and lava and lava froth spurt from the earth.

GEOLOGIC HISTORY

Most of the volcanic features now visible in the national monument developed within the Holocene or Recent Epoch of geologic time—the last 10,000 years. Some flows near Echo Crater and Crescent Butte are older, as are some of the flows north of the highway near Sunset Cone.

As the "skin" of a pahoehoe flow cools, continued movement of molten lava below may wrinkle and fold it as in this photograph.

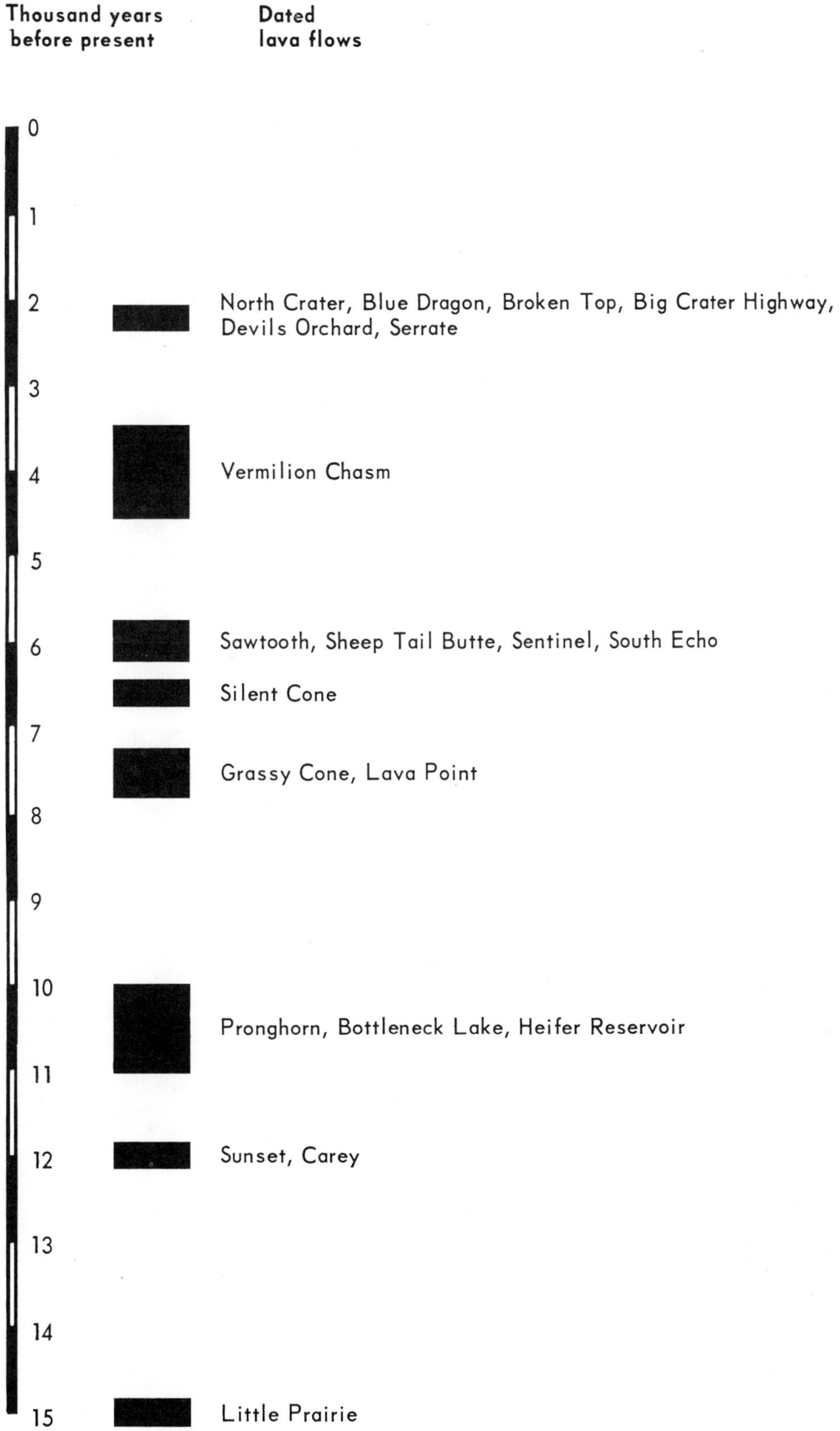

Eruptions at Craters of the Moon occurred during eight periods of activity in the last 15,000 years.

Eruptions began with the opening of the Great Rift across the northwest part of the Snake River Plain, about 15,000 years ago. Along this rift, a series of eruptions built two lines of cinder cones and lava flows that contained fragments of the granitic rocks that underly the area. Most of these flows and cones are gone now, eroded away or covered by newer ones.

After a period of dormancy, new eruptions broke out around 12,000 years ago to form the double chain of cinder cones that survive today—Grassy Cone, Silent Cone, Big Cinder Butte, and the rest. For almost 10,000 years, sporadic eruptions occurred. Sometimes fiery cinders were thrown into the air and fell to earth to form cinder cones. At other times, fluid basalt lava welled out of vents and spread around the cinder cones in black and stormy seas.

The latest eruptions, responsible for all the barren black cinder and lava surfaces now visible in the national monument, took place less than 2,300 years ago. New cones formed; many old ones were reactivated. Vents near Big Crater released flows in four directions. North Crater and Watchman Cone accounted for more. Spatter cones formed along the rift lines. And some of the lava that had earlier engulfed the Great Rift collapsed, so that chains of pitlike craters developed to mark the positions of the fissures. In places, pahoehoe lava surged out from below its own cooling, solidifying skin, leaving behind Needles Cave, Indian Tunnel, and other lava tunnels. The Blue Dragon flow swept rapidly into a forest, engulfing living trees even as it was marked by their seared and falling trunks and branches.

The volcanic field at Craters of the Moon is now dormant, and no eruptions have occurred here for 2,000 years. However, the interval since the last eruption is no longer than the interval between some of the other eruptions, and there is no reason to think that volcanic activity here has ended completely. The next eruption is likely to occur along the Great Rift, as others have done. It will probably be preceded by warning signs such as increasingly frequent small earthquakes, hoarse, low-pitched sounds generated by movement of magma up through the crust, slight tilting of the surface, and the appearance of wisps of

Lava that flowed around a fallen tree shows shrinkage cracks formed as the wood charred. In all likelihood, moisture from the tree helped to cool the lava and preserve the impression of the charred wood.

NPS photo

steam along narrow cracks in the ground. Perhaps you will be here to witness it!

OTHER READING

Anonymous. 1957. *Craters of the Moon National Monument, Idaho.* U.S. Geological Survey topographic map, with text.

Crawford, Vern. 1978. *Craters of the Moon—Life in a Volcanic Landscape.* U.S. National Park Service.

Stearns, Harold T. 1963. *Geology of the Craters of the Moon National Monument, Idaho.* Craters of the Moon Natural History Association, Arco, Idaho.

Devils Tower National Monument

Established: 1906, as the very first national monument
Size: 5 square kilometers (2 square miles)
Elevation: 1,295 meters (4,250 feet) at the visitor center; 1,560 meters (5,117 feet) at the summit of the tower
Address: Devils Tower, Wyoming 82714

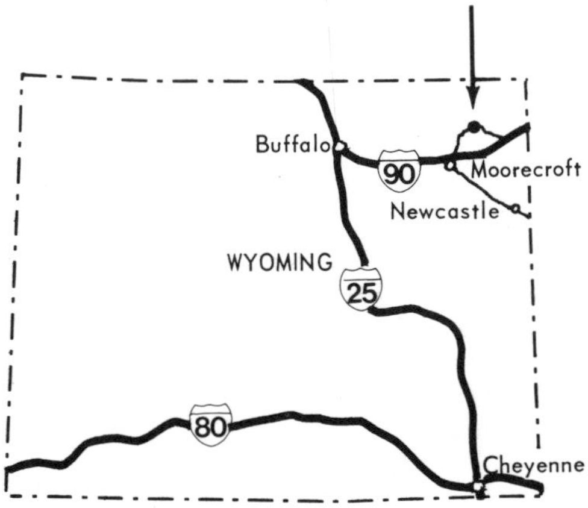

STAR FEATURES

• Devils Tower itself, an enigmatic mass of intrusive igneous rock divided by shrinkage cracks into tall, many-sided columns.

• Soft, easily eroded Mesozoic sedimentary rocks around the base of the tower and along the valley of the Belle Fourche River.

• Visitor center exhibits, trailside displays, and evening talks. The 2-kilometer (1.25-mile) Tower Trail circles the tower, as does the Red Beds Trail, about twice as long but passing through some of the surrounding sedimentary rocks.

See page 32 for additional photograph.

SETTING THE STAGE

Looming like a giant stump above the twisting valley of the Belle Fourche River and the surrounding Wyoming hills, Devils Tower is visible from many kilometers away. Only by coming close to it, though, and looking up at it from below or scrambling among its fallen blocks can one really appreciate its immensity. The tapered columns visible on its flanks are up to 5 meters (15 feet) in diameter, the size of a railroad box car, and they reach 260 meters (865 feet) above the surrounding hills, 390 meters (1,280 feet) above the nearby Belle Fourche River.

The dark gray rock of Devils Tower is an intrusive igneous rock called phonolite porphyry. Phonolite is similar to andesite, composed mostly of feldspar minerals. The "phono" part of its name refers to the musical clank the rock gives off when it is struck with a hammer or another piece of rock. "Porphyry" indicates the texture of the rock, with large, conspicuous crystals of, in this case, white feldspar imbedded in a fine gray groundmass. Little dark green rodlike pyroxene crystals are present also.

Around the base of the tower, below the talus of coarse rock fragments fallen from the tower, red, white, green, and yellow siltstone, sandstone, limestone, and gypsum lie in almost flat layers that dome up slightly toward the tower and then in the last 100 meters (300 feet) or so dip downward toward it, like a broad upside-down saucer with a sag at its center pressed down by the great weight of igneous rock. The sedimentary layers appear on the rolling hills and in the valley of the Belle Fourche River. As you can see, they are much more easily eroded than the hard igneous rock of the tower.

Devils Tower itself reveals an interesting structural pattern. It is not all made up of perfect parallel columns. Its base, rising above the talus of fallen fragments, is a mass of imperfectly formed, twisting columns and bulbous lumps of rock that make a sort of shoulder below the rest of the peak. Joints here are irregular and, in some parts of the shoulder, far apart. Although its composition is the same, the whole nature of the rock seems different, more massive and less structured than the rock above. Up from the shoulder rise the polygonal columns, graceful in their gentle curve, smooth and fairly regular in size. They sweep inward at first and then curve upward, straightening into tapering vertical fluting. Most of

The rock of which Devils Tower is made shows sizeable crystals of white feldspar against a fine gray background.

Jumbled blocks of igneous rock, covered with colorful lichens, make up the talus that surrounds Devils Tower.

Billiant yellow and pink at the top of the Pierre Shale mark the Interior Soil Zone, product of millions of years of weathering.

Pastel tones and rounded landforms identify the Chadron Formation.

"Toadstools" form where resistant layers overlie weak ones. Here a nodular zone protects underlying clay.

Dinosaur National Monument

Near Echo Park, lower slopes of Morgan Formation are topped by high cliffs of Weber Sandstone.

Cliffs of Weber Sandstone, streaked with desert varnish, tower over the confluence of the Green and Yampa Rivers.

John Chronic photo

Layers of sedimentary rock turn up sharply on the north side of Split Mountain Anticline, as seen near Rainbow Park.

Avalanche Creek carved a narrow passage through massive mudstone by whirling boulders and cobbles in a series of potholes. Eventually the potholes joined to make this scenic gorge.

Lincoln Creek's U-shaped valley is seen from the trail over Lincoln Pass between Sperry Chalet and Ellen Wilson Lake. Precambrian metasedimentary rocks wall the valley.

Grinnell Glacier, which feeds Grinnell Falls, is almost hidden by its tan moraine. The white-bordered band of the Purcell sill crosses the Garden Wall just left of Salamander Glacier.

Glacier National Park

Barren moraines and ponds tinted with glacial flour occupy Grinnell Glacier's ice-carved basin. The glacier retreated from this area within the last 100 years.

Sperry Glacier, like most others in this park, is now only a remnant of its former self. Glacier-tinted lakes and barren moraines show its former extent.

Glacier National Park

Avalanche Lake lies below a cirque wall of hard, layered, Precambrian mudstone of the Grinnell Formation. Waterfalls drain Sperry Glacier, out of sight above the cliff.

Crevasses of Grinnell Glacier show up best late in the summer, when the previous winter's snow has melted.

Rocky Mountain National Park

John Chronic photo

Iceberg Lake, shown here as it was in 1949, is now almost dry, probably because ice in its rocky natural dam has slowly melted, allowing lake water to drain through the porous rockpile.

From Bear Lake a trail leads to Dream Lake and beyond. Precambrian granite nearby is marked with glacial striae.

Rocky Mountain National Park

A glaciated valley, its U shape emphasized by clouds, leads to a tiny alpine lake. Trees near timberline seem to hug the ground, with old growth protecting new growth from wintry winds.

There are few volcanic rocks in Rocky Mountain National Park. Those on Specimen Mountain and others near Fall River Pass probably came from volcanoes in the Never Summer Mountains. They are separated from that source now by deep glaciated valleys (left).

Pointed pinnacles near Tower Falls were shaped by wind and rain in coarse breccia and conglomerate of the Absaroka Volcanic Series. A basalt flow above them displays fine columnar jointing caused by shrinkage during cooling.

For more than 100 years, Riverside Geyser has angled its plume over the Firehole River. Eruption through a small vent near the river usually precedes the main display.

A hot spring lines its pool with satiny sinter. Its blue depths contrast with the orange of algae along the rim.

Fountain Paint Pots vary with the season. The mud is thin and watery in spring, thick in late summer.

This hot spring first appeared in May 1978, 15 months before this photograph was taken.

Many fossil trees on Specimen Ridge are still in upright position. Several successive forests are superimposed.

the columns are five- or six-sided; some have four or even seven sides. A short distance below the summit they are cut into small blocks by cross-fractures. There, some columns converge and unite with their neighbors, and the joints become wavier and less regular. The summit of the tower is almost flat.

Columnar jointing such as you see here occurs because molten rock material shrinks and contracts as it cools and solidifies. This type of jointing seems to demand some very special conditions, as not all igneous rock fractures in this way, but what these conditions are is an intriguing and unsolved puzzle. Columnar jointing is fairly common in basalt lava flows, less common in intrusive sills. In terms of the diameter and length of its columns and its remarkable prominence as an erosional remnant, Devils Tower is surely unique.

Talus around the base of the tower consists of immense polygonal blocks, often broken as they tumbled from the tower. A walk on Tower Trail will take you among them. You may be startled to see blocks as large as trucks or boxcars that appear to have fallen gently in the forest without harming the trees—a seemingly remarkable feat until you remember that the rocks fell first and the trees grew later. Older talus, with blocks heavily lichen-covered and interspersed with soil and vegetation, is distinct from younger talus, which shows little lichen or soil development. No columns have fallen in historic time.

GEOLOGIC HISTORY

Precambrian intrusive and metamorphic rocks and Paleozoic marine sedimentary rocks are known in the nearby Black Hills, but none of them surface within this national monument. So we will start our geologic history in Mesozoic time, when the oldest rocks now exposed here were deposited. If you are interested, the older history of this region is given in the chapter on Wind Cave National Park.

Mesozoic Era. During the first half of Mesozoic time, about 225 to 150 million years ago, around 100 meters (300 to 400 feet) of colorful red, white, gray, and gray-green sedimentary rocks were deposited here on floodplains and deltas and along low-lying shores. Because of fluctuations in sea level, deposition alternated with erosion, so marked erosional unconformities—surfaces of erosion or nondeposition—separate some layers. In Triassic time, 225 to 195 million years ago, brick red sandstone and dark maroon siltstone layers accumulated, and gypsum and salt (the latter later removed by solution) were at times deposited as sea water evaporated in shallow bays. Together the sandstone, siltstone, and gypsum make up the Spearfish Formation, usually a slope former but exposed in cliffs and steep-walled gullies where the Belle Fourche River has since cut down rapidly near Devils Tower.

A prominent white ledge of gypsum separates red rocks of the Spearfish Formation from gray, yellow, and gray-green shale and sandstone and limestone of the Sundance Formation. Changing environments in Jurassic time, 195 to 136 million years ago, are responsible for the contrast between these units. Spearfish sediments are red because of oxidation of iron minerals; Sundance rocks are greenish because they were deposited in low-oxygen environments such as marshes or swamps, where the same iron minerals were not able to combine with oxygen.

At localities outside the national monument, thick, tan Lakota Sandstone, also Jurassic in age, lies above the Sundance Formation. The Lakota Sandstone was surely present within the monument area when Devils Tower igneous rock appeared on the scene. A few isolated blocks of hard white quartzite found in two small patches just north of Devils Tower are believed to be baked remnants of this formation.

In Cretaceous time, 136 to 65 million years ago, this region was alternately below and above the sea. Thick layers of marine sediments were deposited here. Late in Cretaceous time the sea withdrew, for all the western part of the continent was beginning to bow upward, affected by new pressures caused by westward drift of the North American Plate as it broke away from Europe and began to ride out over the Pacific Plate.

Cenozoic Era. Early in Cenozoic time these pressures climaxed, creating the Rocky Mountains, well west of Devils Tower, and the Black Hills a short

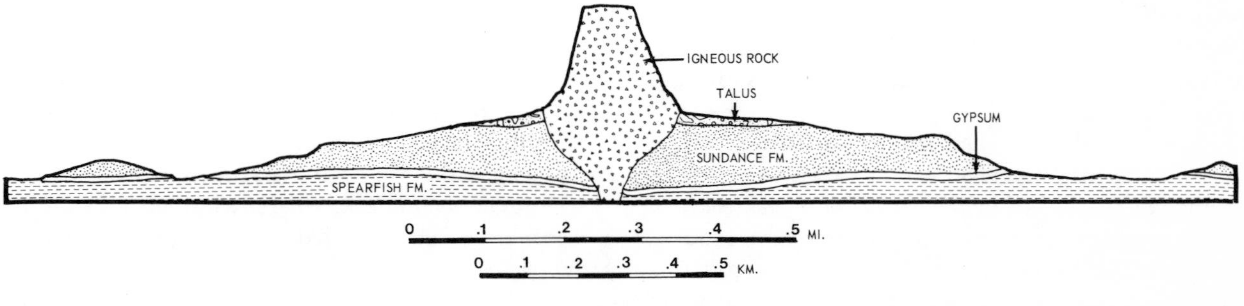

distance to the east. In the throes of this mountain-building, molten magma welled up in scattered localities, often erupting onto the surface, often unable to break through overlying layers of sedimentary rock. Among the igneous masses was that which slowly cooled and crystallized into the phonolite porphyry of Devils Tower.

Many geologists have considered Devils Tower only a remnant of a very thick and once much more extensive sill, an intrusion that spread out between layers of sedimentary rock, or as part of an equally extensive laccolith that domed up overlying rock layers. They visualized the sill or laccolith as extending to and including Missouri Buttes, two less prominent but otherwise similar igneous masses about 6 kilometers (4 miles) north of Devils Tower. A few geologists believed that the tower was a volcanic neck, the conduit of a volcano, albeit of unusual shape and structure. Geologists who studied it agreed that as it formed it was completely covered by layers of rock now removed by erosion, but there has been no real agreement concerning its mode of origin.

Re-examination of Devils Tower and Missouri Buttes within the last few decades has introduced some new ideas. The small amount of talus around the tower and around Missouri Buttes is taken as an indication that the original igneous mass, or masses, were never very much larger than they are today. The similarity of the rocks at Missouri Buttes and those of Devils Tower is interpreted as indicating that these structures, although they arose separately, drew on molten rock from a single large magma chamber far underground. An oil well drilled northwest of Devils Tower, southwest of Missouri Buttes, struck similar rock about 1,400 feet below their known bases, perhaps another manifestation of a common magma chamber. The tower is here, but its story remains an enigma.

Downcutting by the Belle Fourche River contributed greatly to erosion of the sedimentary rock layers around Devils Tower, making it far more prominent than Missouri Buttes, which are away from the river. Weathering and erosion of the tower appear to have been a two-stage process, with the summit of the tower—its uppermost 50 meters or so—being for a long time the only portion exposed. Because of that long exposure, the upper part is far more deeply weathered, with transverse cracks or joints much more prominent than on portions lower down. What caused this two-stage process we can only guess. Perhaps it had something to do with times of immense downcutting by swollen Ice Age streams. Or perhaps downward erosion was for a time delayed by some particularly resistant sandstone layer, or by lava flows from some forgotten volcano. There is even the possibility that the uppermost parts of the columns had more transverse joints to begin with, inviting easier destruction by water, weather, and time.

As the latest cycle of erosion bared the lower part of the tower, coarse, rocky talus developed around its base. With the Belle Fourche River cutting rapidly through soft sedimentary layers, in some places undermining the area just adjacent to the tower, parts of this talus often became landslides, mixing with blocks of sedimentary rock and sliding down toward the river. Continuing differential erosion, removing soft sedimentary rocks and leaving hard igneous rock, made Devils Tower what it is today.

OTHER READING

Anonymous. 1949. *Geologic Map and Section of Devils Tower National Monument, Wyoming.* U.S. Geological Survey.

Dutton, C. E., and Schwartz, G. M. 1936. "Notes on the Jointing of the Devil's Tower, Wyoming. *Journal of Geology,* vol. 44, no. 6, pp. 717–728.

Robinson, Charles S. 1954. *Geology of Devils Tower National Monument, Wyoming.* Devils Tower Natural History Association (originally published as U.S. Geological Survey Bulletin 1021-I).

Dinosaur National Monument

Established: 1915
Size: 854 square kilometers (330 square miles)
Elevation: 1,442 to 2,745 meters (4,730 to 9,005 feet)
Address: Box 210, Dinosaur, Colorado 81610

STAR FEATURES

• A graveyard of the past, a rich dinosaur quarry within a protective exhibit building where visitors can watch as bones are excavated and prepared for study. Portions of more than 300 dinosaurs have been found here.

• Scenic canyons of the Green and Yampa Rivers, unusual in that they cut through the Uinta Mountain uplift rather than flow around it, the easier course.

• Sedimentary, structural, and erosional features clearly exposed because of the arid climate.

• Dramatic Echo Park, where two rivers join amid a setting of steep-walled buttes and confined canyons.

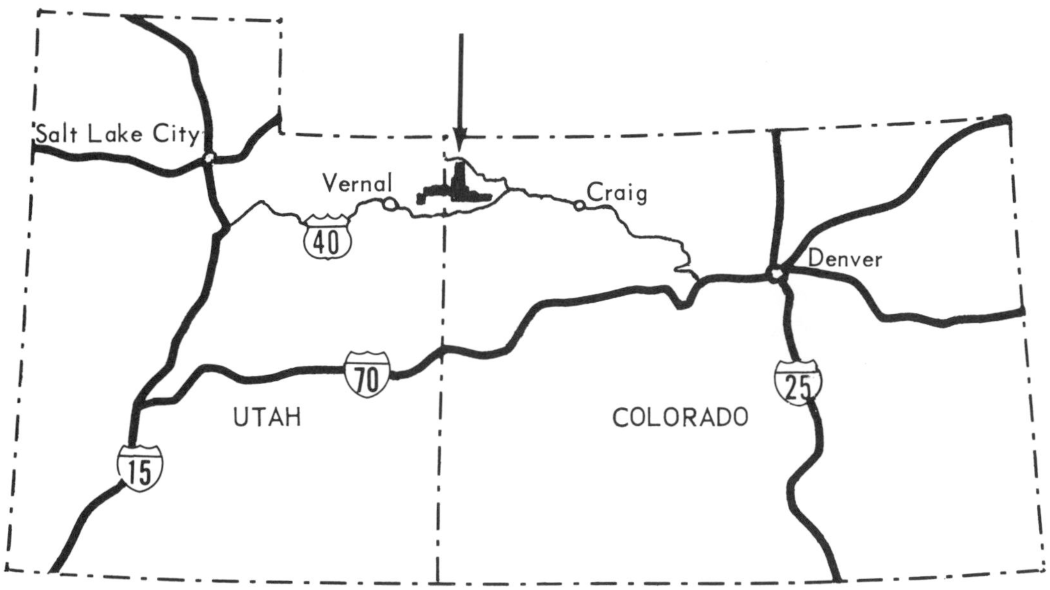

• An interpretive program that includes the Dinosaur Quarry Visitor Center, naturalist talks and walks, slide shows, self-guided nature trails, and trail and roadside exhibits.

See color pages for additional photographs.

SETTING THE STAGE

The canyon country where the Green and Yampa Rivers join is a rugged wonderland of pink and red sedimentary rock, an intricately eroded, almost inaccessible world little influenced by man. Because average annual precipitation is only 23 centimeters (9 inches), vegetation is thin, and the rocks of this monument and the geologic structure of the Uinta Mountains are well displayed. Several impressive anticlines and synclines show up in the layered rocks. They, as well as a series of east-west faults, determine the shape of the Yampa Plateau and the Uinta Mountains. The oldest rocks are exposed in the walls of the Canyon of Lodore, bared by the Green River's downcutting. Successively younger rocks appear on the canyon rims and the flanks of the uplift.

Pennsylvanian Weber Sandstone and redbeds of the Triassic Chinle Formation arch across Split Mountain Anticline.

W. R. Hansen photo, courtesy of USGS

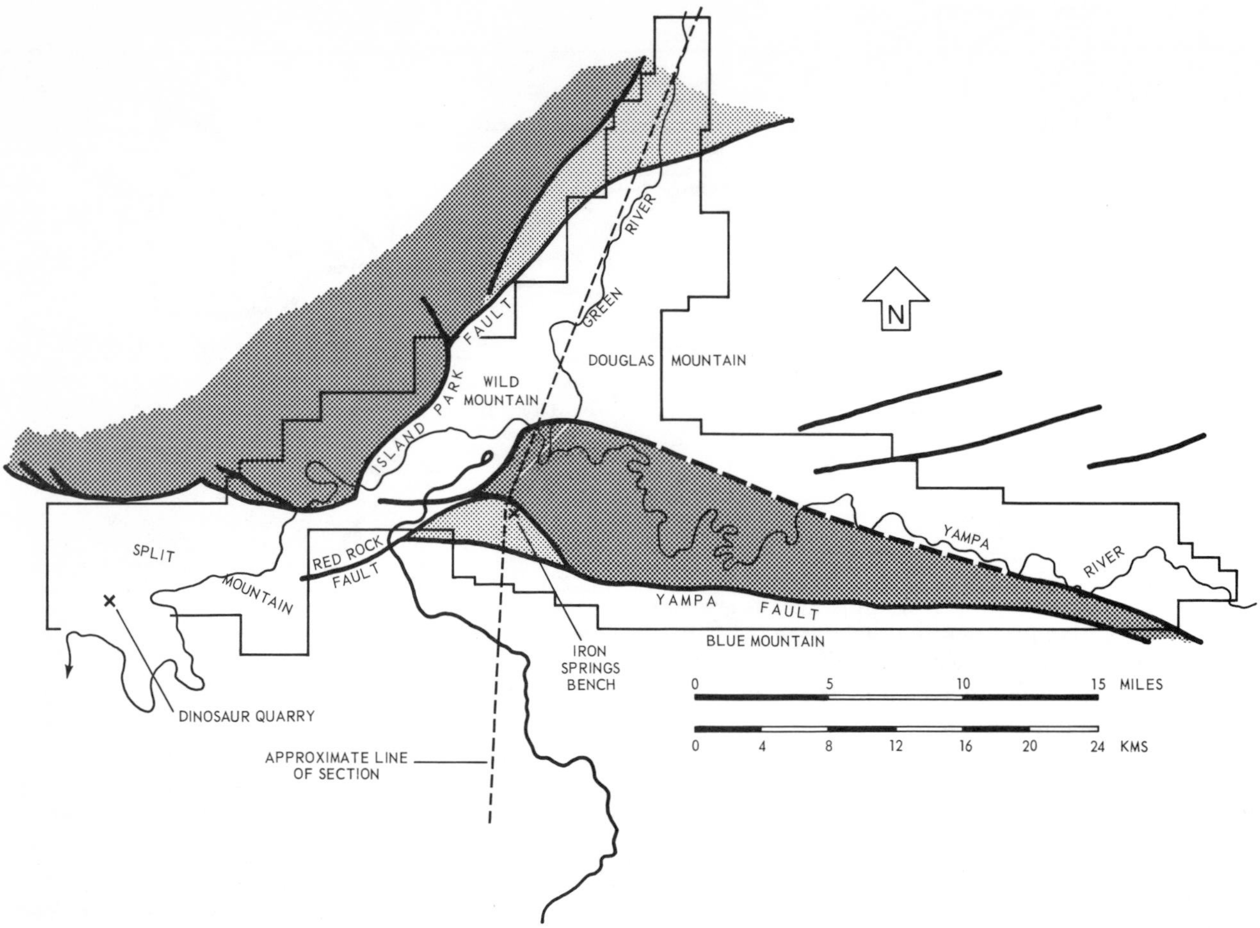

Curving faults outline the geologic structure of the east end of the Uinta Mountains. Down-dropped blocks are shaded.

What brought about the impressive scenery of this monument? And why do the Green and Yampa Rivers come together in the middle of a mountain range? There are a number of contributing factors:

- Many layers of sedimentary rock, some young and not very well consolidated, some far older and hardened into metasedimentary rocks.
- Development of the Uinta Mountains, an east-west range that consists of a single large anticline faulted along both edges and down its center as well, with the central block dropped 600 meters (2,000 feet) or more as a fault-edged graben.
- Almost complete burial of the eastern half of the Uinta Range early in Tertiary time, 65 to about 50 or 40 million years ago, by a thick blanket of silt, sand, and gravel.
- Development of two sinuous rivers across the nearly level surface of this sedimentary mantle.
- Regional uplift of all of Colorado and large parts of adjoining states fairly late in Tertiary time.

Let us see how these factors fit into the history of this area.

GEOLOGIC HISTORY

Precambrian Era. The story begins more than a billion years ago when sand, mud, and limestone layers were deposited in a sea-filled basin that stretched far north into Canada and south to Arizona. Time has hardened those sediments and colored them a deep red by gradually oxidizing iron-rich minerals within them. They are now the quartzite, slaty shale, and marble of the Uinta Mountain Group. They form the central core of the Uinta Mountains and appear in the walls of the Canyon of Lodore and in a few small, deep side canyons along the north edge of the Yampa Plateau. Though life existed when they were deposited, no fossils have ever been found in them here. In Glacier and Grand Canyon National Parks, corresponding rocks contain telltale remains of primitive algae and sponges, and imprints of jellyfish.

Paleozoic Era. Fossil-bearing sedimentary rocks of Paleozoic age tell us that this area was repeatedly flooded by shallow seas and that it rose above sea

Precambrian rocks in the Canyon of Lodore are still recognizable as sandstone, siltstone, and conglomerate. These old metasedimentary rocks extend from Canada to Arizona. They are well exposed in Glacier National Park.

level for some time late in the era. Particularly applicable to the monument story are changes that took place in Pennsylvanian time, 320 to 280 million years ago, when a pattern of rising and falling sea level left deposits of alternating sandstone and limestone layers. These gave way later to a pattern of coastal sand dunes edging a western sea. The sandstone–limestone sequence is now known as the Morgan Formation; the dunes have become the Weber Sandstone, cross-bedded pink and buff-colored rock whose barren slopes are so spectacular along the Yampa Plateau and in Yampa Canyon and parts of the Green River canyons. Its rounded, frosted, even-sized grains and large-scale cross bedding assure us that it is a wind-blown or eolian sandstone.

Mesozoic Era. This era began with a new note—emergence of the land and an environment that alternated between lush, humid tropical jungles, dry deserts of drifting sand, and short incursions of the sea. During this era the region was low and much nearer to the equator than it is now. Red Triassic sandstone and siltstone, pebbly conglomerate, and limy mud were deposited on a low plain where lakes, ponds, and slow-flowing rivers were bordered with vegetation. Some of the rocks contain petrified wood and fossil animal footprints.

During late Triassic and early Jurassic time, desert conditions predominated, probably because the newborn Sierra Nevada far to the west and other new mountains in central Utah were beginning to cut off moisture-bearing winds from the Pacific, as they do today. An incredible quantity of wind-blown sand came to rest here; this arid inland basin must have resembled parts of the present Arabian desert. Tan and pink, fine-grained, cross-bedded sandstone layers now stretch from western Colorado clear to Zion National Park in southern Utah. Though stream and beach deposits are often cross-bedded too, the particularly large cross-bedding in these sandstones and their rounded, pitted, uniform grains identify them as dune sands. Horizontally bedded sandstone and mudstone containing fossils of marine shellfish, evidence of brief incursions of the sea, separate several formations of dune sand.

Late in Jurassic time a rainbow-colored sequence of sandstone, conglomerate, shale, and freshwater limestone was deposited over an equally broad region, a widespreading floodplain at times studded with short-lived, shallow lakes. And in these sediments, now the Morrison Formation, the dinosaur bones of this national monument were deposited and preserved.

Though dinosaurs in abundance have been found at only one site within this monument, in tilted layers on the south side of Split Mountain, they have been unearthed from the same formation at other far-flung localities in Utah and Colorado. The giant reptiles, as well as some of their small relatives, may have perished during seasonal floods that swept across the featureless land.

In Cretaceous time seas swept this area again, coming this time from the east and southeast. Layers of beach sand, lagoon shale and coal, and marine shale overlie the Morrison and its buried dinosaurs. Many fossil shellfish have been found in the thick marine shale: oysters, a variety of snails and clams, and beautiful ammonites, relatives of the octopus and the chambered nautilus. Cretaceous rocks now edge the Uinta uplift and make narrow, upturned hogback ridges outlining the mountain front.

Cenozoic Era. Shortly after the end of the Mesozoic Era, mountain building that had started in the west with the Sierra Nevada and the Utah ranges crept eastward, forcing the sea to withdraw from the center of the continent. About 65 million years ago the Rocky Mountains (including the Uinta Mountains) began to push upward, isolating a spacious interior basin. Erosion of these mountains contributed thousands of meters of sedimentary waste to this basin, enough cobbles, gravel, sand, and lake sediments thick with volcanic ash to cover all but the highest peaks of the Uinta Range.

As time went on, two rivers established courses across the plain of Tertiary sediment. The ancestor of the Green River flowed east for a time into Mississippi drainage, but was diverted by continued rising of the Rockies and headward erosion of a smaller stream in the Uintas, so that it now flows south as a tributary of the Colorado River. The Yampa River developed as a tributary of the Green. Both rivers found going pretty easy on the featureless blanket of Tertiary sediment, and they swung about lazily in looping meanders.

Strengthened by widespread uplift in Miocene and Pliocene time, the rivers finally began to carve down into the thick sediments, still following snakelike meanders inherited from their leisurely past. As they eroded more deeply, they eventually reached the buried mountains. Since by then they were completely imprisoned in valleys of their own making, they had to continue to carve on down into the hard rocks of the Uintas. In the last 12 million years they have lowered their beds at least 600 meters (2,000 feet), retaining their former bends as incised meanders, keeping staunchly to their courses despite the hard Precambrian rock that cores the Uinta uplift. Meantime, their tributaries cleaned away surrounding Tertiary sediments, leaving just a few remnants to remind us that these sands and gravels had at one time covered most of the range.

Pleistocene climate changes that brought glaciation to North America and Europe scarcely touched this area, though valley glaciers developed in the western part of the Uintas. Heavy Ice Age rains, coupled with melting from the glaciers, must have increased the volume of the rivers, speeding up the canyon-cutting process by contributing meltwater and broken rock and sand, an abrasive combination.

BEHIND THE SCENES

Canyon of Lodore. Named by geologist John Wesley Powell during his venturesome first trip down the unexplored Green and Colorado Rivers in 1869, this canyon cuts deeply into the core of the Uintas. It begins at Browns Park, where the youngest rocks in the monument, the Browns Park Formation, lie next to the oldest, Precambrian quartzite of the Uinta Mountain Group. Hard red quartzite walls most of the canyon. Altogether there are about 6,000 meters (20,000 feet) of this ancient rock which, with overlying younger sedimentary strata, represents a time span of nearly a billion years.

Above the Precambrian rocks, visible from Harpers Corner or along the river downstream from Limestone Draw (whose name foretells a change in rock type), are Cambrian sandstone layers. They are separated from the Precambrian rocks by an unconformity, a break in sedimentary sequence between rocks deposited late in Precambrian time and those deposited in Cambrian time. This break represents a time of erosion rather than deposition — many millions of years of uplift and bending and folding and beveling before Cambrian seas crept across the region. And above the Cambrian layers, above another but less profound unconformity, Mississippian limestone forms narrow bands of stepped gray cliffs. Where the Green and Yampa Rivers come together, both flow below cross-bedded, wind-deposited sandstone of the Pennsylvanian Weber Formation.

Dinosaur Quarry. Here, fossil dinosaur bones lie in sandstone layers in the Morrison Formation, a colorful shale and sandstone sequence deposited in

Stegosaurus *greets visitors at the Dinosaur Quarry.*

Jurassic time, around 160 or 170 million years ago, long before development of the Uinta Mountains. The rocks tell us of a broad floodplain with abundant vegetation bordering branching and usually sluggish streams. Plant-eating dinosaurs feasted on the rich vegetation, and meat-eaters preyed upon their fellows. As streams shifted, flooded, and shifted again, some of the dinosaurs perished and were buried in the shifting channel sand. Probably their bodies were washed and tangled and even broken apart by stream currents before they came to rest in shallow bends and bars. The sand that buried them is now sandstone, the bones are fossilized by gradual cell-by-cell addition of silica, and both sandstone and fossils are tipped up steeply at the edge of the Split Mountain anticline.

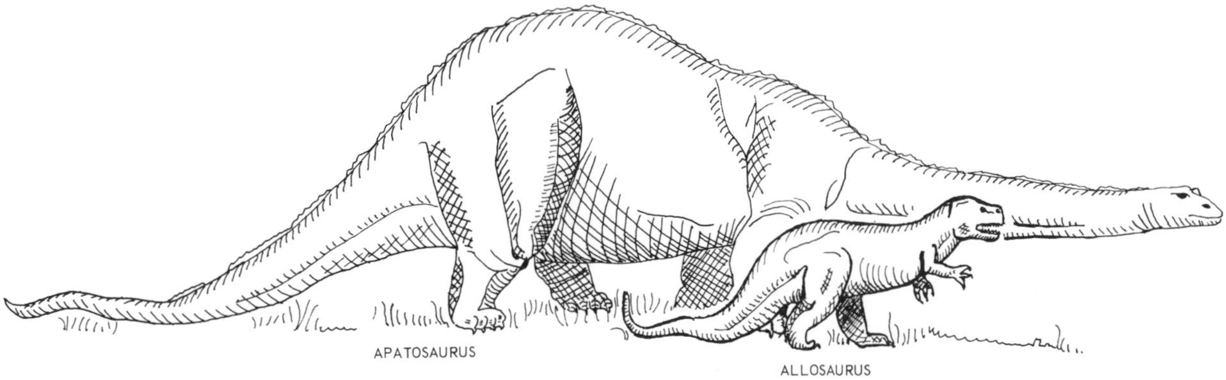

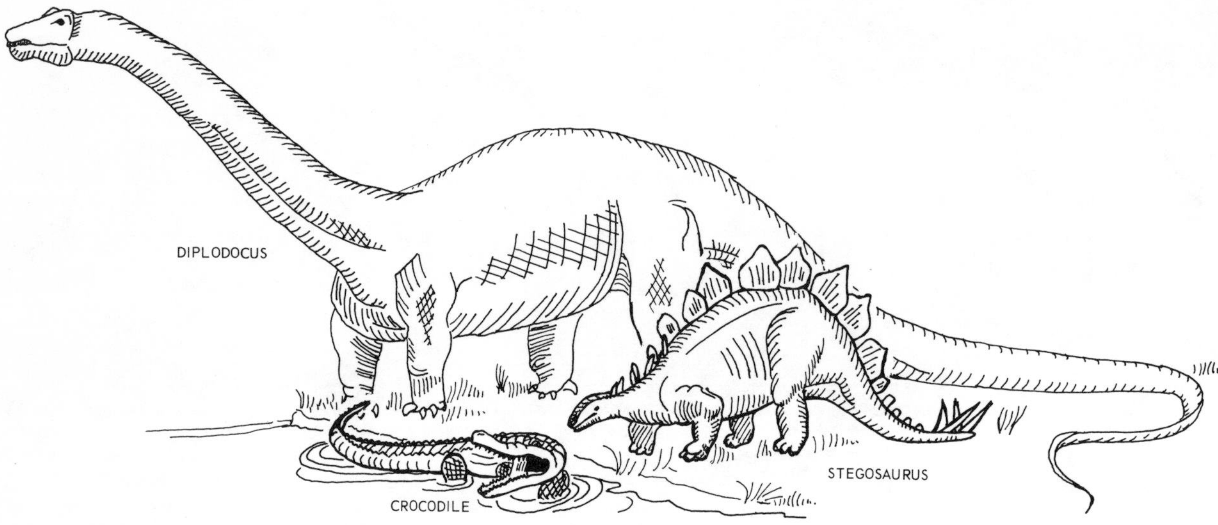

More than 20 complete dinosaur skeletons, as well as many incomplete ones, have come from this quarry since its discovery in 1909. They represent 12 species of dinosaurs, including *Apatosaurus, Diplodocus, Brachiosaurus, Stegosaurus,* and others whose names are even less familiar. Fossil turtles, crocodiles, frogs, and freshwater clams occur here too.

Excavating fossil bones involves careful cleaning of their upper surfaces, painting them with penetrating varnish that strengthens and protects them, and coating them with thick layers of burlap dipped in plaster of paris. After the plaster hardens, rock beneath the bones is carefully removed, the plaster-and-bone block is turned over, and the same treatment is applied to the undersurface. Entire skeletons and hundreds of individual bones were completely removed in this way from this site and shipped to museums to be chiseled out of their plaster casts and studied or exhibited.

Bones are no longer being taken from this quarry. Instead, they are being cleaned off as far as possible and soaked with preserving varnish, so that now they stand out in bold relief from surrounding rock. In this way they give monument visitors insight into some geologic methods as well as a view of a remote page of the geologic story.

Echo Park. Whether you see it from above, from viewpoints along the road to Harpers Corner, or from river level, Echo Park holds special fascination. Steamboat Rock's sharp, jutting prow dominates the confluence of the two rivers. The great rock is part of the Yampa Canyon graben, a large east-west trending fault block dropped down between the Mitten fault (which crosses the Green River just north of Steamboat Rock) and the Yampa fault (which edges Blue Mountain and the Yampa Plateau). A smaller fault block, dropped only half as far, creates the stairstep of Iron Springs Bench between Echo Park and the south canyon rim. The road to Echo Park takes advantage of the break in the cliffs along the Yampa fault, and of the stairstep level provided by Iron Springs Bench, to reach the bottom of the canyon.

Pink and peach-colored cliffs surrounding Echo Park reveal wide sand-dune style cross-bedding in the Weber Sandstone. The same formation occurs on the summit of Blue Mountain, 1,000 meters (about 3,000 feet) higher than the rivers near their confluence.

Many rocky cliffs in this area are thinly coated with dark iron and manganese minerals drawn to the surface of the rock by thousands of years of desert sun and occasional moisture. Prehistoric Indians occasionally chipped through this desert varnish to the light-colored rock beneath, engraving long-lasting petroglyphs.

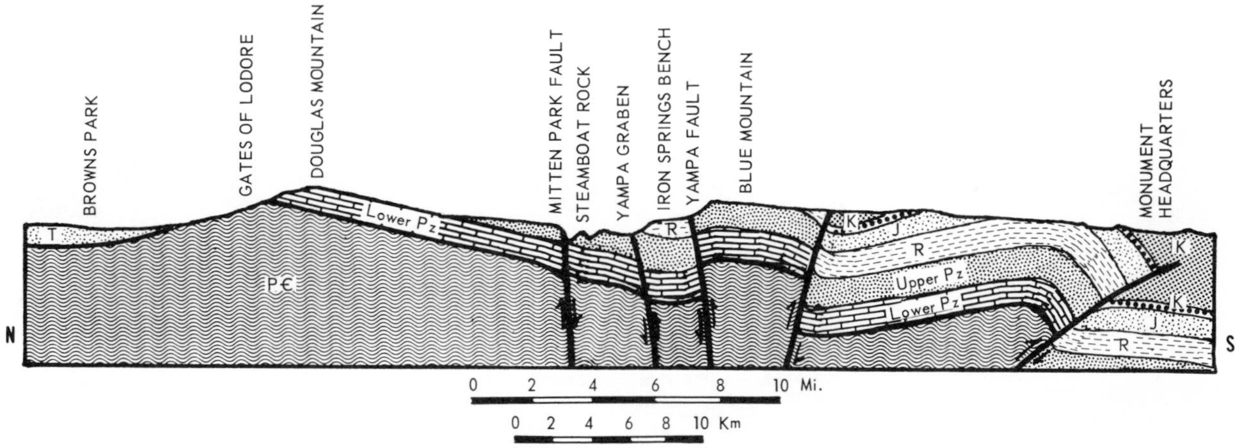

The nature of the faulted anticline of the Yampa Plateau shows up on this cross section from the Gates of Lodore to the Monument headquarters. The vertical scale is exaggerated.

Harpers Corner. The road to Harpers Corner, in the Colorado portion of the monument, passes through a rock sequence that spans 250 million years of geologic time. Starting in Cretaceous rocks near Highway 40, it encounters successively lower, older strata of Cretaceous and Jurassic age. Beyond Mud Springs Draw the road is bordered by cross-bedded pink and buff Weber Sandstone, laid down in drifting dunes of an ancient desert. This formation is the most distinctive one in the monument. Its sweeping slopes, almost devoid of soil and vegetation, are in places capped with patches of red conglomerate and sandstone and white volcanic ash of the Browns Park Formation, at only 20 million years old, the youngest geologic unit in the monument.

Near the south monument boundary, the road crosses the Yampa fault. Cliffs that edge the Yampa Plateau mark its position. Rocks south of the fault, on Blue Mountain, are at water's edge near the Green and Yampa Rivers' confluence.

Viewpoints look out over the rocky wonderland of the Yampa Canyon graben, down-faulted between the Yampa fault on the south and Mitten Park fault on the north and west. Twisting, incised meanders of the Yampa River can be seen, as can the lower end of the Canyon of Lodore along the Green River. Iron Springs Bench, the level area south of and above Echo Park, is a smaller fault block that dropped only about half as far as the rest of the graben.

Just beyond Iron Springs Bench Overlook, the road rises onto Harpers Plateau, climbing up across the sharp south edge, which marks the position of the Mitten fault. That fault cuts north of Steamboat Rock and swings east to edge the north rim of Yampa Canyon graben.

Harpers Corner offers splendid views east along the graben, north to the Canyon of Lodore, and west to Whirlpool Canyon, Island Park, and Split Mountain. It is surfaced with small patches of Tertiary gravel and sand deposited before canyon cutting began.

Island and Rainbow Parks. Accessible only by river or rough dirt road, this open region is in a graben northwest of Island Park fault. Rocks which floor it are much younger than those in the canyon slopes across the river, on the upthrown side of the fault. Colored shales that give Rainbow Park its name are parts of the Morrison Formation, the same rock unit that contains the Dinosaur Quarry. Free here of confining canyon walls, the Green River braids its way around a large bend probably similar to meanders originally formed on the blanket of Tertiary sediment.

Split Mountain and Split Mountain Canyon. As one of the anticlines fringing the south side of the

W. B. Cashion photo, courtesy of USGS

Deeply incised meanders of the Yampa River date back to a time when the river wound across a wide lowland plain of Tertiary sand, silt, and gravel, most of it washed from the Rocky Mountain ranges to the east.

Uinta Range, Split Mountain displays arched layers of sedimentary rock that range in age from Mississippian in the depths of Split Mountain Canyon to Cretaceous in hogbacks that border the mountain itself. Split Mountain is oval-shaped, long in the east-west direction, and "split" diagonally by the Green River as it adheres to a course established in Miocene time. Its tributaries, revitalized by uplift and swollen by Ice Age storms, cleared away loose Tertiary sand and gravel that had completely concealed the surrounding highlands. The south side of Split Mountain and the mouth of its canyon can be seen from the campground; river-runners see both sides of the anticline.

Yampa Canyon. Good views of the Yampa region can be had from the Round Top fire lookout on Blue Mountain and from viewpoints on the road to Harpers Corner. Inner parts of the canyon are accessible by river or, in dry weather, by rough dirt roads.

The Yampa is bordered on its trip through the national monument by Pennsylvanian rocks belonging to the Morgan and Weber Formations. The Morgan is a series of flat-bedded sandstone and limestone layers, some of them red. It is a marine deposit and contains fossil shellfish. The Weber Sandstone walls much of the river's narrow inner canyon, in places overhanging the water as pink cliffs marked with dark swaths of desert varnish. The river follows a twisting, canyon-confined course through meanders inherited from Tertiary time.

OTHER READING

Hagood, Allen. 1971. *Dinosaur, the Story Behind the Scenery.* KC Publications, Las Vegas, Nevada.

Powell, John Wesley. 1875. *Exploration of the Colorado River of the West and its Tributaries.* U.S. Government Printing Office, Washington, D.C.

Powell, John Wesley. 1876. *Report on the Geology of the Eastern Portion of the Uinta Mountains and a Region of Country Adjacent Thereto.* U.S. Geologic and Geographical Surveys of the Territories.

Florissant Fossil Beds National Monument

Established: 1969
Size: 24 square kilometers (9 square miles)
Elevation: 2,530 meters (8,300 feet) at visitor center
Address: Box 185, Florissant, Colorado 80816

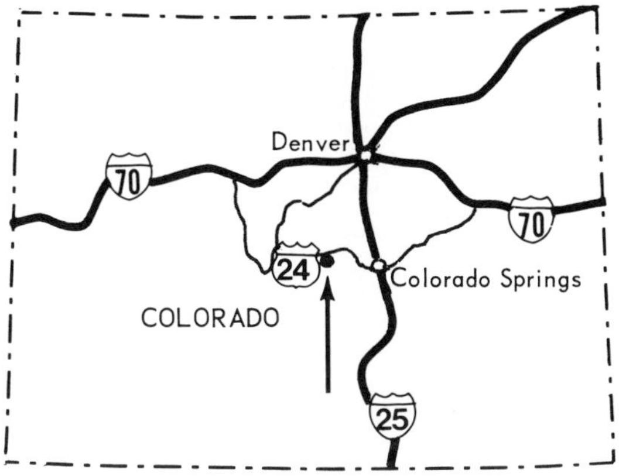

STAR FEATURES

• A fossil forest preserved in volcanic ash. Stumps of large sequoias and many other trees still stand where they grew 35 million years ago.

• Thin-bedded layers of volcanic ash that retain flattened, carbonized remains of thousands of insects and impressions of many leaves, from which fascinating details of the region's history can be gleaned.

• An interpretive program with museum exhibits, naturalist talks, trail leaflets, and explanatory trailside signs.

SETTING THE STAGE

On the rolling granite upland that reaches westward from Pikes Peak, hills of fine, light gray shale tell the story of a volcanic catastrophe. Surrounded on all sides by coarse pink granite similar to that on Pikes Peak, the fine shale seems strangely out of place. In its thin layers, moreover, are impressions of tree leaves of warm-climate woodlands not at all like the cold-climate forests that grow here now. And

F. M. Brown photos

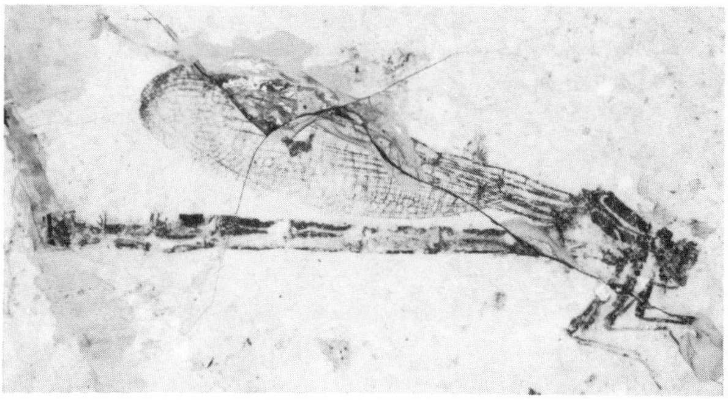

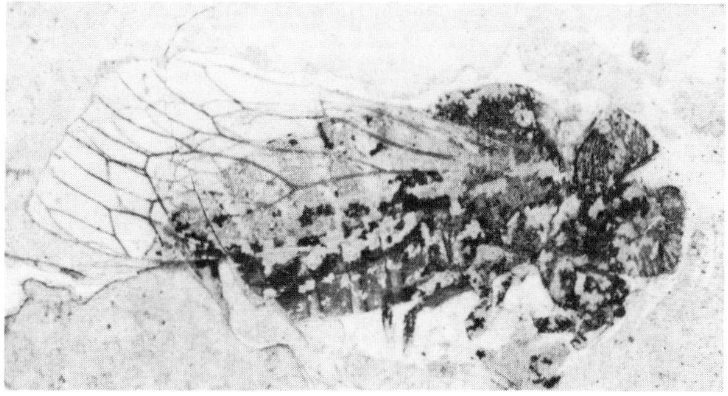

Delicately preserved in fine volcanic ash, a dragonfly, cicada, lacewing, and long-horned beetle give us insight into a past environment: a warm, moist lowland with abundant insect life.

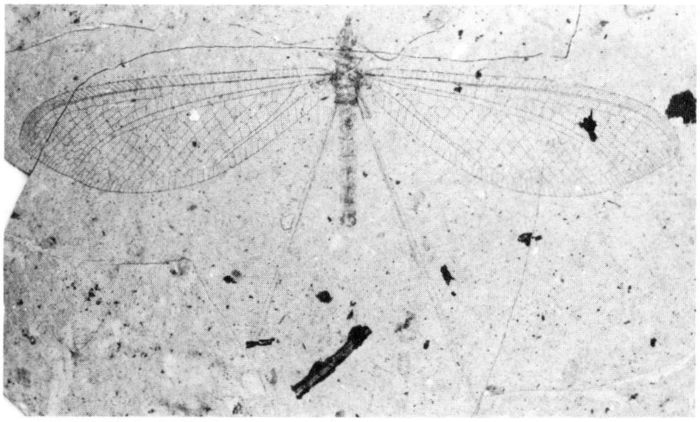

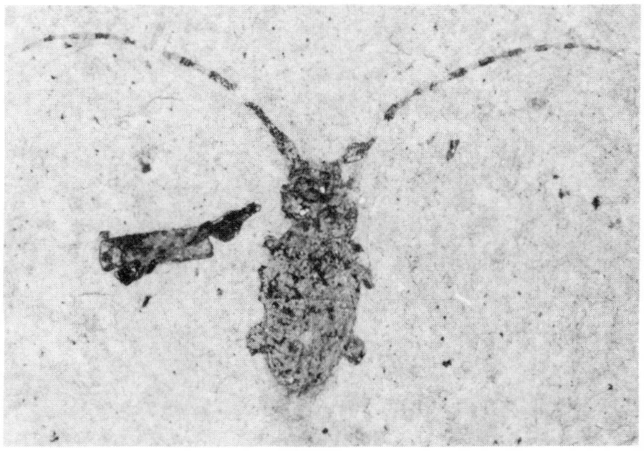

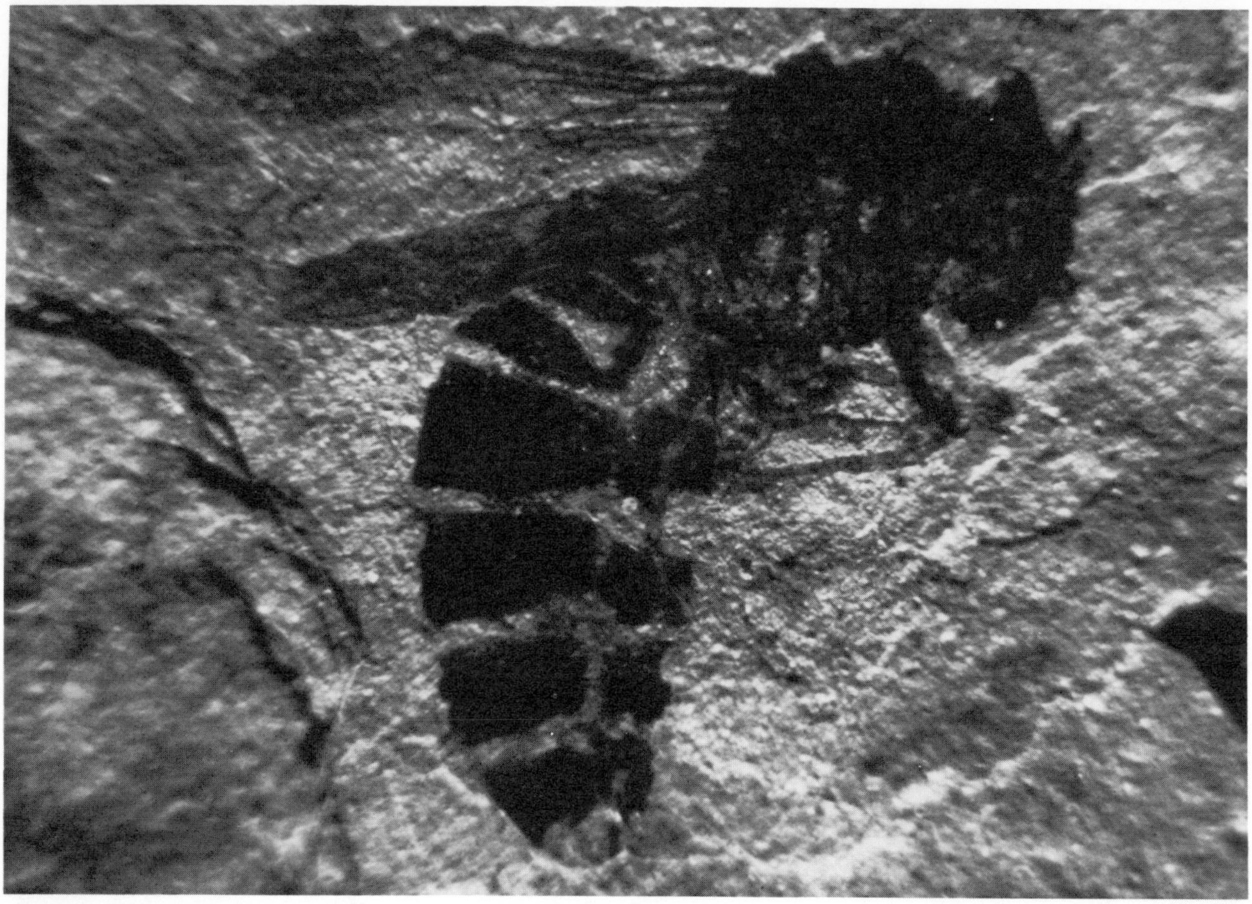

NPS photo

Preserved as a fine film of carbon darkening the light-colored volcanic ash, a bee brings to mind humming summer days and the sweet perfume of flowering plants.

sandwiched between its layers are carbonized remains of thousands of insects and spiders: bees, butterflies, dragonflies, damsel flies, beetles, ants, flies, water skaters, daddy-long-legs, and many other varieties. In places, fossil stumps jut through the shale. Eleven hundred species of insects have been identified in material collected here between 1874, when the deposit was discovered, and 1969, when it came under national monument protection. An opossum and the imprints of bird feathers are known from this deposit also. The fossils occur in an arcuate band of shale extending southwest from the town of Florissant.

GEOLOGIC HISTORY

Florissant's fossils trace back to Oligocene time, about 35 million years ago, but its earlier, more remote history is part of the story of the Southern Rocky Mountains.

This story had its murky beginnings in Precambrian time and in long erosion at the end of that era. Through all of the Paleozoic Era and most of the Mesozoic Era, the region was alternately submerged, buried in sediments, and exhumed. Then, toward the end of the Cretaceous Period, about 65 million years ago, it rose from the sea once again. As the faraway Atlantic Basin opened, as the North American Plate drifted westward, uplift of huge fault blocks built the Rocky Mountains. Again the sedimentary rocks were ravaged by erosion, stripped away from the mountain blocks. Debris from the mountains was strewn out over the Great Plains in a blanket that was continuous with an erosion surface on the mountain mass itself, a pediment now visible as the rolling yet basically horizontal plateau of pink, deeply weathered Precambrian granite that surrounds Florissant and extends well west and north of Pikes Peak.

This pediment surface was originally much lower in elevation than it is now, probably only a few hundred meters above sea level. Because of the lower elevation, it enjoyed a mild climate similar to that of, say, Missouri and Arkansas today. Woods of birch and willow, maple, beech, and hickory trees covered the rolling hills. Here and there clusters of firs were dwarfed by towering groves of tall sequoias. Oddly, a few palm trees were in the woodland as well. Streams, marshes, and ponds attracted flying insects;

The trunk of an immense sequoia, standing where it grew, is mute evidence of the glory of an Oligocene forest.

ants and beetles crawled on the leafy forest floor; opossums nosed about among the roots. A crescent-shaped lake dammed by lava flows completed the picture.

Then, about 35 million years ago, disaster struck. A series of eruptions in a small volcanic field southwest of the lake filled the air with fine volcanic ash. Windswept ash spread eastward as clouds of death, smothering the vegetation, choking streams and ponds and marshes, bringing insects and leaves down into the crescent lake. As the insects and leaves fell, they sank to the lake bottom, where they were quickly covered with airtight layers of ashy mud.

On hills around the lake, thickly falling ash was unstable; during heavy rains, swollen streams cut into it, feeding mudflows that swept among the trees, toppled some, snapped off branches of others, buried small animals, and created a barren, surrealistic scene similar to that created by Mount St. Helens in its 1980 eruption.

For millions of years, groundwater filtered invisibly through the ash, becoming charged with silica dissolved from the fine volcanic material. It redeposited the silica little by little in the porous cells of stumps and fallen trunks. Later, more ash and probably lava flows covered the area again, concealing the crescent lake and preserving its white, ash-filled muds through the passing centuries.

Eventually other geologic forces came into play. In Miocene and Pliocene time, the whole region lifted to its present elevation. The western Great Plains, the Rocky Mountains, and the Colorado Plateaus arched upward as a unit. With uplift came reinforced erosion, and again tumbling streams stripped away layers of ash and lava, laying bare once more the ash beds of the Oligocene lake, with the finely preserved insects and fossil leaves, stumps and fallen logs of the Oligocene woodland.

OTHER READING

Leopold, Estella. 1974. "Florissant, a Photograph in Rock." *National Park Service Newsletter*, vol. 9, no. 1, pp. 1-2.

MacGinitie, H.D. 1953. *Fossil Plants of the Florissant Beds, Colorado.* Carnegie Institution of Washington Publication 599.

Fossil Butte National Monument

Established: 1972
Size: 33 square kilometers (13 square miles)
Elevation: 2,050 meters (6,720 feet) at visitor center
Address: P.O. Box 527, Kemmerer, Wyoming 83101

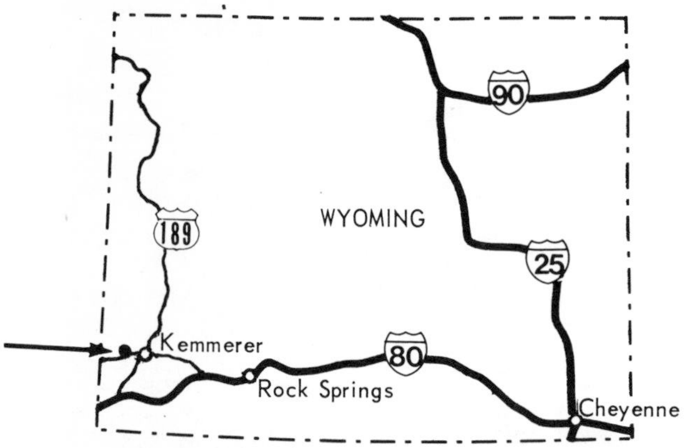

STAR FEATURES

- Beautifully preserved fossil fish, complete in almost every detail. For more than a century, fossil fish have been collected in this part of Wyoming for shipment to scholars, collectors, and museums around the world.
- Examples of intertonguing lake, shoreline, and stream deposits.
- A growing interpretive program which will include a new visitor center, conducted walks, and on-site displays where visitors will be able to watch as fossils are exposed for study and exhibition.

SETTING THE STAGE

The fossil fish of this region occur in fine, gray-white layers of silty limestone in the Green River Formation, a rock unit deposited in the smallest of three expanding and contracting and sometimes merging inland lakes that existed here 52 to 48 million years ago. The formation is now exposed in corrugated cliffs near the tops of buttes and ridges that

Quarries at and near Fossil Butte have yielded thousands of specimens that tell us much about the ancient lake in which the Green River Formation was deposited.

University of Wyoming photo

University of Wyoming photo

Fossil herring given the name Knightia *are by far the most abundant fish in these fossil beds. Many thousands appear to have died during catastrophic changes in lake water temperature and composition.*

border the valley of Twin Creek. In bluffs south of the stream, fossil fish are quarried commercially. Those north of Twin Creek and within the national monument are of course protected now, although they too were quarried prior to 1972. The fish are members of more than 40 species, among them perch, bass, bowfin, herring, gar pike, paddlefish, catfish, and stingray. In the Eocene Epoch, when they were buried here, these were all freshwater fishes, though some now occur only in salt water or have modern saltwater relatives. Some of the rock layers enclose other kinds of fossils, including snails and clams, crocodiles, insects, palm leaves, fern fronds, pollen and spores, other leaf impressions, and even a few tantalizing fragments of birds and bats.

An unusual feature of the rock that encloses these fossils is its very fine layering. Under magnification, paper-thin dark brown bands can be seen to alternate with slightly thicker light gray bands. Geologists have discovered that each pair of layers (which they call varves) represents a single year's deposit. The light layers, which consist partly of calcium carbonate shells of tiny organisms, accumulated in spring and summer, when freshened runoff brought fine silt and life-supporting oxygen to the lake. The dark layers represent fall and winter deposits, when lake temperatures changed and only dead and dying organic material settled to the bottom. Each meter of the deposit contains from 825 to 2,600 varves and therefore represents 825 to 2,600 years of slow deposition. The entire formation contains more than 4 million varves deposited during 4 million years.

In large modern lakes in summer, warm surface water floats above cooler, denser, deeper water. The upper layer, well supplied with oxygen and with a wind-caused circulation pattern of its own, sometimes acts as a seal for the deeper, denser body of cold water. When oxygen in the deeper water is used up, that layer becomes stagnant, fouled with hydrogen sulphide (the "rotten-egg smell" chemical) because of decay of plant and animal material. No forms of life other than certain types of decay bacteria can exist in such stagnant water.

With the coming of fall and early winter, the temperature of the upper layer decreases, the density difference disappears, and the waters begin to mix. Hydrogen sulphide from the foul bottom layer slowly becomes oxidized and harmless. But sometimes the layers mix so rapidly that there is not time for oxidation. When this happens, thousands of fish and other aquatic creatures perish. Such events are thought to be responsible for the masses of fish found in some of the lake sediments of Fossil Butte. Poisoned by hydrogen sulphide, they sank into stagnant pockets where no scavengers or bottom-feeders could attack their dying bodies. As fine mud filtered over them, their skeletons were beautifully preserved, even to delicate fins and fine tail rays. The chemical compounds that composed their skin and bodies were also preserved and, though flattened and dehydrated, their flesh shows up as the impressed outlines of the fish themselves—long and slender, short and flat bodied.

The poisonous effects of hydrogen sulphide may also be responsible for deposits of oil shale encountered in the Green River Formation in this and other Eocene basins. Oil shale may have formed as a muddy ooze made up of the remains of tiny, often one-celled aquatic plants and animals, as well as spores and pollen grains, accumulated in fairly deep lake waters. With time, the ooze was compacted by the weight of overlying sediments. Slow chemical processes then converted the ooze into a waxy petroleum compound called kerogen, which can be distilled to yield petroleum products.

Below the fossil fish beds on the slopes of Twin Creek Valley are colorful red and purple, gray and orange siltstone, sandstone, and gravel layers of the Wasatch Formation. In them are scattered fossils of other kinds of animals that lived in forests and underbrush that surrounded Fossil Lake. Fragments of tortoise shells and bones of a tiny ancestor of the horse have been found, as well as remains of monkeys, snakes, birds, crocodiles, and several small, early mammals. More such creatures may well be discovered in the national monument area as exhibits are excavated, as trails are built, and as the area is explored in greater detail. If during your visit you find any fossils, leave them in place and report your find to a ranger. You may contribute to our knowledge of the life of this area 40 to 50 million years ago!

Small bass called Priscacara *are also common in the thin-bedded lake deposits.*

GEOLOGIC HISTORY

Cenozoic Era. Except for an outcrop of Triassic limestone at the northeast corner of the national monument, and recent stream deposits along Twin Creek and its tributaries, only Eocene rocks are exposed here. Prior to Tertiary time, through the long half billion years of Paleozoic and Mesozoic time, most of western United States was either beneath a shallow sea or lifted slightly above it. A record of that half billion years lies deep under the Tertiary deposits, and beneath it is the even earlier record of Precambrian time.

As the Mesozoic Era neared its end, a widespread sea that covered much of west-central America slowly withdrew. The continent was drifting westward as the Atlantic Ocean widened, and a wave of mountain building that began along the west margin of the continent slowly crept eastward. When it reached the area that is now southwestern Wyoming, huge slices of crustal material were pushed eastward along thrust faults. Movement along one of these faults created a number of north-south "ripples," two of which show up near Fossil Butte as the Tunp Range and Commissary Ridge, on the two sides of the North Fork of Twin Creek. Crumpled Paleozoic and Mesozoic rocks of the leading edge of the thrust sheet can be seen from Rubey Point.

By early Eocene time the structure of the region had become quite complex. New ranges of mountains in Colorado, Utah, and western Wyoming divided the tri-state area into a number of intermountain basins, low areas that soon began to bow downward beneath increasing burdens of gravel, sand, and other debris washed from the mountains. Three of the basins, as we've seen, were occupied by lakes.

Studies of the rock material that filled the mountain-girt basins, and of the fossils enclosed in this material, show that the climate was warm and humid

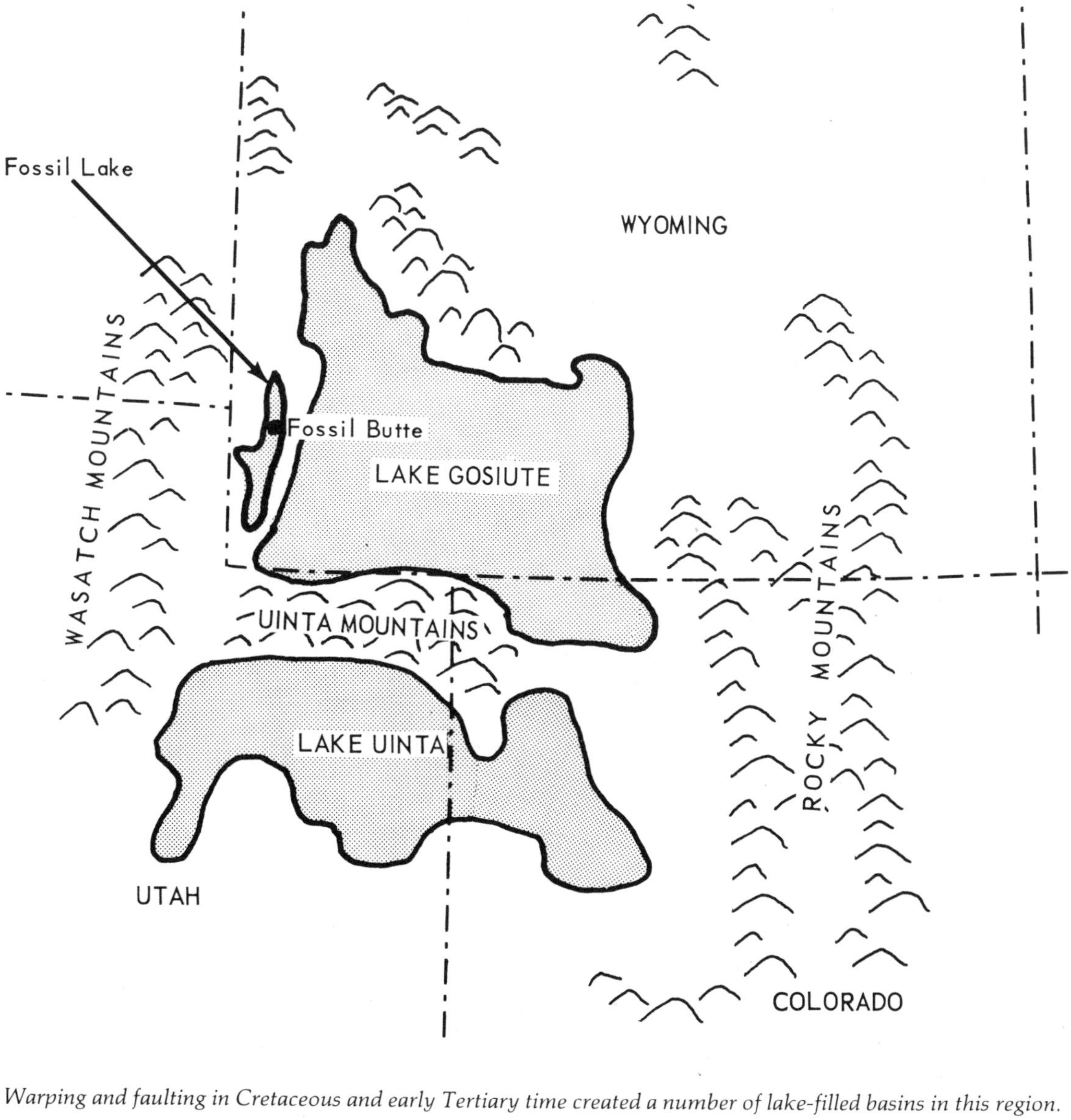

Warping and faulting in Cretaceous and early Tertiary time created a number of lake-filled basins in this region.

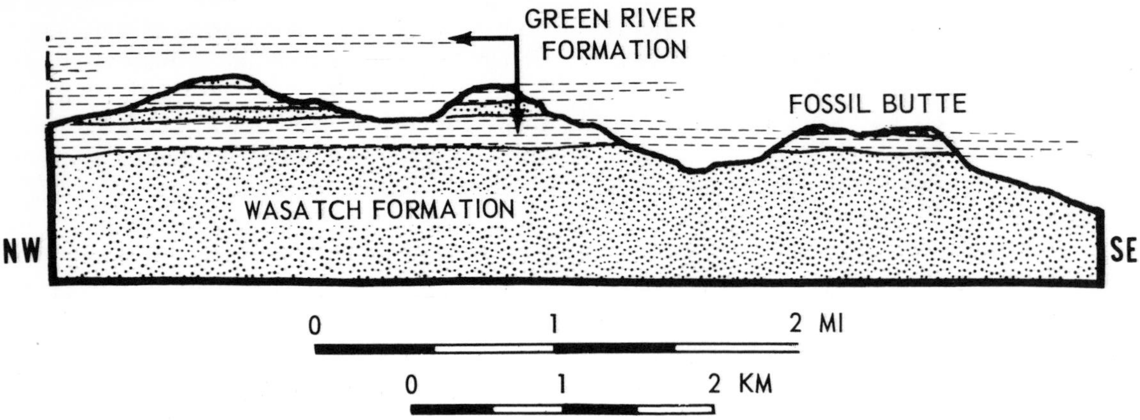

On Rubey Point, intertonguing lake and non-lake deposits define a fluctuating shoreline.

during the time the lakes existed. The basins themselves were at most only 300 meters (1,000 feet) above the sea. Lush woodlands of palm, maple, oak, and beech trees surrounded the lakes, and at times the lake level rose until intervening divides were submerged and the lakes had become one. Strange animals roamed among the trees, ancestors of today's rodents, snakes, and lizards. Some of the earliest members of the horse family—tiny, delicate animals about the size of a small dog—pranced about in the woodlands. Surrounding mountains were forested with spruce, pine, and fir. Willows and cypress, reeds and rushes grew in shallow shoreline marshes. The lakes teemed with many forms of aquatic life: fish, snails, clams, and various aquatic insects and worms. At their margins lived crocodiles and turtles; flamingoes waded in their shallows.

In this humid, semitropical surrounding, both uplands and basins weathered deeply, and rock material decayed into clayey red soil similar to tropical soils known today. Washed into the basins, this soil formed the Wasatch Formation's colorful siltstone and sandstone. The part of the Green River Formation exposed here, above the Wasatch Formation, was deposited in a narrow freshwater lake that geologists call Fossil Lake.

An interesting feature of the Wasatch and Green River Formations is that here they intertongue; that is, thin wedges of one lie above and between thin wedges of the other. Though this feature is not apparent on the south-sloping bluffs near the visitor center, it is clearly displayed north of Rubey Point, the highest part of Fossil Butte. Such a relationship indicates that the two formations were deposited at nearly the same time in two different but adjacent environments—the Wasatch in stream channels and floodplains, the Green River in a lake. As if in confirmation of this pattern, beach deposits have been identified along their contact.

As time went on, the Eocene lakes shriveled and dried, and the silt, sand, and limy layers of lake sediment were buried beneath more mud and silt, sand and gravel. Early in Pliocene time, uplift of the whole Rocky Mountain region revitalized streams and rivers, and they carved ever-deeper channels in the soft, poorly consolidated Tertiary sediments. Finally, the old lake deposits with their many fossil fish were exposed to view along the valley of Twin Creek.

OTHER READING

Bradley, W. H. 1936. "The Biography of an Ancient American Lake." *Scientific Monthly*, vol. 42, pp. 421-430.

Bradley, W. H. 1948. *Limnology and the Eocence Lakes of the Rocky Mountain Region.* Geological Society of America Bulletin, vol. 59, no. 7, pp. 635-648.

Hesse, C. J. 1939. "Fossil Fish Localities in the Green River Eocene of Wyoming." *Scientific Monthly*, vol. 48, pp. 147-151.

Glacier National Park

Established: 1910
Size: 4,100 square kilometers (1,584 square miles)
Elevation: 948 to 3,190 meters (3,110 to 10,466 feet)
Address: West Glacier, Montana 59936

STAR FEATURES

• Rugged redrock mountains with scenic peaks, sharp ridges, blue lakes, and sparkling waterfalls—all products of geologic processes.

• Alpine glaciers hugging shadowy cirques, contrasting with angled summits and straight, deep valleys imprinted by more extensive glaciers of the past.

• Sedimentary rocks deposited a billion years ago—colorful mudstone, limestone, and sandstone layers hardly changed since they formed. At roadside and trail's edge they display ancient mudcracks, ripple marks, and raindrop impressions, as well as some of the world's oldest fossil plants.

• Evidence of gigantic forces that disrupted these ancient rocks and slid them eastward over far younger strata.

• An interpretive program that includes two visitor centers, roadside exhibits, conducted and self-guided hikes and walks, and campfire talks.

See color pages for additional photographs.

SETTING THE STAGE

Glacier National Park is named not just for its 50 small modern glaciers, which have developed in the last 3,000 years, but for earlier, more extensive ones that shaped its canyons, whittled its pointed peaks, and scoured its upland basins. Everywhere in this national park the imprint of glaciers is evident. Angular matterhorn peaks, cliff-girt cirques and sharp-crested arêtes, U-shaped valleys, slender waterfalls that plummet from hanging valleys, and

Clearly exposed where it cuts diagonally across the flank of Wynn Mountain near Many Glacier, the Lewis overthrust fault (arrow) separates Cretaceous rocks below the fault from Precambrian rocks above it. Recognized by geologists many years ago, this great fault was not really well understood until recently.

An unnamed hanging glacier clings precariously to a steep ravine above Ellen Wilson Lake. Its moraine is at lower left. Surrounding red Precambrian rocks are part of the Grinnell Formation.

Billion-year-old ripple marks are common in the ancient sedimentary rocks of Glacier National Park.

Cabbage-like stromatolites show up in roadcuts along Going-to-the-Sun Road.

rocky moraines that dam narrow finger lakes are telltale signs of mountain or alpine glaciation.

Among this park's most attractive features are the red and gray-green layers of Precambrian metasedimentary rock that make up its mountainsides, and the festive red and green pebbles of lakeshore and streambed. These rocks—mudstone and siltstone compacted and hardened through time, and sandstone become quartzite—are about a billion years old.

In most Precambrian rocks, details of their origins are lost in metamorphism and recrystallization. Not so here. Every cliff and slope and rockslide reveals astonishing sedimentary details. Here are ripple marks made by moving water and waves; there are mudcracks and raindrop impressions showing that at times the mud, deposited perhaps on some vast floodplain, dried out. Cabbagelike fossils called stromatolites reveal that blue-green algae, most primitive of seaweeds, grew as slimy scum in sunlit seas. Even the reds and greens of the rock, colors due to oxides of iron, are clues to atmospheric or marine conditions when these rocks were formed.

But ancient rocks carved by recent glaciers are not the whole story of Glacier National Park. A third factor, mountain building, lifted these great stone pages to our view. Movement began about 70 million years ago as part of the upheaval that lifted the Rocky Mountains. The remarkable thing here (and elsewhere in the Northern Rockies) is that as the ancient metasedimentary rocks and the thousands of meters of younger limestone, sandstone, and shale that were then above them were lifted, several huge slabs broke loose and slid eastward for 55 kilometers (40 miles) or more. They ended up on top of much younger rocks, a clear reversal of the customary youngest-on-top sequence. Thus Glacier National Park is in a slab of billion-year-old Precambrian metasedimentary rocks that now overlie Cretaceous shale scarcely more than 70 million years old.

The surface on which the Precambrian block slid over younger rock is the Lewis thrust fault, or overthrust fault. The Precambrian slab that makes up the Lewis and Livingstone Ranges in the park is some 120 kilometers long and more than 30 kilometers wide (75 by 19 miles), and it belongs farther west.

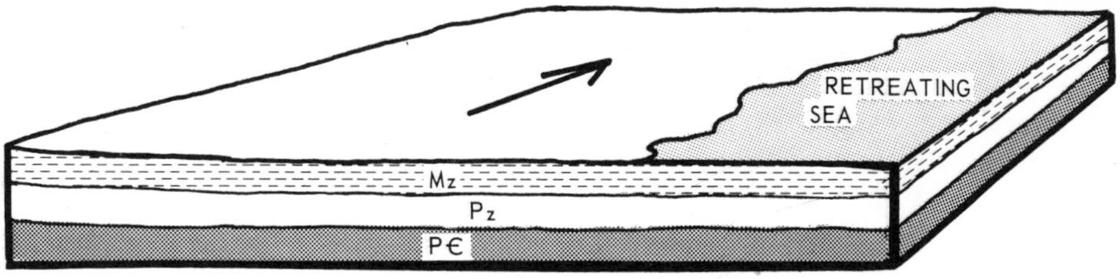

① *As the Mesozoic Era ended, the sea withdrew from this region, leaving thick deposits of marine shale and mud.*

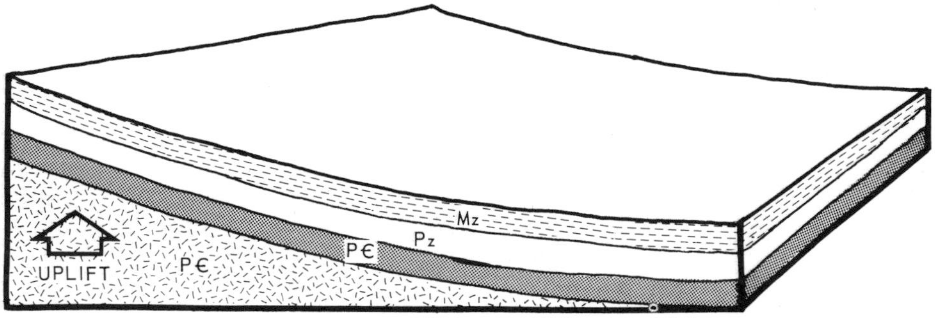

② *Uplift far to the west caused instability in Precambrian, Paleozoic, and Mesozoic sedimentary strata.*

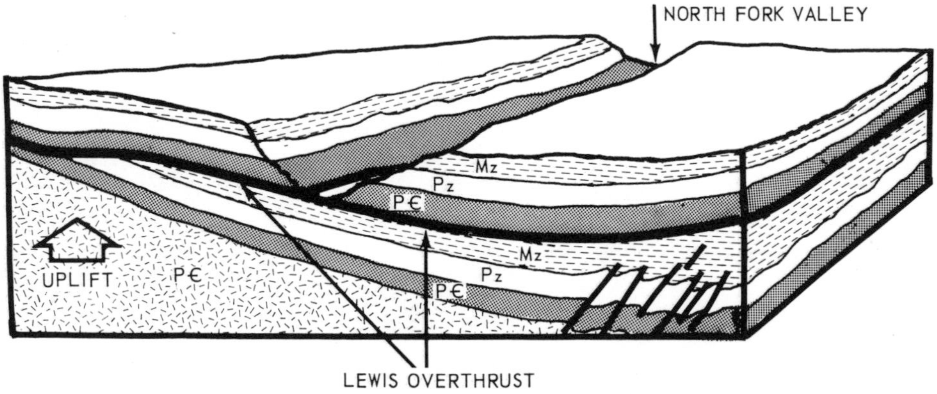

③ *Titanic blocks of sedimentary rock slid eastward along the Lewis overthrust, crumpling some of the soft Mesozoic sediments and probably faulting underlying layers. The Lewis overthrust turned up at its eastern edge.*

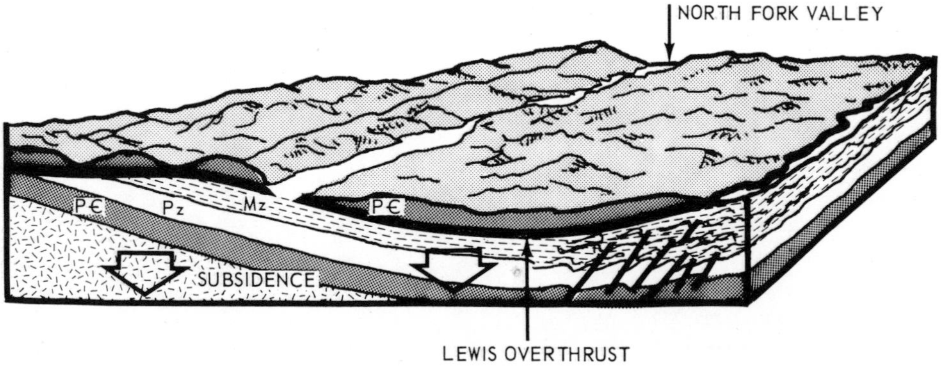

④ *Long years of erosion pared away overlying strata and carved Precambrian rocks into the scenic mountains of Glacier Park.*

When it slid into its present position, this slab must have been 5 to 8 kilometers (3 to 5 miles) thick — piled high with strata that ranged in age from Precambrian to Cretaceous. Geologists once thought it had been pushed by some powerful force from the west, but there was nothing farther west on which to pin the blame. And how could such a slab be rigid enough to survive such shoving without crumpling? Now most geologists regard the movement as downhill sliding, very slow-motion tobogganning, under the relentless pull of gravity. Gradual uplift of a broad arch about 150 kilometers (100 miles) west of the park established an eastward slope surfaced with Cretaceous mud and silt. As the slope became steeper, rock layers near the top of the arch broke loose and tobogganned eastward, probably not all at once but little by little over many millions of years. This sort of mass movement does seem hard to believe, but the evidence is here. Southeast of Many Glacier you can put your hand right on the Lewis overthrust and see Precambrian rocks above it and Cretaceous ones below it. The sliding becomes more believable when we remember that soft, slippery, newly deposited Cretaceous clay probably acted as a lubricant for the moving slab.

As the sliding mass pulled away from the crest of the western arch, wide gaps tore open behind it. These gaps still exist as the North Fork and Flathead Valleys west of Glacier Park. The separation of Precambrian rocks across these two valleys tells us that the overthrust block moved eastward about 55 kilometers (40 miles).

GEOLOGIC HISTORY

Precambrian Era. Except for Cretaceous shale and sandstone in the eastern part of the park, almost all sedimentary rocks of Glacier Park date from Precambrian time. They seem to have been deposited roughly a billion to 600 million years ago, during the long interval known in most of the world as a time of erosion. Erosion was in fact widespread during that

Sand-filled mudcracks mark some layers of the Grinnell Formation, indicating short-term environmental fluctuations that allowed water-deposited mud flats to dry out.

time, lengthy erosion that reduced much of what is now North America to a flat, featureless plain. Here the products of some of that erosion — the mud, silt, and sand — seem to have come to rest.

What was this part of the world like a billion years ago? Was the atmosphere similar to what we know today? Did the same processes prevail? Are there modern counterparts to the ancient environments in which this rock formed?

At least tentative answers to these questions are in the rocks themselves. Geologists feel fairly sure that late in Precambrian time, when the rocks were deposited, plant and animal life was confined to lakes and seas. Blue-green algal scums were food for soft-bodied, shell-less invertebrate animals that were to evolve explosively into the many shell-bearing forms of Paleozoic time. But on land, no living thing existed. No plants grew, and no animal had yet, as far as we know, left its trail on the muddy shore. Think how the absence of plants influenced the forces of erosion! Every raindrop splatter loosened sand and silt. Every unimpeded rivulet cut into the earth.

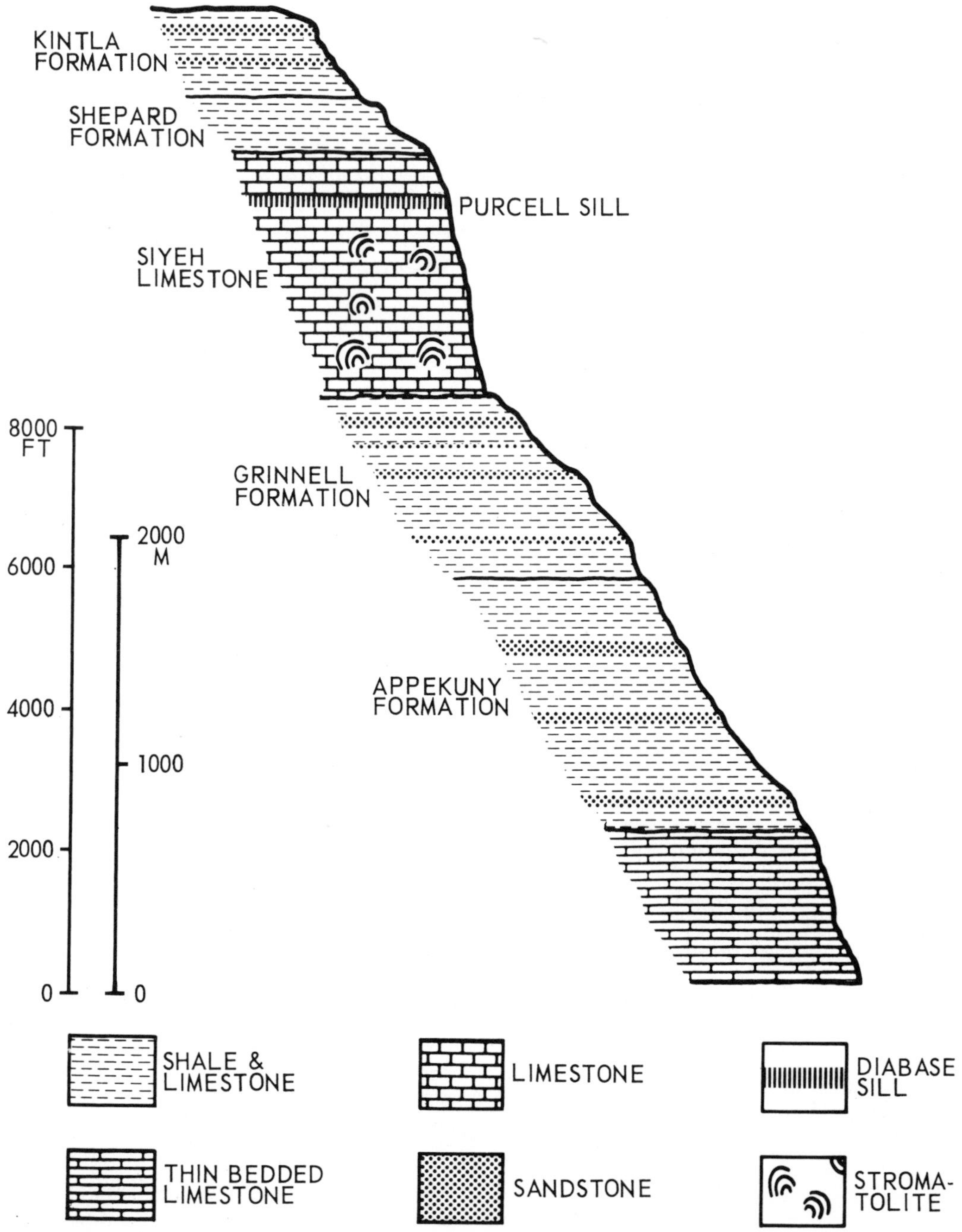

Each stream and river attacked rocks unprotected by leafy canopies or fallen trees or tangled roots. With every storm, mudflows swept across the barren land, settling clay, silt, and sand on far-off floodplains or broad deltas near the sea. Tides much greater than those we know today* flooded the shores, swirling up mud and carrying it out to sea. A barren, lifeless Sahara, an Amazon in flood, a broadly shelving Gulf Coast—put them together and move them back in time. And without land plants to utilize carbon dioxide or to release oxygen, the atmosphere was probably not at all as we know it, and would not have supported air-breathing animal life.

Some of the Precambrian formations in this area, particularly the Altyn and Siyeh Limestones, are unequivocally marine. Others, such as the Appekunny and Grinnell Formations, were deposited under conditions alternately wet and dry, perhaps on tide flats or river floodplains near sea level, perhaps on low-lying land that was periodically submerged by slight crustal movements. In any case, none of the rocks are coarse-grained; by their very fineness they indicate the absence of mountains or even hills in areas nearby.

Not long after the Siyeh Limestone was deposited, molten magma rich in iron minerals forced its way up through the Precambrian layers. In places it filled vertical fractures to harden into dikes. Elsewhere it spread horizontally between layers of limestone as the Purcell sill, now apparent high on mountain cliffs as a prominent dark line sandwiched between bands of limestone bleached and marbleized by heat from the intrusion. At the time the Shepard Formation was being deposited, magma erupted onto the sea floor, where it took on the pillowlike appearance of lava flows that erupt under water. The pillow lava can be seen today near Granite Park Chalet, north of Logan Pass. The dikes and sill and pillow lava have about the same chemical and mineral composition and come probably from the same source, but the dikes and sill, which cooled slowly, are coarsely crystalline black diabase, and the pillow lava is its fine-grained equivalent, basalt, because of its faster cooling.

Dating of radioactive minerals in the diabase of the Purcell sill shows that it is about 1,080 million years old. If the basalt flows in the Shepard Formation are the same age, then all the Precambrian formations below them are more than 1,080 million years old, and all those above are somewhat less than that.

Some of the diabase dikes contain copper minerals. Late in the 19th century these attracted prospectors and miners. The boom was brief, and faded before the area became a park.

Paleozoic Era. For 350 million years after the end of the Precambrian Era, this area was repeatedly submerged by shallow seas. Limestone, mudstone, and sandstone layers deposited in these seas extended completely across the region that is now the national park, as well as over areas farther west that were to become the Lewis overthrust slab. By rights, then, these Paleozoic rocks should be present both below and above the present mountains. However, they were eroded off the overthrust slab, probably after overthrusting occurred.

During Paleozoic time, both plants and animals became important components of the geologic scene. Marine fossils are abundant, for the seas teemed with shell-secreting invertebrates, fishes, and highly advanced seaweeds that took the place of the simple algae of Precambrian time. During the Paleozoic Era, both plants and animals ventured onto the land, but there is no record of land dwellers in the marine sediments of this region.

Mesozoic Era. In Glacier Park no record exists for Triassic or Jurassic time or for the early part of the Cretaceous Period. The absence of a sedimentary record is taken to mean that this part of the continent was above sea level, as was much of the rest of the continental interior, subject either to nondeposition or to erosion.

The sea returned late in Cretaceous time, between 100 and 70 million years ago. Thick deposits of clay and silt accumulated once more—the sediments destined to play a role as lubricants for the Lewis overthrust.

Close to the end of Cretaceous time, uplift of the Rocky Mountains began, and the earth's crust west of the park tilted eastward. With the tilting, the once flat-lying sedimentary rocks began to move, sliding downhill along the overthrust fault. As the sedimentary layers moved east, gaps that opened behind them became the ancestral Flathead and North Fork Valleys.

Cenozoic Era. The climate in the interior of North America seems to have been arid and desertlike during most of Cenozoic time. Rainfall was not adequate to support lush vegetation, nor was it sufficient except during sudden floods to remove the sand and rock that day-to-day processes like frost action loosened from the mountains. Thus a sloping apron of debris gradually gathered around the mountains, stretching eastward onto the flat continental interior and, farther west, filling up the pulled-apart valleys, accumulating there to depths of 1,000 meters (3,000 feet) or more. Surviving remnants of these coarse sediments exist today. Their rounded cobbles and

*A billion years ago the moon was a good deal closer to the earth than it is now and exerted a far greater tidal pull. If the earth was also spinning more rapidly, as geologists and astronomers now believe, tides were not only greater but more frequent.

pebbles and their colorful sand are clearly derived from the distinctive Precambrian rocks of the Lewis and Livingstone Ranges.

By the end of Miocene time, 12 million years ago, the mountains must have resembled today's desert ranges of southern Arizona and New Mexico, half buried in their own debris. Only their highest summits projected above broad, gently sloping sand and gravel aprons.

Sometime in Miocene time, probably about 10 million years ago, the Rocky Mountain region from Canada to New Mexico began to lift once again, arching upward as one broad unit until it attained its present elevation. Uplift changed the climate, causing lower temperatures and increasing precipitation. As stream gradients and stream runoff increased, running water cut down into the sand and gravel deposits of earlier Tertiary time. Streams were augmented also by worldwide climate changes that came about at the end of the Pliocene Epoch, 3 million years ago, when rising precipitation and/or falling temperatures brought North America and Europe to the doors of the Ice Ages.

During each of four continental Ice Ages, streams became torrents and rivers became churning floods, devastating the land and sweeping away what remained of the loosely consolidated gravel of the previous 60 million years. On the local level, the Rocky Mountains don't seem to have been heavily touched by glaciation (at least not south of the Canadian border) before the last of the four known advances of the continental ice sheets. No positive evidence exists of any mountain glaciers earlier than about 200,000 years ago, although there may have been earlier ones whose marks were destroyed by those that followed. During the last great Ice Age, though, the mountains in the park were three times burdened with ice. From cirques high on mountain crests, long alpine glaciers flowed down stream-cut valleys, sometimes merging with others, sometimes traveling alone. Reaching the foot of the mountains, they spread out as piedmont glaciers which in turn flowed westward into the pulled-apart valley of the North Fork, southward beyond the present park boundaries, and eastward to meet the advancing edge of the vast continental ice sheets.

Glacial striae mark ledges of the Grinnell Formation near Sperry Chalet. The glacier moved from right to left, rounding upstream surfaces and breaking away or plucking downstream surfaces.

By the end of Pleistocene time, 10,000 years ago, glaciers and the streams they spawned had bared the core of the mountains. They had bitten deep into Precambrian metasedimentary rocks of the core, tooling the pointed peaks, narrowing the arêtes, and deepening the major valleys. About 6,000 years ago the ice melted, retreated, and finally disappeared altogether. Small new glaciers came into being in the cirques of their predecessors about 3,000 years ago.

BEHIND THE SCENES

Avalanche Gorge and Avalanche Lake. The trail to Avalanche Lake begins close to a narrow, red-walled gorge where Avalanche Creek has carved deep potholes through massive red mudstone of the Grinnell Formation. The creek's source is Avalanche Lake, 3 kilometers (2 miles) up the trail. There, streams of meltwater from Sperry Glacier (out of sight behind the skyline) plunge in slender filaments over a splendid curving precipice. The rockbound amphitheatre is one of the loveliest sights in the park, and one of the most interesting geologically. On the cliffs are exposed mudstone layers of the Grinnell Formation, here twisted in folds, there broken by faults, and tinged deep red where they are wet with spray. Along the lakeshore, fragments of these rocks display features characteristic of the park's Precambrian metasedimentary rocks: ripple marks and cabbage-head stromatolites in layers deposited in water, mudcracks in layers that dried out. You may also see rocks marked with bands of flat, narrow pieces of mudcracked clay lifted by moving water and redeposited gently before they disintegrated.

Garden Wall. This slim arête, almost straight on its western flank, took shape as glaciers whittled relentlessly at both sides of a high ridge. In places it is so thin that there are windows in it. Its cliffs are marked with the dark horizontal stripe of the Purcell sill, bordered with white marble. The diabase sill is made up chiefly of crystals of black pyroxene and is spangled with white feldspar crystals.

Going-to-the-Sun Road. With the access it affords to high country along the Continental Divide and the crest of the Lewis Range, this highway offers an unusual transect of the park's geology. Starting in the Appekunny Formation on the west side of the park or in the Altyn Formation on the east side, the road climbs through successively younger formations to Logan Pass, where mudstone of the highest Precambrian unit, the Kintla Formation, caps nearby peaks. Many of the sedimentary details of these rocks show up near the highway or at the numerous vantage points. Watch for ripple marks, mudcracks, raindrop impressions, and big cabbage heads of stromatolites that are as much as a meter (a yard) across. Just below Logan Pass, the Purcell sill is at roadside level,

Seen edgewise, mudcracks appear as dark brush strokes on rock faces. They may have been deposited on tidal flats.

a thick band of black diabase sandwiched between whitened, marbleized layers of limestone.

The road travels through or within sight of a variety of glacial features: U-shaped valleys of Saint Mary and McDonald Creeks, ice-planed uplands of Logan Pass, the delicate filament of Birdwoman Falls plummeting from a hanging valley, many ice-sharpened peaks, and the Garden Wall arête. Sexton Glacier, on Going-to-the-Sun Mountain, is visible from Siyeh Pass. Lateral moraines, usually densely forested, edge many valleys. Oval, glacier-scoured roches moutonnées (literally "sheep rocks") hump from valley floors.

Landslides large and small are common along oversteepened walls of glacial valleys, especially where parts of old lateral moraines, no longer supported by ice, break loose and slide into the canyons. Landslides can often be distinguished by their hummocky surfaces, by the cirquelike scarps from which they slide, and by changes in vegetation density. One is visible across McDonald Creek from the Loop.

Granite Park (via Highline Trail). The trail from Logan Pass to Granite Park skirts the west face of the Garden Wall and crosses the Purcell sill, where dark diabase and contrasting white marble can be examined closeup. Fossil algae show particularly well in the marble bands.

Granite Park faces southwest and is fully exposed to the afternoon sun. Thus, despite the fact that this western side of the mountains gets more snowfall than the eastern slope, no glaciers have existed here in recent times. As a result of its lack of glaciers, this side of the Garden Wall is relatively straight, whereas the other side is deeply scalloped by glacial cirques.

Granite Park is one of several high erosional platforms that remain from the Tertiary Period. In late Miocene or early Pliocene time, the mountains were buried to the level of this platform by a sea of rocky gravel. Most of the exposed sedimentary rocks here belong to the Siyeh Limestone (weathers tan) or to the Kintla and Shepard Formations (dark red).

There are good exposures of Purcell pillow basalt in Granite Park. Misidentified as granite, they are responsible for the name of Granite Park. They contain little or no quartz (in contrast to granite) and are much darker than granite. Because the pillow basalt cooled rapidly by contact with water, it is finer-grained than diabase sills and dikes derived probably from the same subterranean source.

Grinnell Glacier. This glacier is the largest in the park and is also the easiest to reach—a 5-kilometer (3-mile) hike from the upper boat dock on Lake Josephine. Like other glaciers in the park, it is much smaller now than it has been in the recent past. High-piled, barren moraines indicate its former dimensions. Early records and annual surveys show that it shrank rapidly between 1887, when it was first explored, and 1950. It now seems to have stabilized. Ice within the glacier moves 10 to 15 meters (30 to 50 feet) a year, with each winter's new snow (some of it whipped across the Garden Wall by curling gusts of wind) approximately balancing each summer's melting.

Features of the glacier show up best in late summer, when the previous winter's snow has melted from most of its surface. For your own safety, observe these features from solid-rock vantage points, or join a naturalist-conducted tour. Don't go out on the ice on your own.

Crevasses form in brittle ice near the surface as it is carried along by moving ice below. Dirty gray zones visible on the surface and in crevasses mark annual growth increments. Near the head of the glacier is the firn line, a color change between this year's clean white snow and older ice. Notice, too, the cirque wall behind the glacier, part of the Garden Wall arête. The Garden Wall is thin and sharp here, only a couple of meters (yards) thick near the top.

Bedrock near and below Grinnell Glacier was scoured clean when ice covered it, and grooved and scratched as rocks imbedded in ice were dragged across it. As the glacier melted back, some of these rock tools were dropped on the bedrock surface; many of them are marked with scratches or striae too. Ponds near the glacier are whitened by fine rock flour produced in the grinding process. Grinnell Lake owes its unusual peacock blue to smaller amounts of this glacial flour.

On cliffs above the glacier, a white-black-white stripe marks the Purcell sill. The sill in places shifts position, moving from one level to another within the strata of the Siyeh Formation. Fragments of glittery black diabase from the sill can be found near the glacier and along the trail.

Lake McDonald. This lake occupies a deep, glacier-scooped trough in stony Tertiary gravel. Howe Ridge and Snyder Ridge, parallel to the lake, are the great glacier's lateral moraines. The lake is dammed partly by an old moraine and partly by outwash gravel from another large glacier that flowed from the northwest down the original valley of the North Fork.

The lake is 15 kilometers (10 miles) long, 2 kilometers (about 1.3 miles) wide, and about 120 meters (400 feet) deep.

Logan Pass, Hanging Garden, and Hidden Lake. Glacier-scoured Siyeh Limestone forms the surface at Logan Pass. It displays numerous large stromatolite heads here. Dark red mudstone of the Shepard and Kintla Formations caps nearby peaks. Just below the pass in either direction, the Purcell sill is exposed near the road.

Many more stromatolites outcrop along the self-guiding trail from the visitor center to the Hanging Garden and Hidden Lake overlook. Here, too, are abundant examples of ripple marks and mudcracks in the Shepard Formation. Glacially striated rock and a small, desolate moraine, its glacier now melted away, are visible on the east side of Mount Clements. The trail leads on to a viewpoint overlooking Hidden Lake, Avalanche Basin, and Sperry Glacier. The magnificent mountain wilderness of southern Glacier Park is also visible from here.

Logan Pass and Hidden Lake Pass are both on the Continental Divide, the winding ridgeline that separates eastward (Atlantic) drainage from westward (Pacific) drainage. Mountains along the divide are among the highest in the park. Many of them shelter small glaciers, which from this distance are best located by their barren, light brown moraines.

Many Glacier and Swiftcurrent Lake. Many Glacier Hotel and nearby Swiftcurrent Lake are departure points for trails leading to Lake Josephine, Grinnell Lake, Grinnell Glacier, Iceberg Lake, and other sites of geologic interest.

Just east of Many Glacier, U.S. Highway 89 crosses the Lewis overthrust, where tan Precambrian Altyn Limestone (which also surrounds the hotel parking lot) overlies much younger Cretaceous rocks. One of the best exposures of the fault is on the slope of Wynn Mountain southeast of here; the fault's slender scar cuts diagonally across the mountainside.

Valleys draining into Swiftcurrent Lake are all glaciated, U-shaped, and occupied by strings of lakes dammed by moraines or sloping, resistant layers of Precambrian rock. At their heads can be seen the cliffs of the Garden Wall, marking on this side an almost continuous line of cirques. Many of the cirques shelter small glaciers, among them Grinnell and Swiftcurrent Glaciers. A hike up any of these canyons will show you at close range the sedimentary features of the Precambrian rocks as well as glacial features that give the park its name.

Saint Mary Lake. Like other finger lakes of Glacier Park, Saint Mary Lake occupies a long, narrow, glacier-scooped valley bordered by lateral moraines. The eastern part of the lake basin was cut into Cretaceous sandstone and shale. The western part, above the narrows, is in buff-colored Altyn Limestone and greenish mudstone of the Appekunny Formation. Between the two is the Lewis overthrust fault, easy to pinpoint because resistant Precambrian rocks rise like a wall above the fault line. Though the fault slants down westward, it is near enough to horizontal that its trace runs west up every valley and east again on every ridge. A quick method for distinguishing near-horizontal and near-vertical faults is based on this very characteristic. Near-vertical ones tend to run in straight lines cross country or across a geologic map, while near-horizontal ones follow the contours fairly closely.

The lake is about 18 kilometers (11 miles) long, 1 kilometer (0.5 mile) wide, and 83 meters (285 feet) deep.

Sperry Glacier. Almost everything said above about Grinnell Glacier could be repeated here. Orange-tipped posts mark a safe route across the moraine to the main mass of the glacier. Largest in the park in 1900, the glacier shrank rapidly between then and 1950. Annual snowfall bands are well displayed late in the summer when the year's new snow has melted back. At that time, too, one can approach the bergschrund, a deep crevice where ice moves away from the cirque headwall (or in this case, the side wall).

Moraines below the glacier give an idea of its former extent. They are impressive piles of rock for a small glacier that has existed for no more than 3,000 years. Think of the quantities of debris that older, larger, longer-lived glaciers discarded! Small ponds among the moraines are whitened with varying quantities of glacial flour. An interesting feature here is the large expanse of bare rock smoothed off during the glacier's advance. Many of the rounded ledges bear glacial striae, as do most of the small, angular rocks scattered freely across them—rocks used as tools by the moving ice.

Sunrift Gorge. Not just a narrow channel carved by a stream, Sunrift Gorge came into existence when a large block of Precambrian rock slid a few feet downhill along a tilted bedding surface, leaving behind a straight, narrow, rock-walled cleft. Baring Creek took possession of the cleft for a direct route through a rock mass that obstructed its way down the mountainside. Surrounding red and green strata are transitional between the mostly green Appekunny Formation and the mostly red Grinnell Formation.

Trick Falls. There are really two falls here, one above the other. When runoff is high in spring, the upper falls completely hide the cave opening from which the lower falls emerge. As runoff lessens, the upper falls appear as a narrow, ribboned veil that suddenly widens where it is joined by water of the lower falls. Still later in the season the upper stream disappears.

Contorted strata of the Grinnell Formation bend sharply upward on the side of Edwards Mountain.

Two Medicine Lakes. Like other finger lakes in Glacier Park, these three lakes lie in deep glacial troughs and are dammed by moraines. Many glacial features can be observed in their valley. The Lewis overthrust fault runs along the change in slope from rolling hills of Cretaceous shale to steep-sloped mountains of Precambrian metasedimentary rock.

The region abounds in hanging valley waterfalls, and lovely forested trails lead to most of them. Both Appistoki Falls Trail and Two Medicine Lake Trail cross creeks ravaged by destructive floods in 1964 and 1975, when heavy rainfall melted snowpack in the mountains and rainwater and snowmelt joined to surge down mountainsides, uproot vegetation, and tumble tons of rock, sand, and gravel down their channels. Recovery from the effects of such floods is slow. The flood-disrupted streams illustrate well the power of running water and the rapidity with which rocks—even large boulders—are rounded even though they were not tumbled far from their original sites. Crescent chatter marks on their surfaces result from impact with other boulders. Despite the mad rush of the swollen streams, some sorting is evident —large boulders and cobbles accumulated in some parts of the channel, pebbles and sand in others.

Green and red gravel along the shores of Two Medicine Lake is derived largely from the Appekunny Formation. Because Upper Two Medicine Lake is surrounded by red Grinnell Formation, shore gravels there are much redder.

Along all the trails in this area, Precambrian sedimentary rocks display their billion-year-old ripple marks and mudcracks. Raindrop impressions are less common.

OTHER READING

Alden, W.C. 1953. *Physiographic and Glacial Geology of Western Montana and Adjacent Areas.* U.S. Geological Survey Professional Paper 231.

Alt, David. D., and Hyndman, Donald W. 1973. *Rocks, Ice, and Water—the Geological Story of Glacier National Park.* Mountain Press, Missoula, Montana.

Brooks, A., and others. 1974. *Glacier and Waterton Lakes National Parks.* National Parkways.

Dyson, J. L. 1960. *The Geologic Story of Glacier National Park.* Glacier Natural History Association.

Dyson, J. L. 1962. *Glaciers and Glaciation in Glacier National Park.* Glacier Natural History Association.

Ross, C. P. 1959. *Geology of Glacier National Park and the Flathead Region of Northwestern Montana.* U.S. Geological Survey Professional Paper 296.

Ruhle, G. C. 1957. *Guide to Glacier National Park.* J. W. Forney, Minneapolis, Minnesota.

Grand Teton National Park

Established: 1929
Size: 1,256 square kilometers (485 square miles)
Elevation: 1,920 to 4,197 meters (6,300 to 13,770 feet)
Address: P.O. Drawer 170, Moose, Wyoming 83012

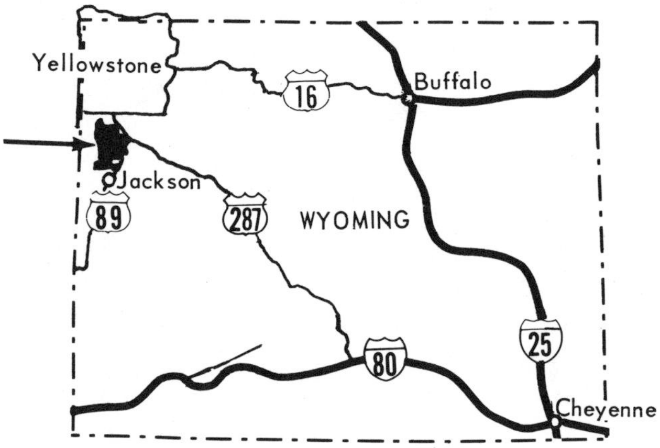

STAR FEATURES

• A stately parade of blue-gray peaks towering a breathtaking 1,200 to 2,000 meters (4,000 to 7,000 feet) above the valley floor of Jackson Hole, itself mostly within park bounds. Geologically young but chiseled from some of North America's oldest rocks, these spectacular mountains rose by vertical movement along a major fault zone.

• Lakes, tiny rockbound gems nestled among frost-riven crags, and larger moraine-dammed lakes at the eastern foot of the range.

• A few present-day glaciers, high above timberline, clinging to deep recesses and precipitous slopes.

• Many hiking trails offering pages of Nature's own textbook of mountain building and geologic structure.

• The distinctive imprint of mountain glaciation, some of it on a very large scale.

• The sinuous, braided course of the Snake River, whose trenched inner valley opens to view the glacial outwash deposits of Jackson Hole.

The Buck Mountain fault zone passes close to the rugged, almost vertical west face of Grand Teton. Precambrian rocks between it and the Teton fault zone rise much higher than those in the western part of the range.

• Visitor centers, museums, guided and self-guided walks, and roadside vistas where some of the principal geologic features are explained.

SETTING THE STAGE

The bold rock mass of the Teton Range rises 1,200 to 2,000 meters (more than a mile) above the cobble-strewn floor of Jackson Hole. The silver-gray peaks ascend abruptly, without foothills, a feature that lends them an air of unreality, like fairy-tale mountains. In places, dark dikes project from the cliffs or erode into deep grooves; elsewhere the precipices are finely drawn with white and light gray veins. The altitude to which the range has been raised, the steep, straight fault scarps that define the east and in some places the west edge of the line of peaks, and the compact, resistant nature of the rocks add to their ruggedness. Frigid conditions during the Ice Ages helped to create the alpine landforms for which the Tetons are acclaimed.

East of the Teton Range lies the open expanse of Jackson Hole, its almost level floor stony with stream-rounded glacial debris. The Teton fault zone, marked by the straight eastern edge of the mountains, separates valley and precipice. Along it, the mountains heaved upward as if hinged somewhere to the west. In a complementary movement, as if hinged to the east, the valley sank many thousands of meters. Taking the movement of both blocks into account, total movement reaches about 10,000 meters (30,000 feet), but erosion whittling the peaks and filling in the valley conceals much of this range of movement now.

Mount Moran's prominent black diabase dike, 50 meters (150 feet) wide, also cuts the summit of the lower, forested ridge. The small light cap on Mount Moran is not snow but Cambrian sedimentary rock.

A cross section of the mountains reveals the positions of major faults.

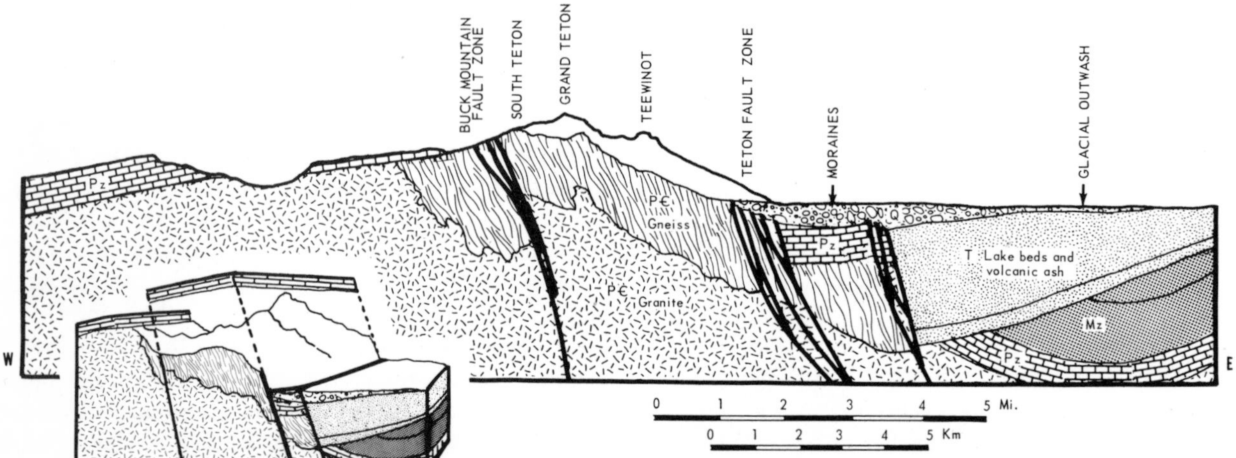

Displacement along the Teton fault zone began 8 to 10 million years ago, not as one or even a few abrupt and earthshaking cataclysms, but as often-repeated sporadic jolts spread at uneven intervals over millions of years, with an average movement of 10 centimeters (4 inches) per century. The long-drawn-out process that elevated the Tetons is still going on today, as is shown by a clearly visible fault scarp that cuts across alluvial fans (which we know are geologically recent) at the bases of Rockchuck Peak and Teewinot. Lake sediments in Jackson Hole, dating from times when downdropping of southern Jackson Hole impounded the Snake River, show increasing tilt with age. And the valley floor, instead of sloping toward the Snake River as we expect in a normal drainage situation, tilts westward to the very edge of the mountains, where Fish Creek and some poorly drained marshes mark the fault zone and the line of maximum movement.

Processes that have shaped the Tetons have been strongly influenced by the westward dip of the fault block in which they are sculptured. The range as a whole is asymmetrical. The highest peaks are set far east in a wedge between the Teton fault zone and an older, almost parallel break called the Buck Mountain fault. Streams cascading down the steep east slope have always had far greater eroding power than more leisurely streams of the gentle western slope. As a result they cut deeper, steeper canyons, canyons that worked headward, "pirating" more and more of the west slope's drainage area, pushing westward the divide between eastward and westward drainage. An asymmetrical ridge, more continuous than the main line of the peaks but not nearly as high or spectacular, forms the present drainage divide. It is well west of the highest peaks.

Water trickling into joints in fractured rock expands when it freezes, gradually widening joints and breaking the rock apart.

Landforms on the two sides of the range differ as well. In the east parts of the range, tough, hard Precambrian granite and gneiss are at the surface, for all overlying softer rock has long since eroded away. The granite is highly jointed, and the gneiss contains layers and bands of schist. Weathering of mica in the gneiss and schist and breakup of the much-jointed granite by frost wedging have produced the rugged grandeur that you see. The work of frost, abetted by that of rain, hail, and snow, is superimposed on landscape roughed out by glaciers—deeply gouged U-shaped valleys, pointed matterhorn peaks, razor-backed arêtes, and high hanging valleys.

The tilted sedimentary rocks of the gentler western slope have not been as thoroughly fractured nor as highly elevated. Glacial features are still apparent though not as prominent. Since stream erosion is less dynamic, the landforms are less vertical: linear cliffs and benches dictated by hardness or softness of sedimentary layers, sloping cuestas that extend west beyond the park boundary to the Teton basin.

Jackson Hole is also in large part a manifestation of the Ice Ages. Here deposition, rather than erosion, held sway. True, a number of sharply rising hills and a few low ridges are ice-rounded remnants of fault blocks. But other prominent features—terraces so regular that they appear man-made, scattered lakes and the moraines that dam them, fields of potholes or kettles—are features of deposition. The valley as a whole slopes southward and westward. A line of lakes, concealed by thick forests growing on glacial-moraine dams, lies below the steep face of the Tetons. Jackson Lake was the largest and deepest of these even before construction of the dam raised the water level and increased the lake area.

The floor of Jackson Hole is a cobble-strewn plain on which are visible, from above, interwoven patterns of overloaded glacier-fed streams. The terrace levels represent successive stages of glacial activity and glacial melting in the Teton–Yellowstone region and in the highlands to the northeast. In contrast to the poorly sorted, sandy, silty glacial moraines, which support dense forests, the outwash gravel of the terraces consists of rounded cobbles and pebbles washed almost free of silt and clay. These deposits hold little water and support only a thin cover of grass, sagebrush, and other drought-tolerant plants.

GEOLOGIC HISTORY

Precambrian Era. Sharply chiseled Precambrian metamorphic and intrusive rocks in the Teton facade are similar to those that underlie the continents. Gneiss, intricately banded and streaked with schist, is the oldest rock present and is indeed one of the oldest rocks in North America, formed about 3 billion years ago. Probably deposited originally as sedimentary and volcanic layers on the floor of an ancient sea, these rocks were buried deeply under thousands of meters of overlying layers for hundreds of millions of years. Long after they accumulated, they were heated and squeezed, folded and recrystallized, until positive traces of their earlier origin were all but erased. Only contorted folds of gneiss and schist and occasional stringers of marble and serpentine remain.

Gneiss and schist are thought to form at depths of 7 to 14 kilometers (5 to 10 miles) below the surface and at temperatures as great as 600°C (1000°F).

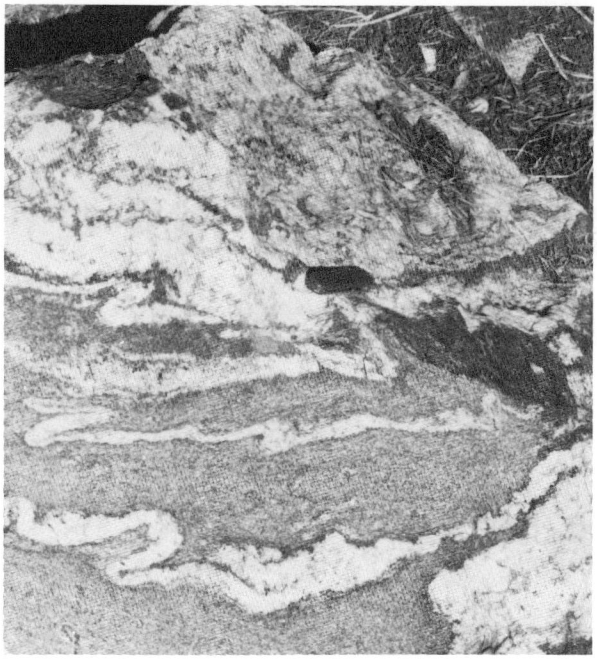

Streaks and squiggles in Precambrian gneiss show that rock flows like taffy under immense pressure and high temperature.

Granite of the central Tetons has a fine-grained salt-and-pepper texture.

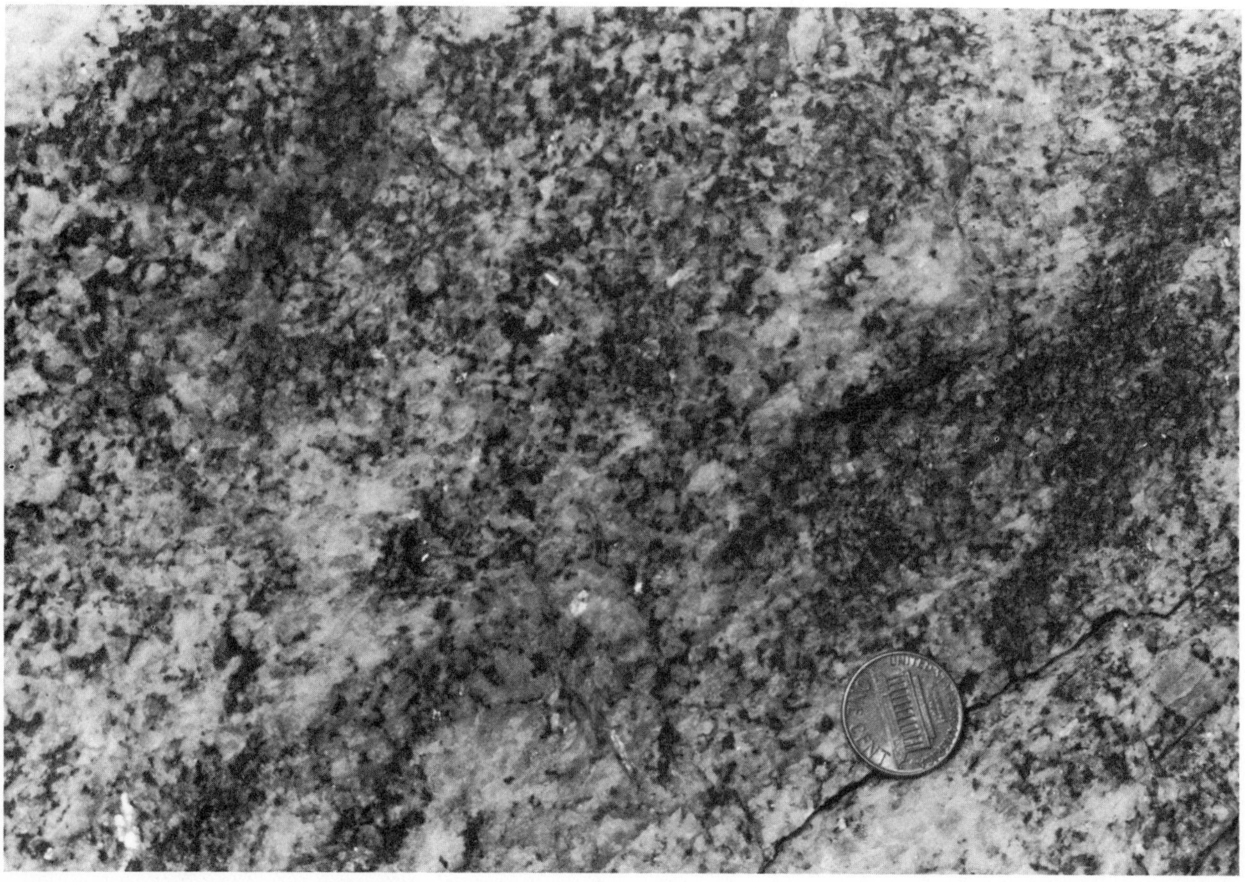

Under these conditions, rock flows stiffly without breaking, like taffy or sun-warmed tar (both of which are brittle when cold). Folded and wiggling patterns in the rock result from such flow. You can see many fine examples of these in the Tetons.

Half a billion years after they were formed, the metamorphic rocks became host to intrusions of molten magma rising from deep inside the earth. Forcing or melting its way into the metamorphic rocks, the magma cooled and crystallized slowly into a large, irregular granite mass and a fine, white lacework of pegmatite dikes. These are visible today in the central Tetons, especially in the Cathedral Peaks cluster. The granite is light gray and fine grained, with small interlocking quartz, feldspar, biotite, and hornblende crystals giving it an uneven salt-and-pepper texture. Pegmatite in the dikes resembles the granite but is coarser grained. Both can be seen along canyon trails.

After more hundreds of millions of years, 1.3 billion years ago, new fluids found their way into vertical fissures that cut through both the gneiss-schist and the granite. Darker in color, these fluids cooled to become prominent diabase dikes that now slash like saber scars across Grand and Middle Tetons and project like a wide wall down the east face of Mount Moran. The diabase is less resistant than the granite of Grand and Middle Tetons, but more resistant than the gneiss and schist of Mount Moran, which explains its different erosion style on the different peaks. Youngest of the Precambrian rocks, the diabase is like basalt in composition, but since it cooled slowly its crystals are large enough to be seen without magnification.

As far as we can tell, the rocks of the Tetons saw no further alteration for more than 700 million years after intrusion of the black dikes. We know that the region was lifted and exposed to erosional processes that obliterated all mountains and all higher rock layers, if there were any. By the end of Precambrian time the area had become a vast, austere, almost featureless plain devoid of vegetation (land plants had not yet evolved) and probably not far above sea level. The closest modern parallels are the glacier-scoured interior of eastern Canada and the flat, nearly featureless plains of Australia and Siberia.

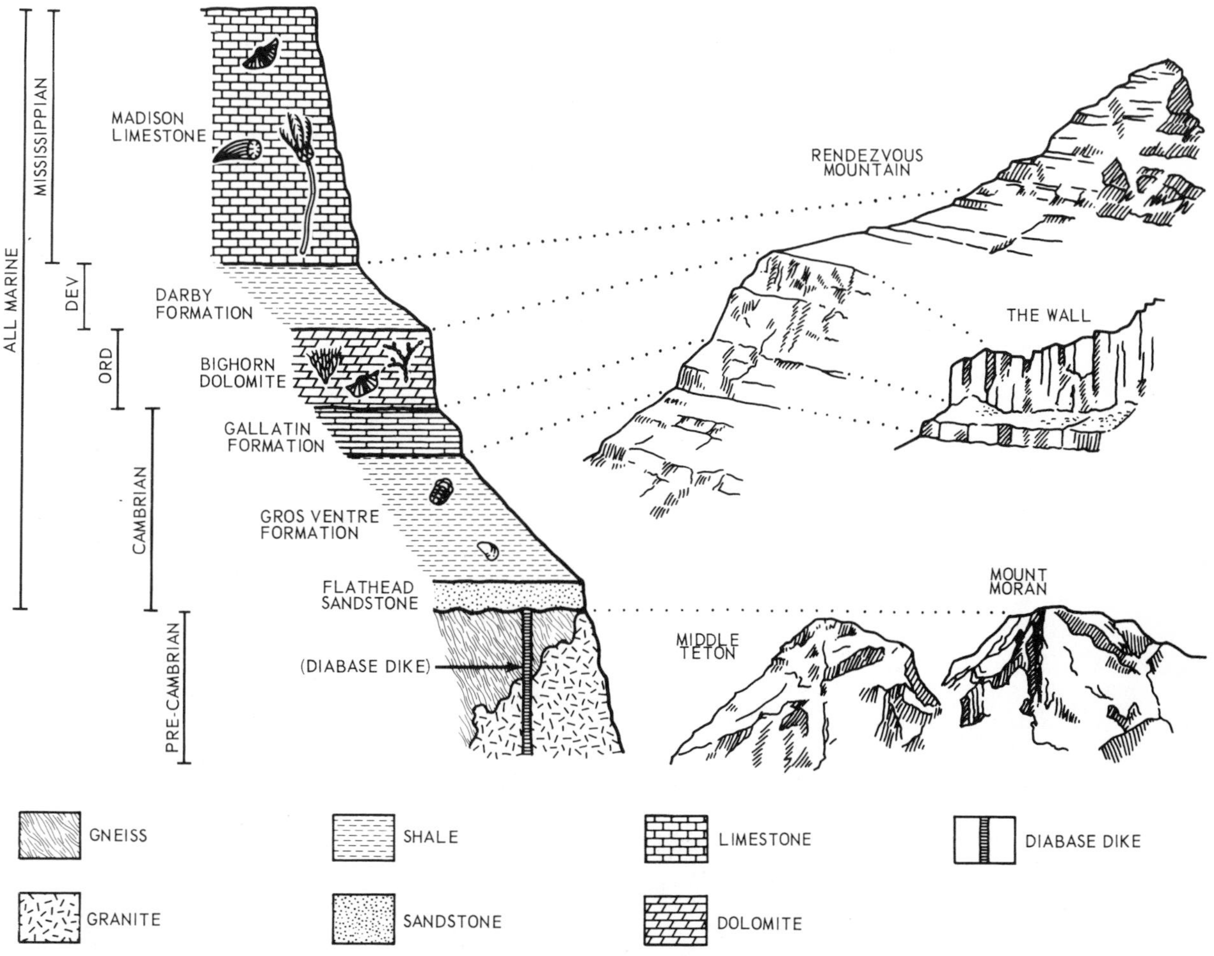

Paleozoic Era. Sedimentary rocks of the Tetons, visible in northern, southern, and western parts of the range, show us that the region sank beneath the sea early in Paleozoic time. Near the summit of the Teton Village tram and in the "back country" of Alaska Basin and the Teton Crest Trail, Paleozoic rock layers lie on the beveled Precambrian surface, a westward-tilted record of the continuing history of the region. These marine shales, sandstones, limestones, and dolomites are rich in fossils: mollusk and brachiopod shells, corals, bryozoans, trilobites, and occasional fish remains which we can recognize and correlate with Paleozoic fossils elsewhere to pinpoint the age of each formation. Here you can see in profile and in well exposed sequence Cambrian, Ordovician, Devonian, and Mississippian rocks—all of the lower Paleozoic systems except Silurian, which either was never deposited here or was carefully and completely skimmed off by erosion. These pages of stone tell us of repeated subsidence of the land, of influx of sand and mud from beaches and estuaries, of warm and tranquil seas in which an extraordinary variety of animals crawled and burrowed and swam, of deep-water deposition of pure, clean limestone, of storm waves that loosened and rounded and redistributed fragments of rock, of occasionally oily, turbid, or stagnant water lethal to fish and other organisms.

Pennsylvanian and Permian rocks were deposited in this region as well, but they have been stripped away from the area in the park. Where they do exist, in Idaho and in the mountains east and south of Jackson Hole, they show continued submersion and then gradual shallowing of the sea.

Mesozoic Era. No Mesozoic rocks are present in the Tetons, but from surrounding areas we know that the Mesozoic was a time of alternating marine and nonmarine environments. At times, desert dunes bordered shallow evaporating pans. At least once, a warm, shallow sea teeming with mollusks covered this region. At times reptiles and amphibians scavenged for food on wide tidal flats; at other times dinosaurs roamed torrid swamps and marshes.

Toward the end of the Mesozoic Era a wave of mountain building swept eastward from California, almost certainly in response to the westward drift of the continent. The area north and west of the Tetons rose in a broad arch. Rivers and streams, strengthened by uplift, stripped from the arch the thick Mesozoic and Paleozoic sedimentary rocks as well as thousands of feet of red and green Precambrian quartzite that had covered its northern end. At about the same time another northwest-trending arch developed across what is now the Jackson Hole–Teton area. Then, for the last time, the sea retreated.

In the western Tetons, Paleozoic sedimentary rocks erode into characteristic cliffs, ledges, and slopes.

Cenozoic Era. Crustal unrest continued during the early part of the Tertiary Period. Tall mountains rose and deep basins subsided. In the Teton area, Precambrian rocks were pushed upward several thousand meters along a great reverse fault, the Buck Mountain fault, whose trend paralleled for the first time the trend of the present Tetons. Rock debris from the many mountain ranges was washed into nearby basins. To it were added, beginning in Eocene time, blankets of volcanic ash from newly erupting volcanoes in the Yellowstone region to the north. These processes continued for many millions of years until by Miocene time both folded and faulted mountains, much reduced from their former size, were virtually buried under hundreds of meters of rock debris and ash.

Eight to ten million years ago, during the Pliocene Epoch, movement began along the Teton fault. As the Tetons were pushed up, Jackson Hole sank. This motion dammed a big freshwater lake where lake limestone and shale and fine volcanic ash accumulated, burying shells of freshwater mollusks and occasional bones and teeth of beaver and other mammals.

Simultaneous broad-scale uplift affecting most of the Rocky Mountain region brought the area gradually to its present elevation – and brought about a corresponding cooling of its climate. Proliferating volcanoes of the Yellowstone region began to die out, though not before titanic volcanic explosions had showered the area with more thick deposits of ash, and new volcanic activity around the explosion area had covered the northern Tetons and nearby parts of Yellowstone with lava.

Sinking of the Jackson Hole block and uplift of the Teton block continued throughout Pleistocene time. New lakes formed as Jackson Hole continued to sink; subsequent faulting has now lifted tilted lake deposits above the valley floor level on Blacktail Butte.

But the most memorable features of the Pleistocene Epoch were the great glaciers, their causes unknown but their distinctive imprint easily recognized in the sculpture of the Tetons and infilling of Jackson Hole. The most widespread glaciation in this region is

Two Ocean Lake is surrounded by moraines of this region's second glacial stage. At least 35,000 years old, these moraines have developed a much thicker soil layer than have third-stage moraines.

dated at about 150,000 years ago. Broad, slow-moving rivers of ice from the mountainous region north and northeast of Yellowstone Park came together to flow south through Jackson Hole, overriding Signal Mountain and other mid-valley buttes, grinding and gouging a path through the Snake River Canyon into Idaho. In many places this giant glacier was at least 600 meters (2,000 feet) thick; it was the largest to invade Jackson Hole. Its tributaries in the Tetons carved and straightened earlier stream-cut gorges and chiseled the peaks into angular matterhorns. When it melted, it left a barren pavement of red quartzite boulders that today reveal its origin in faraway mountains on the other side of the Yellowstone volcanic plateau.

The second glaciation 70,000 to 54,000 years ago was less austere. A tongue of ice swept from eastern Yellowstone Park into northern Jackson Hole, where it met and joined mountain glaciers from the Tetons. Moraines from this glacier now surround Two Ocean and Emma Mathilda Lakes, and part of its great sheet of outwash carpets the southern half of Jackson Hole.

The third and last glaciation, only 30,000 to 13,000 years ago (man was already in America), added most of the final scenic touches to the present park area. Mountain glaciers sharpened the intricate peaks and narrow arêtes, smoothed and striated the walls of Teton canyons, and deposited relatively small moraines along the west edge of Jackson Hole, where they now encircle Taggart, Phelps, Bradley, Jenny, and Leigh Lakes. Glaciers from Moran Canyon and canyons farther north merged into a piedmont glacier where Jackson Lake is now. Burnt Ridge and Jackson Lake moraines mark its southernmost advance. Outwash deposits extend south to Blacktail Butte and in places are pocked with kettles (locally called potholes) where large blocks of ice incorporated in the outwash debris slowly melted.

Present glaciers in the Tetons are not just unmelted remnants of these last glaciers. A warm-temperature cycle occurring 6,000 years ago is thought to have destroyed all the glaciers of that time. The little glaciers here today may date from the Little Ice Age of the 13th Century A.D., when European glaciers

Phelps Lake at the mouth of Death Canyon is dammed by high lateral and terminal moraines of a mountain glacier.

Trapper Lake is one of many small ponds occupying icemelt depressions or kettles in glacial moraines.

are known to have increased in size. Several of the present glaciers can be reached by trail. They range to about 1,100 meters (3,500 feet) in length and 335 meters (1,100 feet) in width. To qualify as glaciers rather than icefields they must show evidence of movement, which usually requires that they be at least 30 meters (100 feet) thick. Coarse, rocky terminal moraines below them testify to recent movement.

BEHIND THE SCENES

Amphitheatre Lake and Surprise Lake. High on the east flank of Grand Teton, these two tiny tarns typify the alpine lakes that occupy scooped-out glacial cirques. Look for glacial striae on rock faces nearby. The lake waters, once pale with finely ground rock flour, are now clear, indicating that there is no longer any moving ice above them.

Cascade Canyon. Deeply U-shaped in cross section, Cascade Canyon is an outstanding example of the way a mountain glacier straightens, scours, and deepens its canyon. The change from smoothed rock to angular rock high on its walls defines the highest level to which this canyon was filled with ice.

Glaciers forming in cirques now occupied by Lake Solitude and Schoolroom Glacier united to flow into the great body of ice that filled Jackson Hole during the first glaciation. Unable to quarry the resistant granite of the Teton fault block as rapidly as the larger glacier from the Yellowstone region could erode the soft, unconsolidated valley fill, the original Cascade Glacier joined the larger one high above the floor of Jackson Hole. When the ice retreated, its valley was left as a hanging valley with a tumbling cascade at its lower end. During the third glacial advance, an icefall plunged over the rim where Hidden Falls are now. Reforming below, the ice spread out as the piedmont glacier that deposited the Jenny Lake moraine.

The canyon owes its stepped floor to ponding of a string of lakes in depressions scoured by the glaciers. Infilling behind beaver dams and low recessional moraines helped to create the fertile canyon floor.

If you hike up Cascade Canyon, be sure to examine the granite, gneiss, and schist exposed on its walls and talus, and observe the magnificent veining on the cliffs.

Glacially smoothed lower canyon walls contrast with angular, nonglaciated cliffs above. Horizontal banding of the ancient gneiss is partly concealed by staining caused by rain, snowmelt, and lichens.

Teewinot and Mount Owen, as well as other peaks of the Cathedral Group, are continually sharpened by frost.

A recent fault scarp, visible as a dark zone of denser vegetation, offsets the alluvial fan at the base of Teewinot.

Cathedral Group. Attacked on all sides by Ice Age glaciers, the Precambrian granite mass of the central Tetons was sharpened into the turrets and spires of today's great clustered peaks—South, Middle, and Grand Teton, Teewinot, and Mount Owen. The rock of which these giants are formed is fine gray granite intricately laced with quartz veins and pegmatite dikes, some of them many meters across. Both Middle and Grand Teton are sliced by single dark vertical diabase dikes; since the diabase weathers more readily than surrounding granite, the dikes are hidden deep in saber-slash ravines.

Trails which climb the face of the Cathedral Group offer many excellent views of major geologic features of the park. They look down on moraine-dammed lakes along the mountain front and reveal the abrupt change from forested moraines to sagebrush-covered outwash plains. Granite bordering the trails often bears glacial striae. At the base of Teewinot is a change in slope that defines a fault scarp recent enough to cut an alluvial fan—evidence that these mountains are still growing. The hike to Surprise and Amphitheatre Lakes is well worth while if you are in good condition.

Death Canyon. This canyon is the best place in the Tetons to see at close hand the metamorphic and intrusive igneous rocks that make up the core of the Tetons: banded gneiss, schist, and granite. The trail approaches the canyon across the high lateral moraine of a glacier that occupied it in Ice Age time, and it looks down on Phelps Lake, dammed by the steep arch of its terminal moraine. The volume of rock in these moraines is impressive, and it resulted only from the least extensive last glaciation. Once into the canyon there is banded gneiss composed chiefly of quartz, feldspar, flaky black mica or biotite, and black rodlike crystals of hornblende. Banding is due to variations in the proportions of these four minerals. Amphibolite, a dark rock composed mostly of hornblende, is also present. Schist is easy to distinguish because it splits along parallel layers of mica crystals. In talus slopes by the trail you may come across blocks of marble, a metamorphic rock originating as limestone.

Evidence points to the origin of these rocks as sedimentary and volcanic layers deposited in the sea. However, the pressures and temperatures to which they were afterward subjected destroyed almost all the original sedimentary and volcanic features; only the banding remains.

Watch for augen gneiss, a rock that contains hundreds of peering "eyes" (*augen* in German). The center of each bright eye is a cluster of magnetite crystals, rich in iron. As iron was drawn into the crystals, the area surrounding each cluster was depleted of dark minerals and now appears white.

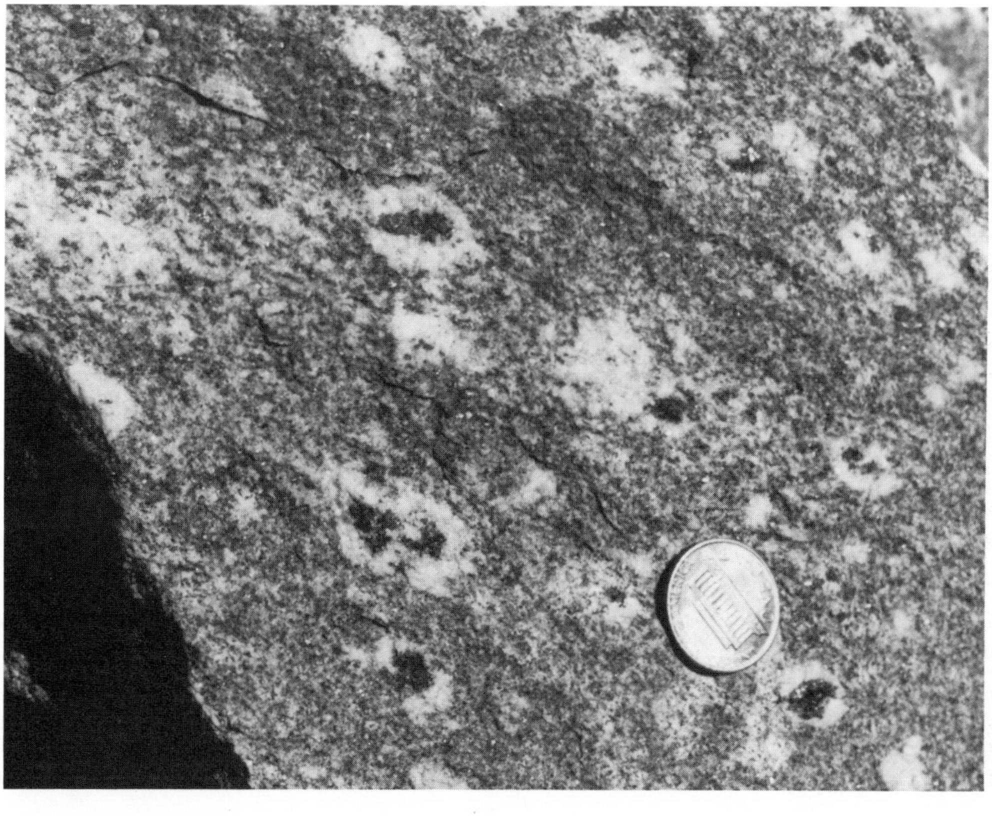

Bright "eyes" or augen peer out from augen gneiss. This sample is quite near the Death Canyon trail.

Fine fracturing and patterned pegmatite veining are well displayed in Granite Canyon. Here, a fault offsets two parts of a pegmatite vein.

The rock glacier crawling toward Granite Canyon is not as active as it once was. Parts of it are now forested.

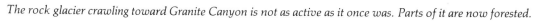

Grand Teton. The view from the summit of Grand Teton is, of course, the grandest view around. All the geologic features of the range and of Jackson Hole are laid out below — the U-shaped canyons, high cirques and little lakes and glaciers that now occupy them, the dark dikes slashing Grand and Middle Teton and Mount Moran, the flat-floored valley intricately traced by ancient glacier-fed floods, tree-covered moraines, the winding channel of the Snake River, and to the west the sloping sedimentary rocks of the west side of the Tetons.

Granite Canyon. Near the south end of the park, Granite Canyon is walled partly with granite, as the name implies, and partly with banded gneiss and schist. Many examples can be seen along the trail (see Death Canyon for rock descriptions). The canyon itself is not as strongly shaped by glaciation as canyons farther north, though there are moraines at its mouth.

About three miles into the canyon, a large rock glacier creeps down the south slope. Great jumbled rock masses such as this, lubricated by ice and water, crawl downhill in much the same manner as true glaciers. Parts of this one have stabilized long enough to become forested.

Paleozoic sedimentary rocks typical of the western slope of the Tetons reach farther east here, reflecting the southward plunge of this end of the range. You will come across them just above the point where the canyon forks. Cambrian Flathead Sandstone and Gallatin Limestone, Ordovician Bighorn Dolomite, and Mississippian Madison Limestone are the cliff formers. Don't be dismayed if there seem to be too many cliffs — they are repeated by faulting.

Jackson Hole. The downdropped block of Jackson Hole is filled with rock debris washed, gouged, and rasped off the Tetons to the west and other mountains to the northeast and east. The boulder-strewn plain, terraced as glaciers came and went in the mountains, is composed of outwash gravels. Most forested areas are moraines.

The steep-sided, ice-scoured buttes that rise from the valley floor are fragments of Paleozoic rock and whitish Tertiary lake deposits raised and tipped by faulting. The old lakes formed when the downward motion of the valley and the upward motion of mountains to the south ponded the ancestor of the Snake River.

Jackson Lake. This lake occupies a deep depression in the glacial outwash of Jackson Hole. It is rimmed on the south with moraines of a single piedmont glacier formed as glaciers from Moran and Snowshoe Canyons and other canyons of the northern Tetons fused and spread out at the base of the mountains. The lake is deepest — 130 meters (400 feet) — close to the mountains, where these merging glaciers accumulated and turned south. Jackson Lake dam, built in 1916, added 12 meters (39 feet) to the depth of the lake.

Jenny Lake. Like Leigh, Bradley, Taggart, and Phelps Lakes, Jenny Lake is a legacy of the last glaciation. It occupies a depression behind the moraine of the glacier that flowed down Cascade Canyon. A small delta now builds outward on the west side of the lake, where Cascade Creek, coming down the hanging valley that is Cascade Canyon, tumbles and splashes over the rocky rim as Hidden Falls. Walk to Inspiration Point for the best view of the lake.

Lake Solitude. Lying in a shallow basin below the steep-walled cirque at the head of the north fork of Cascade Canyon, Lake Solitude typifies small alpine lakes of the Tetons. It is surrounded by glacially smoothed and striated granite of the core of the central Tetons. Diminutive granite islands, as well as outcrops around the lake itself, display smooth, rounded upstream surfaces and angular, near-vertical downstream faces, features often used to diagnose the direction of movement of glaciers and ice sheets of the past.

U-shaped canyons are legacies of mountain or alpine glaciers.

Lake Solitude's rocky islets indicate the direction of ice flow, from right to left in this photograph.

Cambrian sedimentary rocks of the west slope of the Tetons crop out above the cirque headwall northwest of Lake Solitude. Banded gneiss shows up well on the headwall, also.

Mount Moran. North of the granite mass that makes up the central Tetons, Mount Moran is composed of gneiss and schist. These rocks contribute to its massiveness for, unlike the granite of the Cathedral Group, they are not heavily fractured and do not develop into frost-sharpened spires and crags. In some places the gneiss is quite intricately folded in light and dark patterns, but for the most part it is layered and streaked with broad light and dark bands that reflect its probable origin as flat-lying marine sediments and volcanic flows. In places it is interlayered with gray marble (once limestone) and with discontinuous masses of serpentine that may once have been lava flows.

A patch of Cambrian sedimentary rock—the Flathead Sandstone—forms a small, moundlike cap on Mount Moran, indicating that the beveled surface of the mountaintop is a remnant of the widespread erosion surface formed at the end of Precambrian time. This same surface is a prominent feature in Grand Canyon and several other national parks and monuments.

The most prominent feature on Mount Moran is the great vertical diabase dike. The largest of several in the Tetons, it is about 50 meters (150 feet) thick

The Teton Range as seen from Signal Mountain defines a low arch. Paleozoic sedimentary rocks, which once extended completely across this area, are now present only at the north and south extremities of the Tetons, on their western slope, and in small patches on top of Mount Moran, Traverse Peak, and Doane Peak.

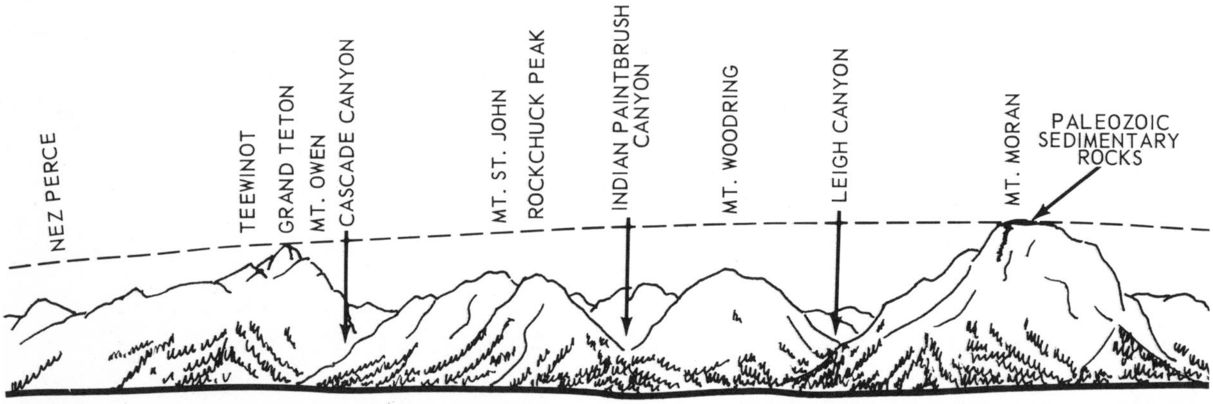

and has been traced about 10 kilometers (7 miles) westward from Mount Moran. It cuts across many light-colored pegmatite veins, which therefore must be older, but is itself truncated by the Precambrian erosion surface, which therefore must be younger. Since Mount Moran's metamorphic rock erodes a little more easily than the diabase of the dike, the dike forms a high wall jutting from the mountainside.

Falling Ice Glacier and Skillet Glacier hang like pendants on the precipitous side of Mount Moran. Their moraines are just visible as grayish piles of rock, though that of Falling Ice Glacier turns immediately into a talus slope.

Oxbow Bend. Not far below the Jackson Lake dam, an old meander loop of the Snake River has been abandoned by the main stream. Without strong flow, this bend is now marshy in places and bedecked with low islands, a wildlife haven. Oxbow lakes like this are common features of old, slow-moving rivers that have very low gradients. Although the Snake is not old, its gradient is quite low here because the river has difficulty cutting down through the ridge near Moran.

Signal Mountain. This little peak, accessible by road, offers an excellent view of Jackson Hole and the mountains that surround it. Twelve kilometers (8 miles) to the west, the Tetons tower above Jackson Lake. Notice that the mountain summits describe a gentle arc from north to south, an arc approximating the upward bowing of the northwest-trending anticline of Pliocene days. Both the northernmost and southernmost summits are patched with Paleozoic sedimentary layers that have been eroded off the highest central part of the Tetons.

To the south, sage-covered outwash gravel floors Jackson Hole. This flat surface is crossed by forested moraines, and the Snake River winds along a channel eroded in the glacial debris. To the east and southeast rise the Mount Leidy Highlands and the Gros Ventre Range, older mountains composed largely of the same sedimentary layers, both Paleozoic and Mesozoic, that must once have arched across the Tetons. Northward and northeastward rise the Yellowstone volcanic plateau and older volcanic rocks of the Absaroka Range.

Snake River. A float trip down the Snake River will take you close to the river-dissected terraces of Jackson Hole, with cobbles and pebbles of igneous and metamorphic rock rounded and sorted by outwash streams. Both rounding and sorting by size are clues to deposition by running water. What must have been the strength of the ice-fed floods that spread all this debris below the melting glaciers?

Of successive terrace levels, the uppermost are the oldest. Lower levels formed as the Snake River and its tributaries, swinging broadly from side to side, first carved into an old level and then formed new floodplains below. These in turn were dissected during another period of downcutting. Sand and gravel bars and shifting channels indicate that the present river is supplied with far more rock material than it can possibly carry.

Teton Glacier. An off-trail hiking permit is required for the climb from Amphitheatre Lake to Teton Glacier. With good binoculars the glacier can be examined from the valley floor.

Squeezing down a narrow chasm between Grand Teton and Mount Owen, this glacier does not have a typical arcuate cirque. The steep headwall took shape as glacial ice repeatedly froze to the rock and then, moving, pulled some of it loose from the mountain mass. At the lower end of the glacier is the piled

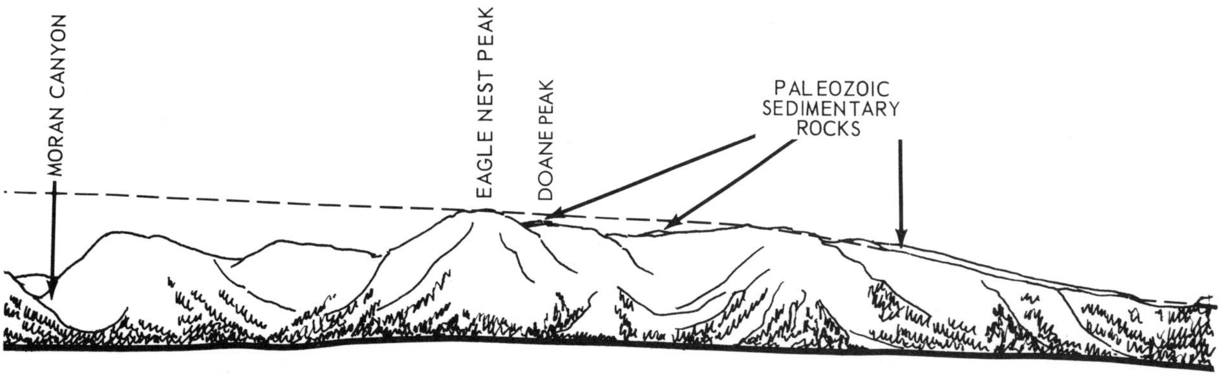

rubble of the terminal moraine, an unsorted, jumbled, new-looking mass of angular rock debris. A hundred years ago the glacier came right to this pile; in the last 50 years it has melted back to its present position. Even though the glacier "retreats," its ice continues to flow downhill at a rate of just over 10 meters (30 feet) a year.

Delta Lake, downcanyon from Teton Glacier, gets its pale green color from fine rock flour produced as glacier movement grinds rock against rock.

Precambrian granite in the crags above Teton Glacier is part of the mass that intruded the central Tetons more than two billion years ago. The jagged, much-jointed cliffs display many examples of frost wedging.

Teton Village aerial tram. Though outside the national park, this tram will deposit you right on the park boundary atop Rendezvous Mountain 1,265 meters (4,150 feet) above the floor of Jackson Hole. As you ascend, look north along the base of the mountains to see the line of undrained, marshy ground that marks the position of the Teton fault. This is the lowest part of the valley, and from here the valley slopes *up* toward the Snake River!

Atop Rendezvous Mountain are Paleozoic sedimentary rocks: marine sandstone, shale, limestone, and dolomite. Use the stratigraphic diagram to identify them, and watch for fossils. The Rendezvous Mountain trail, which curves west, north, and then east into Granite Canyon, passes among these rocks and gives an excellent downhill transept of Teton rocks and structure.

OTHER READING

Anonymous. 1970. *Grand Teton National Park.* Reverse of U.S. Geological Survey topographic map of Grand Teton National Park.

Crandall, Hugh. 1978. *Grand Teton, the Story Behind the Scenery.* KC Publications, Las Vegas, Nevada.

Love, J. D., and de la Montagne, J. 1956. *Pleistocene and Recent Tilting of Jackson Hole, Teton County, Wyoming.* Wyoming Geological Association guidebook, Field Conference for 1956, pp. 169-178.

Love, J. D., and Reed, John C., Jr. 1968. *Creation of the Teton Landscape.* Grand Teton Natural History Association, Moose, Wyoming.

Great Sand Dunes National Monument

Established: 1932
Size: 149 square kilometers (58 square miles)
Elevation: 2,377 meters (7,800 feet) at visitor center
Address: Box 60, Alamosa, Colorado 81101

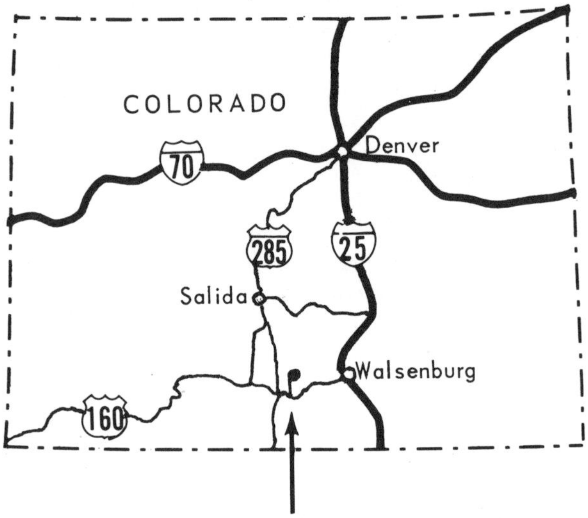

STAR FEATURES

- Large wind-deposited sand dunes that display many features of both modern and ancient wind-blown sand: cross-bedding, ripple marks, sand avalanche paths, animal tracks, and buried vegetation.
- A setting within an arid intermountain basin bounded by volcanic mountains and a youthful fault-block range.
- A seasonal stream and its interesting interplay with the dunes.
- Interpretive activities that include a visitor center, self-guide trails, guided walks, and evening programs.

SETTING THE STAGE

Colorado's Great Sand Dunes, nestled close under the Sangre de Cristo Range in a protected corner of the San Luis Valley, rise 240 meters (almost 800 feet) above the sloping valley floor. Though 2 kilometers (7,000 feet) above sea level, the San Luis Valley is almost totally surrounded by high, rugged mountains. To the east looms the jagged fortress of the Sangre de Cristo Range, its face marking a large, recently active fault zone, its towering peaks reaching elevations of 4,200 meters (14,000 feet). Across the valley to the west lie the San Juan Mountains, born in the thunder of volcanic eruptions. To the north and northwest the two ranges converge. To the

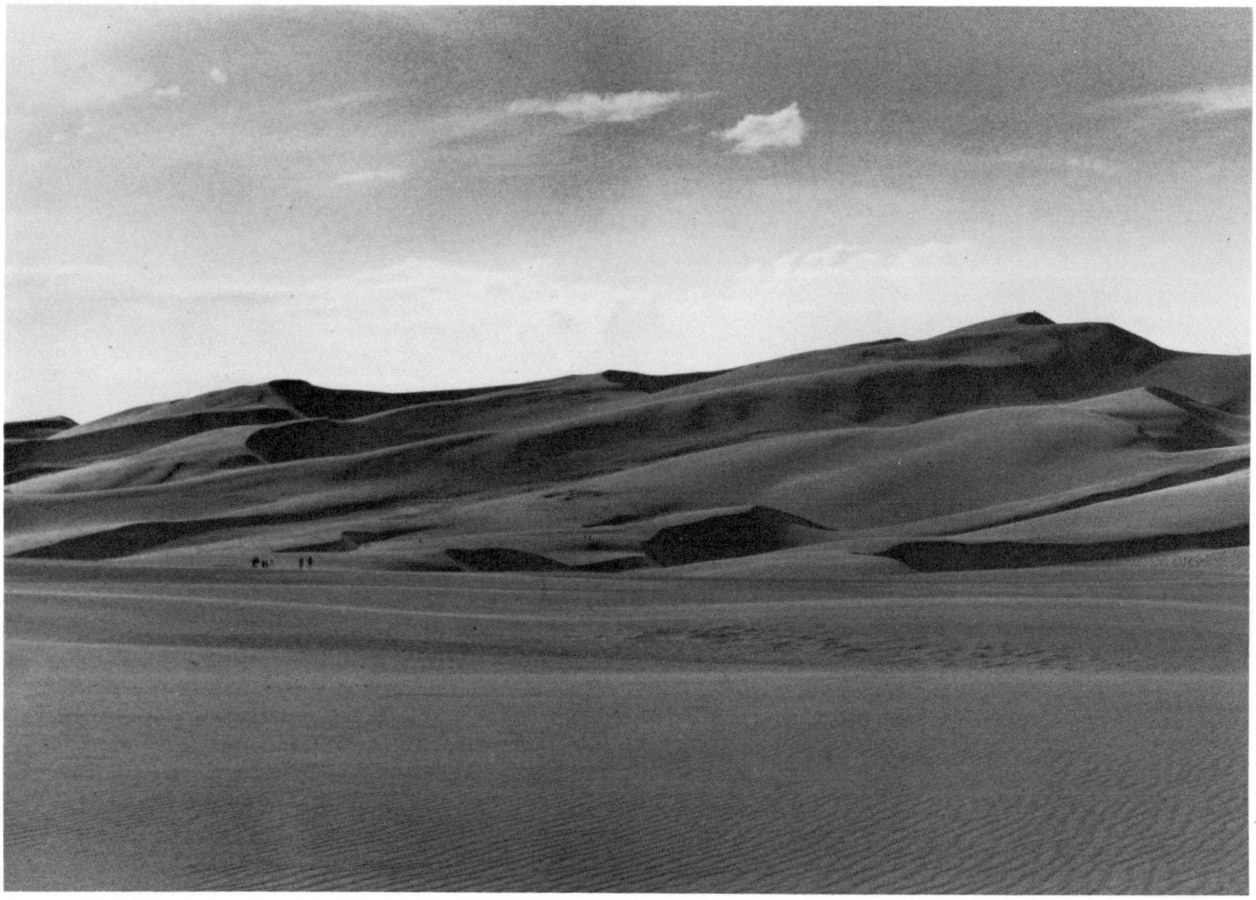

Despite occasional reversals in wind direction, the Great Sand Dunes are markedly asymmetrical, with long, gentle southwest slopes and steep northeast faces.

south the valley is open, but even there the horizon is interrupted by clustered cinder cones, lava-capped mesas, and volcanic domes.

Why are the dunes here, crowded against the Sangre de Cristos, tucked into the angle where Blanca Peak (Sierra Blanca) bulges westward from the abrupt mountain bastion? Here, special ingredients vital to dune formation come together. There is sand. There is wind. And there is a sheltered place where wind-carried sand can come to rest.

Prevailing winds in this region blow across the San Luis Valley from the southwest. They are at times no more than mild breezes, scarcely rippling the sagebrush and grasses of the valley floor. But in spring and early summer they increase in strength. Winds vital to sand dune growth must move with speeds greater than 7 or 8 meters per second (15 miles an hour). Gusting across the valley, such winds raise clouds of dust and whirls of sand from the valley floor, carrying the dust in suspension, bouncing sand grains along the ground surface. There is plenty of sand. With average annual rainfall measuring only 23 centimeters (8 inches), vegetation is sparse in the San Luis Valley, and large expanses of soil remain dry and unprotected by plant roots or branches. Moreover, the valley holds thick deposits of sand and silt washed from the mountains that ring it. The greater share of this material, distinctly volcanic in origin, comes from the San Juan Mountains to the west. Most of the tiny, rounded sand grains of the dunes have mineral compositions like those of volcanic rocks, with only trifling additions of quartz and feldspar sand derived from nonvolcanic rocks of the Sangre de Cristo Range. The high proportion of volcanic sand gives these dunes a darker cast than most dune and beach sand. (Because the dark grains soak up solar radiation, the dunes can become quite hot in summer, too hot at midday for barefoot enjoyment.)

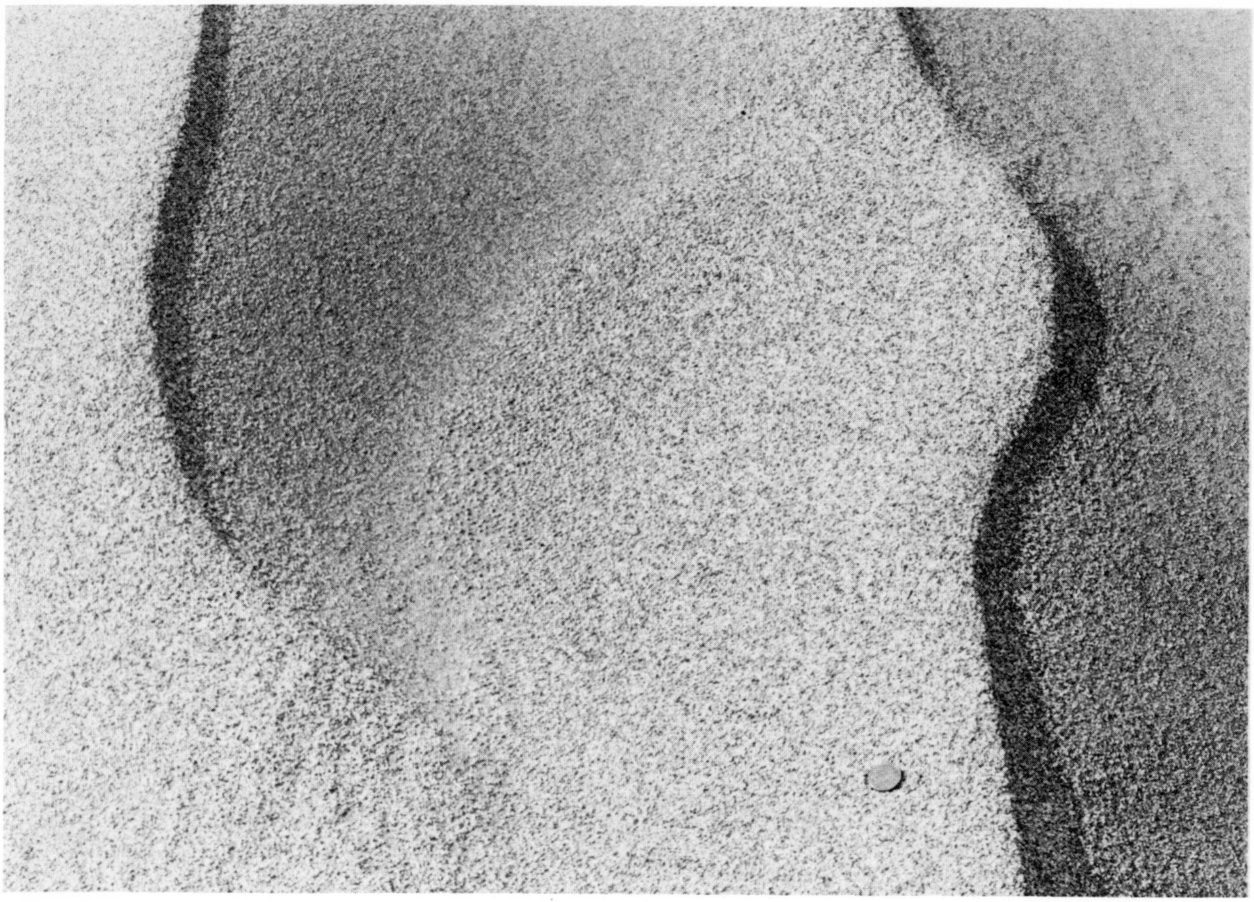

Grains of dark and light sand are blown into undulating ripples on the dunes. Sand grains are rounded and lightly frosted by collision with other grains.

As strong southwest winds with their combined burden of sand and dust approach the Sangre de Cristos, they funnel toward three low spots in the sharp-edged barrier of the range: Mosca, Music, and Medano Passes. Tumbled into eddies by their encounter with the mountains, the rising winds carry suspended dust on over the mountain passes. But they cannot lift the larger, heavier grains of sand high enough to get them across the range. So over countless centuries sand has accumulated, grain by bouncing grain, near the mountain front in a large pocket somewhat sheltered by the projecting mass of Sierra Blanca. Here the drifting sand, perpetually rearranged by the wind, has piled up in dunes.

The dunes have long, gentle windward slopes and steep leeward faces. Sand grains blown up the upwind slope gradually bounce their way to the dune crest. There they are dropped just beyond the dune crest, on the upper part of the sheltered downwind face. The addition of more and more sand grains gradually oversteepens the lee face. When it becomes steeper than about 34 degrees (the angle of repose for most wind-blown sand), masses of the sand begin to avalanche, to slide downhill.

In most dunes these processes — movement of sand by bouncing (or saltation) up the windward slope and by avalanching down the leeward slope — go on indefinitely, so that sand skimmed from the windward side is moved regularly to the leeward side, with a net result of slow downwind creep of the entire dune. But here in Great Sand Dunes another factor comes into play. Wintry storms drive down the eastern side of the mountains and sweep across the passes from the northeast to temporarily reverse the drift of the dunes. These winds gather sand from Sangre de Cristo streambeds as well as from the steep lee faces of the dunes and move it *westward* over the crests, building sharp little reverse crests or counterdunes on every ridge. The northeast winds thus seem to cancel out some of the downwind drift and to hold the dunes back from the mountains.

The result of the interplay between southwest and northeast winds is a fairly stable but unusually high-piled dune mass, with the main dune crests and ridges scarcely changing in shape or position with passing years.

As new sand is added from the valley floor or from the Sangre de Cristo streambeds, the dunes increase

E. D. McKee photo

When winds reverse, counterdunes appear along dune crests. Reversing dunes tend to build higher and higher as new sand is added.

Medano Creek, broad, shallow, and often dry near the dunes, fights a never-ending battle against encroaching sand.

in height. Three flowing streams from the Sangres interfere, however, with any increase in area, regulating the position and size of the dune field. Medano Creek on the south and Sand Creek with its tributary Cold Creek on the north curve around the dunes, dampening the sand near their banks, undercutting the dampened sand to form small cliffs, and carrying away dry sand that cascades down the dune slopes. Though these streams flow only in spring, when runoff is high, they play an important part in limiting the size of the dune field. Nevertheless, the dunes gradually deflect the streams from their former courses, so that all three streams now follow arc-shaped paths defining an oval dune area. Some sand drifts across the streams when they are dry, building small dunes southeast and northeast of the main dune mass. Much of the water from these streams actually travels under and through the dune sand, sinking into the gravel of the valley floor or emerging in springs and seeps on the west side of the dunes.

Aerial photographs or the shaded relief maps available at the visitor center show that several distinct types of dunes develop here in response to variations in wind direction and sand supply. Most of the large dunes are transverse dunes, long sinuous ridges lying at right angles to the prevailing wind. Along the sides of the dune mass, where the wind is still strong but the supply of sand is less abundant, there are a few crescent-shaped barchan dunes, their two arms or horns pointing downwind. Where vegetation has partly stabilized low dunes, as in the area near the entrance road, parabolic dunes develop, with long, plant-anchored arms stretching upwind from narrow but active dune noses. Several star dunes, with crests radiating from a central high point, have been identified in the northern part of the

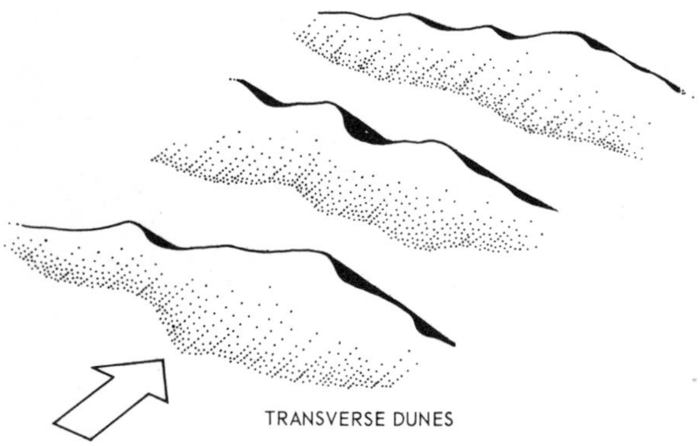

TRANSVERSE DUNES

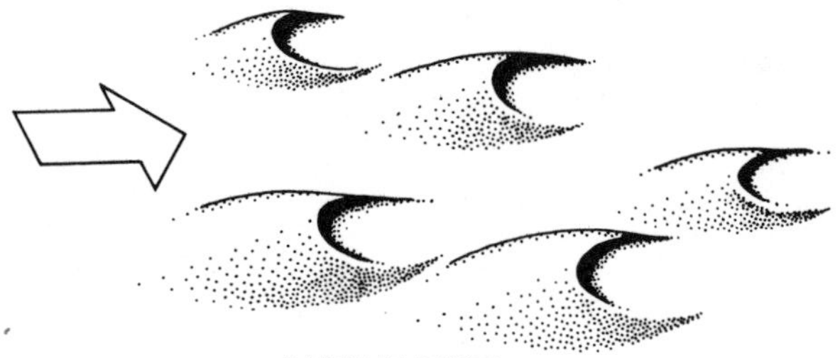

BARCHAN DUNES

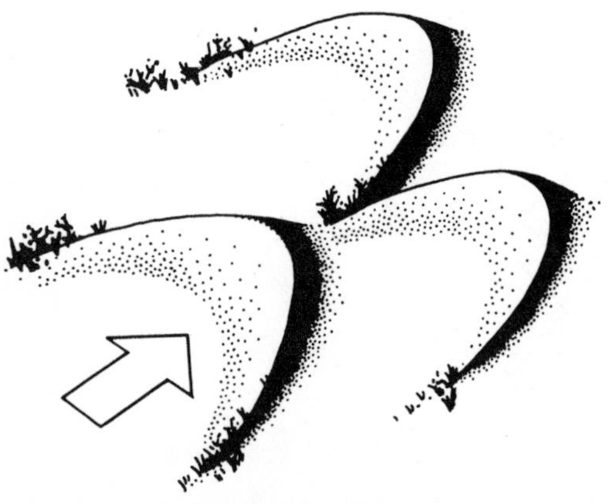

PARABOLIC DUNES

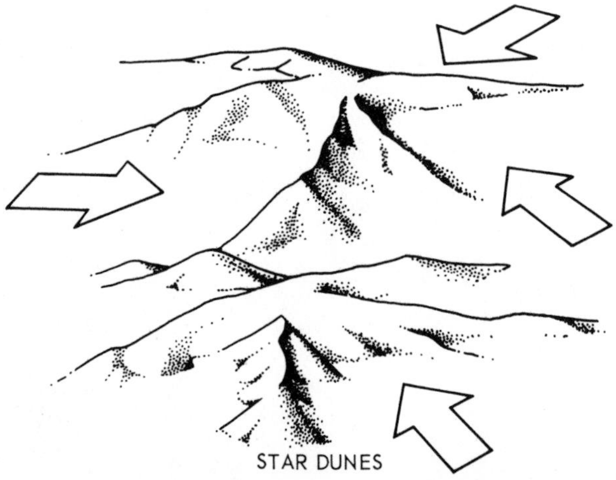

STAR DUNES

Courtesy of E. D. McKee

Along the edges of the dunes and in the partly forested dunes south of Medano Creek, blowouts are common.

dune field where the wind apparently swirls in unusual eddies that shift direction right around the compass.

Examine some of the sand surfaces—the long, ripple-marked windward slopes, the steep lee slopes with their slumps and avalanches. After rains, the sweeping cross-bedding of wind-deposited sand may show up festooning windward surfaces. Along Medano Creek are stream-formed ripples that differ in shape and sand grain size from the wind ripples of the dry dunes. On sandbars and near stream banks you will see animal tracks and trails in the sand. Since most dune-dwelling animals avoid sun-heated sand by hunting and foraging at night, look for their tracks early in the day before the morning winds dry them and smooth them over. Trails that look like the treads of tiny tractors are beetle tracks. Snails leave shallow, glistening grooves. Mouse tracks hop in fours across the sand, usually starting and ending in the shelter of shrubs and grasses. Lizard footprints border S-shaped furrows marked by dragging tails. Birds, deer, coyotes, rabbits, dogs, and people all leave distinctive tracks.

Studies of dune areas such as this one enable geologists to identify and understand older dune deposits preserved as sedimentary strata. Many of the dune forms and patterns described above have been recognized in dunes deposited millions of years ago, long since hardened into sandstone. There is a particular abundance of these eolian (wind-deposited) sandstones in southwestern United States, where desert conditions existed during much of the Mesozoic Era

Mouse tracks, arcs drawn by blowing grass, and the conical holes of "doodle bugs" are but a few of the many telltale records of life on the dunes.

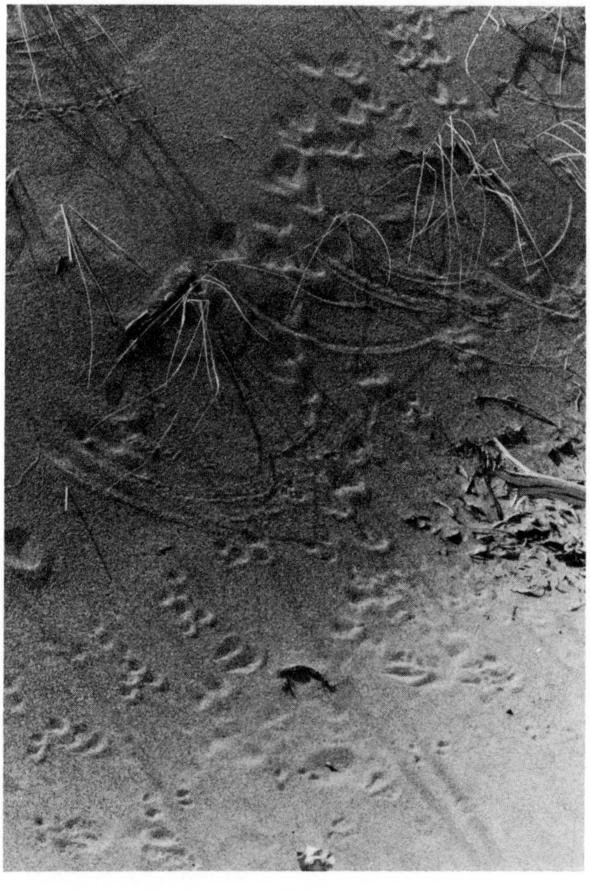

Deke Schnabel photo

Left: *By wetting and trenching modern dunes, as in this photograph, scientists study patterns of dune cross-bedding. They can then recognize ancient dunes now preserved in the rock record.*
Below: *Dunes of Paleozoic time remain today as the Weber Sandstone in Dinosaur National Monument.*

Once the sand grains are cemented together by calcium or silica minerals deposited by groundwater, dune sandstone seems to be particularly strong, strong enough to hold up as tall, vertical cliffs. Recognized by fine, even-sized, rounded and frosted sand grains and long, steeply sloping cross-bedding, eolian sandstones are responsible for some of the Southwest's most spectacular scenery, the cliffs of Colorado, Dinosaur, and Canyon de Chelly National Monuments and of Canyonlands, Arches, Grand Canyon, and Zion National Parks.

GEOLOGIC HISTORY

The history of the Great Sand Dunes begins with the birth of the Rocky Mountains at the beginning of the Cenozoic Era. Areas now occupied by the San Juan and Sangre de Cristo Ranges were arched upward to form anticlines—an almost circular dome for the San Juans and a narrow linear fold for the Sangres. Then, during millions of years, erosion whittled at these ranges, laying them bare to their very cores.

Around 40 million years ago, the San Juans began to rise once more, not as an anticline but as a cluster of volcanoes. Erupting again and again, the volcanoes spewed towering clouds of volcanic ash and churning rivers of molten lava. These volcanoes were active off and on for 30 million years, sometimes collapsing into their own subterranean magma chambers partly emptied by incredible outbursts of lava froth and volcanic ash.

Sometime between 28 and 10 million years ago, new unrest in the earth's crust lifted much of western United States—a region that included all of Colorado and most of its neighboring states. Central portions of this region were raised more than 1,500 meters (5,000 feet) above their former positions. Both the San Juan and the Sangre de Cristo areas were affected by this uplift, but the San Luis Valley was not. It is a part of the Rio Grande rift, a long, slender wedge of land faulted along both edges that seems to have remained at about its former elevation. Geologically, such a fault-edged block is a graben. Faults that edge the valley on the west are now covered with lava flows and river deposits, but on the east side of the graben the Sangre de Cristo rampart rises steeply along the line of the fault. Movement on this fault has occurred within the last thousand years.

The Rio Grande graben is much deeper than the San Luis Valley of today. During the last 10 or 20 million years, it has been filled with layer upon layer of sand, silt, and gravel eroded from the encircling mountains, as well as with layers of volcanic lava and ash from the San Juans. More than once the valley has held lake waters. Much of the infilling must have occurred during Pleistocene time, when both ranges gave birth to valley glaciers that transported vast quantities of rock debris toward the valley. Gradually, however, the glaciers receded. In Colorado the last of them disappeared about 10,000 years ago—after the arrival of man. Man must have seen their demise as a mixed blessing. The climate became warmer and more bearable, but it also became drier. With increasing aridity, the San Luis Valley lost its once-heavy mantle of vegetation, and large areas of bare soil began to be exposed to the elements. Winds sweeping across the valley plucked grains of sand from the valley deposits and moved them northeastward, funneling toward the few low spots in the Sangre de Cristo barrier. And so the Great Sand Dunes were born, less than 10,000 years ago, one of the youngest geologic features in our national parks.

OTHER READING

Johnson, Ross B. 1971. *The Great Sand Dunes of Southern Colorado.* New Mexico Geological Society guidebook, San Luis Basin.

Meek, G. P. 1960. "Great Sand Dunes of Colorado." In *Guide to the Geology of Colorado,* Rocky Mountain Association of Geologists, pp. 127-129.

Jewel Cave National Monument

Established: 1908
Size: 5 square kilometers (2 square miles)
Elevation: 1,614 meters (5,294 feet) at visitor center
Address: Hot Springs, South Dakota 57747

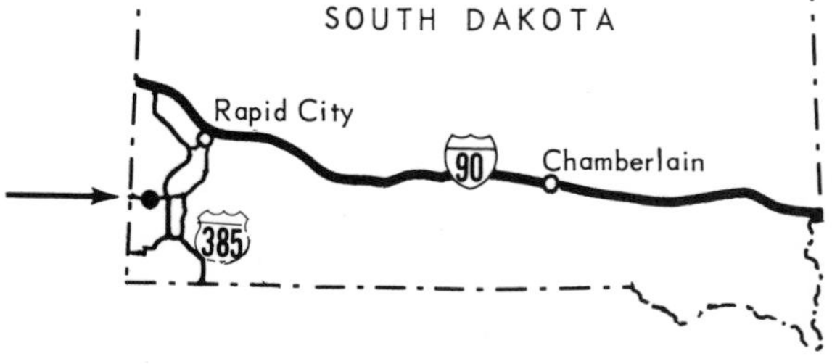

J. and H. Conn photo, courtesy of South Dakota Highway Dept.

Finger-sized calcite crystals — mostly nailhead spar — line the walls and ceilings of Jewel Cave.

STAR FEATURES

- A complex, three-dimensional labyrinth of narrow corridors, most of which follow sets of parallel rock joints. Since 1959 (when it was still called a "small cave") more than 100 kilometers (64 miles) of passages have been explored and mapped.
- Unusual crystalline forms of calcite and gypsum cave ornaments.
- Excellent displays in the visitor center, with strong emphasis on geology. Maps of the cave are available here.
- Guided cave tours through a well lit area that was opened in 1972. Historic candlelight tours use the old entrance, and spelunker trips explore less known parts of the cave.

SETTING THE STAGE

Like Wind Cave, this cavern is a fascinating network of intricately branching passages in limestone of the Pahasapa Formation, deposited in a shallow sea about 300 or 320 million years ago, during the Mississippian Period. Here the limestone has been subjected to the same pressures from overlying deposits, the same fracturing during uplift of the Black Hills, and the same solution by groundwater as Wind Cave. Both caves remain at the same year-round temperature of 8°C (47°F). Both display walls decorated with boxwork, and neither has much in the way of stalactites and stalagmites. Here the similarity ends.

Jewel Cave's passages trend northeast-southwest,

J. and H. Conn photo, courtesy of South Dakota Highway Dept.

Dripping water, lime-charged by its passage through limestone, creates these flowstone draperies.

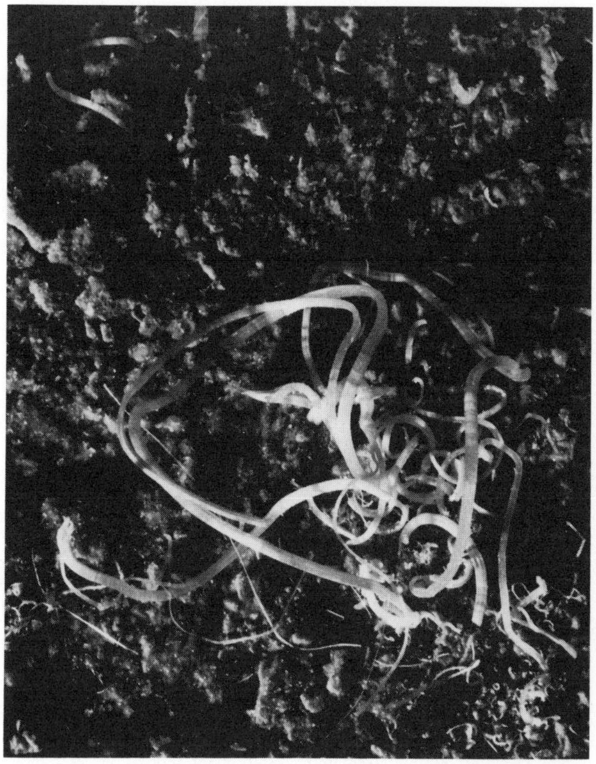

J. and H. Conn photo

Delicate gypsum "flowers" are curved, twisted crystal growths of satiny gypsum so delicate a finger's touch will break them.

while Wind Cave's passages trend northwest-southeast. Jewel Cave's walls and ceilings, unlike those of Wind Cave, are coated thickly with calcite crystals. Individual crystals vary in diameter from about pencil-thin to finger-thick and are mostly squeezed together into a thick layer. Sharp-pointed crystals are often called dogtooth spar, and duller ones nailhead spar — two forms of the mineral calcite.

GEOLOGIC HISTORY

The geologic story of Jewel Cave is similar to that of Wind Cave. For a discussion of the origin of these caves, see Wind Cave National Park.

After solution of limestone carved this cavern, lime-bearing water remained in the cave and gradually deposited crystals of pure calcite on the walls and ceilings. The crystals are layered or zoned in a way that suggests that water flooded and retreated from the cave at least five times. Today, Jewel Cave is moister than Wind Cave. Pools of water remain, with paper-thin calcite rafts forming as escape of carbon dioxide into the air lessens the water's ability to hold calcium carbonate in solution.

The boundary between calcium carbonate solution and deposition is a narrow one. Some geologists believe it to be a matter of water temperature, which in turn is controlled by cave temperature and climate changes at the surface. Since the cave's history runs back through Pleistocene Ice Age time, when cold, wet climates alternated with warm, dry ones, this interpretation seems likely to be correct. Certainly, abundant water slightly charged with carbonic acid, moving rapidly, dissolves limestone. Slow-moving water, on the other hand, supersaturated with calcium carbonate, tends to redeposit it.

During the very last flooding, streams brought clay and silt into the cave and deposited them along with new calcite, dulling the crystal surfaces. When the water finally receded — though of course it may come again someday — large portions of the crystal layer were left without support and fell to the cave floor as breakdown. None of the breakdown is recent, and the vaulted ceilings are secure and safe, much stronger than man-made ceilings of homes, schools, and offices.

Some of Jewel Cave's walls are coated with "popcorn," more scientifically called globularites. These

Dave Schnute photo

Fine frostwork of slender aragonite crystals ornaments a ceiling. Like water, calcium carbonate has several crystal forms; aragonite is one of them.

J. and H. Conn photo

Jewel Cave's narrow passages line up along limestone joints that in a wetter climate invited penetration by groundwater.

features are also known to be deposited under water or right at the interface between water and air. Water-deposited frostwork, helictites, and rare gypsum needles and "flowers" also occur here.

Below surface streams Jewel Cave is wet and dripping, and cave ornaments are growing: slender, hollow soda straws, small stalactites, stalagmites, and fanciful flowstone draperies. Ornaments grow extremely slowly, about 2 centimeters (1 inch) each 100 years. Dripping has started under the new visitor center parking lot, where rain and snowmelt concentrate in runoff gutters, so in a hundred years we can expect to see the small beginnings of new ornaments.

The powdery black dust abundant at certain levels in this cave is manganese dioxide. This compound occurs on some limestone surfaces as delicate and decorative many-branched markings known as dendrites—not "fossil ferns," but branching crystals. Spelunkers who have crawled through cave passages wear the black smudges as proud badges of exploration.

Manganese and iron are present in small quantities in the Pahasapa Limestone, and are concentrated as the limestone is dissolved away. Iron minerals appear as splotchy patches of red and yellow rust, as well as delicate shadings of yellow and pink in some parts of the cave. Watch also for sparkling red surfaces coated with crystals of scintillite, a quartz-calcite mineral colored with iron.

OTHER READING

Conn, Herb and Jan. 1977. *The Jewel Cave Adventure.* Wind Cave National Park and Jewel Cave National Monument Natural History Association.

Thompson, James B. (no date). *The Geology of Jewel Cave.* Wind Cave National Park and Jewel Cave National Monument Natural History Association.

Rocky Mountain National Park

Established: 1915
Size: 1,067 square kilometers (412 square miles)
Elevation: 2,440 to 4,345 meters (8,000 to 14,256 feet)
Address: Estes Park, Colorado 80517

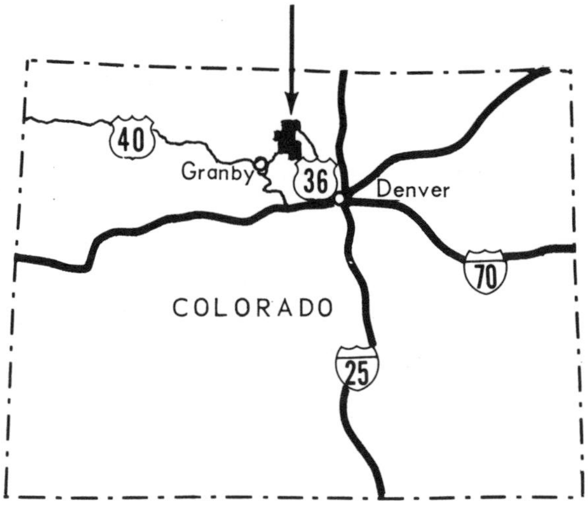

John Chronic photo

Rocky Mountain National Park's ancient uplands show the imprint of alpine glaciation in their high cirques and U-shaped valleys.

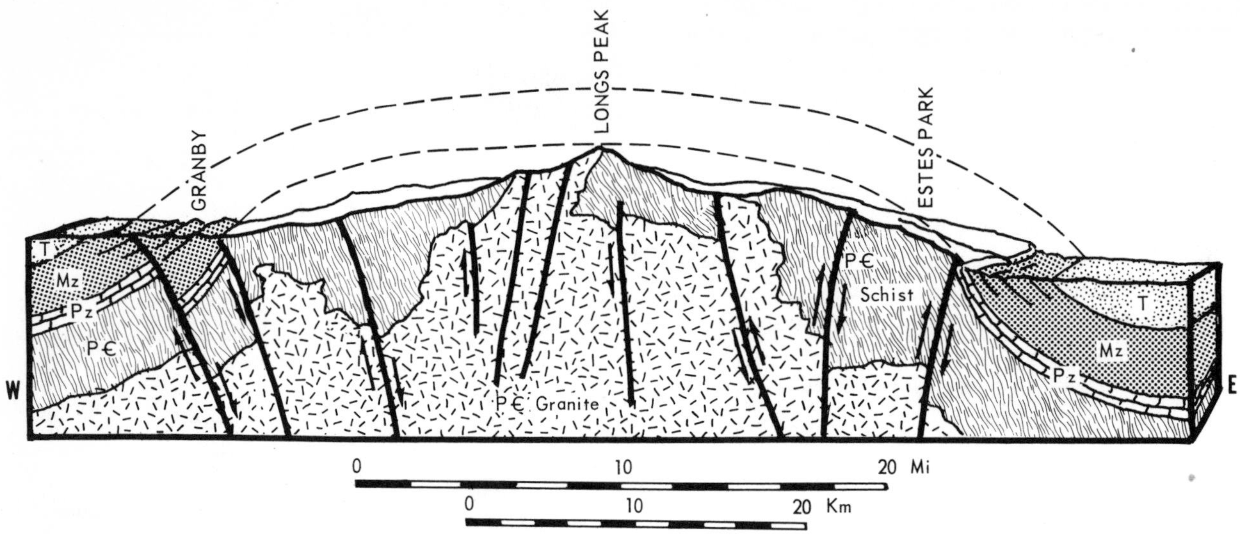

The Front Range is an upthrust block of Precambrian rock bordered by steeply tilted sedimentary rocks now eroded from the top of the faulted anticline.

STAR FEATURES

• Spectacular mountain scenery: towering peaks, cliff-girt canyons, and rolling uplands more than 3,600 meters (12,000 feet) above sea level. The scenic features of this park, geologic in origin, illustrate many stages in the building of the Rockies and their wearing down by processes of erosion.

• Some of the oldest rocks in North America: Precambrian gneiss, schist, and granite that were the roots of ancient mountain systems.

• Evidence of extensive alpine glaciation, as well as several small modern glaciers and many features developed by frost action.

• Intricate networks of joints and faults that in many cases regulate patterns of erosion and shapes of landforms.

• Trails galore, and an above-timberline highway from which can be seen geologic features of alpine terrain.

• Trail and roadside exhibits, campfire talks and slide shows, guided walks, self-guide leaflets, and two visitor centers.

See color pages for additional photographs.

SETTING THE STAGE

The Front Range of the Colorado Rockies extends as a long, narrow range from the Wyoming–Colorado border southward beyond Colorado Springs, a distance of about 290 kilometers (180 miles). Its steep cliffs, smoothly sculptured highlands, and stark summits are made of extremely old granite, gneiss, and schist. One cannot be long in Rocky Mountain National Park without observing these ancient crystalline rocks in speckled shades of white and gray and black, often sparkling as their quartz, feldspar, and mica crystals catch the sun.

These rocks are Precambrian in age and, broadly speaking, fall into two groups. The gneiss and schist are the oldest, approximately 1,750 million years old. The granite is younger, having intruded here 1,450 million years ago. Rocks similar to these are known to underlie much of the continent; here they are lifted high, a prominent and highly visible part of the mountain scene.

Like many other ranges of the Rockies, the Front Range is a large faulted anticline. Its core of ancient rocks is lifted along two nearly parallel fault zones. Additional faulting between the zones is complex and hard to decipher, but several major faults and many minor ones are known. Sedimentary layers that at one time lay horizontally above the Precambrian rocks were bowed up across the faulted core as the mountains rose. They probably never draped over the edges of a Precambrian block like blankets across a bed, as suggested in the diagram, but rather were attacked by erosion as soon as the mountains began to rise. They are gone now from the summits, though their upturned edges embroider the foot of the mountains (outside the park) as ranks of hogbacks that extend in an almost unbroken line from Wyoming to New Mexico.

This 1750-million-year-old gneiss, deformed by heat and pressure, may have originated as sea-floor mud and sand.

Fine-grained granite is recognized by its even "salt-and-pepper" appearance. This granite is part of a large body of magma—perhaps the contents of an entire magma chamber—that cooled slowly far beneath the surface.

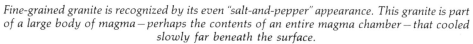

The most obvious features in the park result from erosion and deposition by moving ice—by glaciation. Moving glaciers scour away loose debris like boulders, sand, and soil encountered along stream valleys, and then attack the solid rock itself. At their heads, ice freezes hard to the rock; then, as each glacier moves away it pulls with it whole blocks of rock, quarrying a steep-walled, horseshoe-shaped cirque. Moving down pre-established stream courses, glaciers use the rocks they quarry as tools, huge, ice-imbedded rasps and files, to rip off spurs and to gouge and groove solid canyon walls. Thus they widen, deepen, and straighten pre-existing canyons, leaving the telltale marks of their passing.

Rocky Mountain Park is a hiker's paradise, with many splendid trails. Some are arduous, but there are easy ones, too—delightful walks among spruce and aspen, past chattering streams and wind-ruffled lakes. Even short strolls are rewarding and lead to new understanding of the nature and natural beauty of these mountains.

GEOLOGIC HISTORY

Precambrian Era. The story of Rocky Mountain Park began 1,750 million years ago with metamorphism of the oldest rocks in the park—gneiss and schist. Previous to that time, some sort of rocks existed of course, probably sandstone and shale deposited in an ancient sea, with liberal amounts of volcanic lava flows and beds of volcanic ash. Deeply buried, partly melted by high temperature and immense pressure, squeezed and distorted and broken by mountain-building forces, these rocks are now so changed that they are no longer recognizable as sedimentary or volcanic rock layers. We know very little about the ancient mountains of which they were a part, only that they did not have the same north-south trend as the present Colorado Rockies.

About 300 million years after the rocks had recrystallized into gneiss and schist, masses of molten magma worked their way up into the older rock. Intrusion of the granite seems to have been as much a process of remelting as of actual physical injection. The granite surrounds and interfingers with the gneiss and schist as if it had melted its way, liquifying, distorting, and fusing with the older rock. Probably new and different mountains were formed at the time of the intrusion. We don't know much about these ranges either, for they were worn away during a long period of erosion at the end of Precambrian time.

Paleozoic and Mesozoic Eras. For more than 500 million years after the end of the Precambrian Era, the eroded surface of the Precambrian rocks was at times below and at times above sea level. We learn this from rocks outside the boundaries of the national park, particularly along the east and west edges of the Front Range, where upturned layers of sedimentary rock fill in the geologic story. Though these rocks should range in age from Cambrian to Cretaceous, as they do in some areas, close to the Front Range all the early Paleozoic units are missing. It is apparent from their absence and from the coarse nature of Pennsylvanian rocks that now tip up against the Precambrian mountain core that mountains also existed here in Pennsylvanian time. These ranges, really a few tall islands in the Pennsylvanian sea, are referred to as the Ancestral Rocky Mountains. Where they rose, all the sedimentary layers laid down earlier—fossil-bearing limestone and shale and sandstone deposited in shallow seas—were stripped away by erosion. Coarse red gravel and sand were deposited along both sides of the islands, where they hardened into coarse conglomerates that now tilt up against our later Rocky Mountains. Once created, the islands yielded little by little to the relentless attack of disintegration and erosion, until by Cretaceous time, seas once more crept across the land where they had been.

Cenozoic Era. The present Rocky Mountains came into being at the end of the Mesozoic Era, somewhere around 65 million years ago, during a mountain-building episode known as the Laramide Orogeny (named for the Laramie Range just north of Rocky Mountain National Park). Almost all of western North America (and South America too, for that matter) was influenced late in Mesozoic and early in Cenozoic time by a wave of unrest that started on the west coast and slowly crept eastward. The Sierras took shape in Jurassic time—first of the mountains to rise. Then mountain building migrated inland, first to the Basin and Range areas of Nevada and Utah, then to the Wasatch Range of Utah, and finally to the Rockies.

The process of faulting and uplift of the Rockies dragged on for nearly 55 million years. Movement occurred sporadically along faults that edged the giant blocks. Some blocks rose; others fell. Rocks near the fault zones were bent and often shattered, so that today they are cut by a multitude of joints. Igneous material rose along the joints to create dikes and mineral enriched veins. And even as uplift occurred, erosion began to wear the mountains down.

At first, the rock material washed from the mountains accumulated nearby, on the plains to the east or in intermountain depressions to the west. In the course of 30 million years, an unbelievable quantity of boulders, cobbles, pebbles, sand, and silt was dumped onto the plains and between the mountains, thousands of meters of rock and gravel fill, until even

Felicie Chronic photo

Rolling upland surfaces of Rocky Mountain National Park date back to late Eocene time, when the mountains were hardly more than rolling hills.

the highlands themselves were nearly covered with their own debris. By late Eocene time the Front Range, as well as most of the ranges west and southwest of it, consisted of rolling mountains that rose only 1,000 meters (3,000 feet) or so above the vast sea of debris. Each stage of uplift enabled rivers and streams to renew their attack—to deepen their canyons for a time, to round the highlands once again.

But in Miocene and Pliocene time, about 26 to 10 million years ago, a new pattern supplanted the old. Crustal forces of a new kind—different from the localized forces that had previously broken the crust and lifted narrow slivers of it to produce the Rockies—elevated a vaster area, all of Colorado and Wyoming and much of every neighboring state, forming a broad upland region. Around the margins of the upland, uplift was not great, but near its center in Colorado, uplift reached 2,000 meters (6,000 feet) and more. Highlands that had been 1,000 meters (3,000 feet) above sea level were raised until they were 3,000 meters (9,000 feet) in elevation; mountains of 2,500 meters (nearly 8,000 feet) became Colorado's "Fourteeners"—a name that defies the metric system.

With renewed vigor, streams and rivers this time attacked not only the mountains but the thick, unconsolidated aprons of debris that had been deposited around them. Rocks and sand, gravel and clay were swept toward the east, where they contributed to the building of the Mississippi River's vast floodplain and delta, and to the drainage of the Colorado River on the west, where rushing waters, tooled with rock debris, etched deep gorges through horizontal rocks of the southwestern plateaus.

Erosion in the Rockies was sped up also by the coming of the Ice Ages. In Pleistocene time, alpine glaciers formed in the Rockies on the flanks of high peaks and ridges near the Continental Divide and crept slowly down pre-existing stream valleys. When they melted at the end of Pleistocene time, they left behind high, arcuate cirques, deep, straight U-shaped valleys, and gouged and striated rock surfaces. At their lower ends the tongues of ice deposited untidy piles and ridges of angular, rocky rubble in lateral, terminal, and recessional moraines. Small lakes and tarns now shimmer in ice-carved basins right in the cirques or in the depths of the glaciated valleys.

In this part of the Rockies, there is evidence of

John Chronic photo

Between moraines of the second and third glacial advances, Horseshoe Park is floored with flat-lying lake sediments. This view is downstream from Trail Ridge Road.

three glacial advances and retreats, all of them within the last (Wisconsin) advance of the great ice sheets of northern North America. The oldest of the three left the lowest moraines, which are now so deeply weathered and badly decayed as to be hardly recognizable. The second advance left moraines that are still distinct: pronounced ridges covered with gray-brown soil and dark forests of lodgepole pine. The third advance ended less than 10,000 years ago, after man had come to North America from Asia, and it left moraines characterized now by sandy soil and fresh-looking boulders. In the warming phase that followed the last advance, the glaciers melted away completely.

Tiny glaciers that nestle in high cirques today are perhaps harbingers of another glacial cycle. They are thought to have come into existence within the last 3,000 or 4,000 years. At present they seem to be shrinking, for they are not as large as they were in photos taken half a century ago. Glacial advances and retreats are never smooth and uninterrupted, and these small glaciers fluctuate with short-term climate cycles that may be superimposed on some greater pattern of climate change. We have not been around long enough to tell what the greater pattern means.

Only recently, within the last 10,000 years, have the denuded crags been gentled by soil development and the growth of forests. Frost still labors in the mountains, prying rocks from cliffs, lifting and loosening boulders and soil, and sometimes creating strange patterns in the rocky alpine tundra.

BEHIND THE SCENES

Bear Lake. A natural lake, this is one of several that lie in basins formed by glaciers that crept down Tyndall Gorge. Although most of the lakes occupy shallow bowls scooped from solid rock, Bear Lake is dammed with glacial debris of a large lateral moraine, and seems to perch high on the side of the main valley. Coarse, bouldery rubble of the moraine can be seen along the lakeshore and in roadcuts near the parking lot. Along with visible rocks, pebbles, and sand, it contains quantities of fine clay-sized rock flour ground in the millstone of rock rasping against rock.

Upstream is the steep-walled, U-shaped valley down which the glacier came. Hallett Peak's sheer

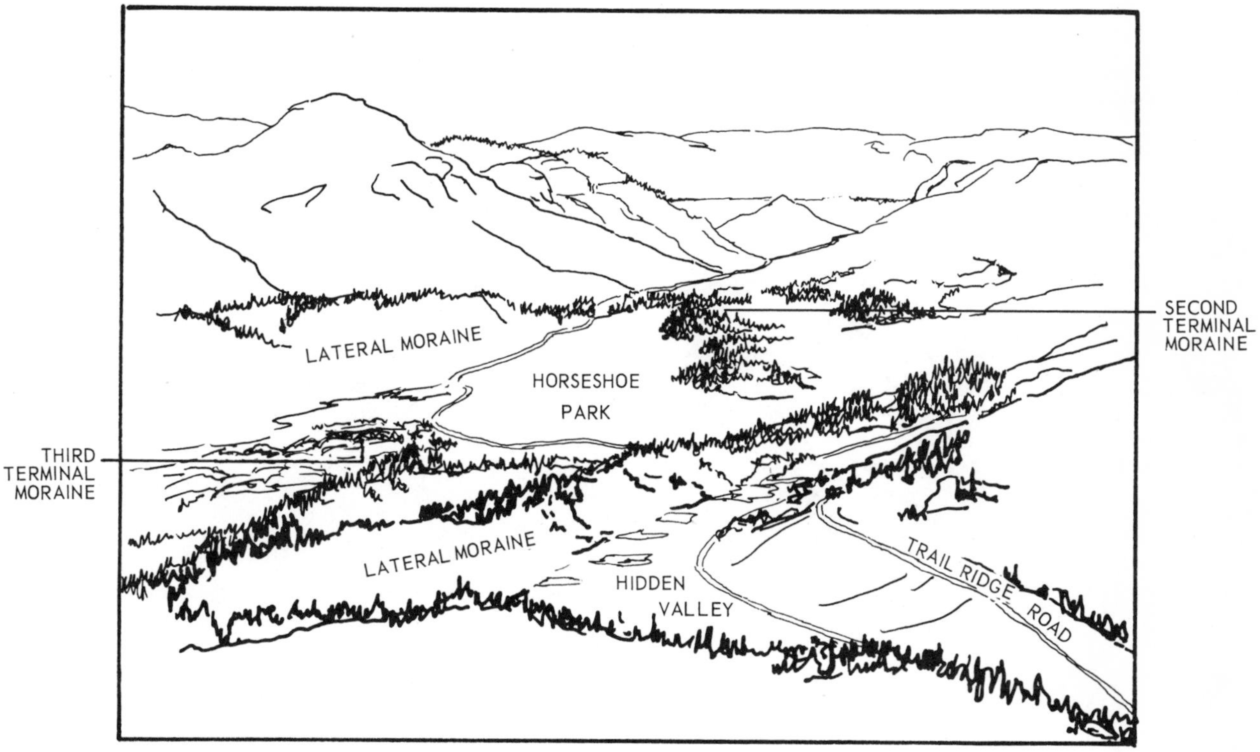

Horseshoe Park from a higher vantage point, showing both the second and third terminal moraines.

face is an indicator of the slow might of its ice. Rock breaking off along vertical joint planes dictated the angular shape of the mountain. Barren, rounded rock surfaces above Bear Lake are just as the ice left them; look at them carefully to find striations left by the glacier's rasping rock tools.

The cirque at the head of the valley is occupied by Tyndall Glacier, a small newcomer rather than a descendant of a Pleistocene predecessor.

Both granite and gneiss are exposed near Bear Lake. Strong banding identifies the gneiss. Coarse-grained pegmatite veins cut through both gneiss and granite. These veins contain the same minerals as both the other rocks, primarily quartz, feldspar, and mica.

Lichens that coat many rocks here initiate the processes that turn rock into fertile soil. Acids released by their metabolism help to break down mica grains, freeing the quartz and feldspar crystals that you see accumulating below old rock surfaces. Moisture freezing between the grains also helps to break the rock apart.

The flat summits of Hallett Peak and Flattop Mountain have puzzled geologists; they are now thought to date back to late Eocene time and to be remnants of the rolling upland surfaces created on the newborn but not yet very high Rockies. Soil taken from a test pit on Flattop Mountain is of a type that could only develop in a low-elevation, warm, humid climate.

Fall River Road. Built between 1913 and 1921, this one-way road is unsurfaced but passable in passenger cars that are in reasonably good condition. Guide leaflets are available near the end of the pavement.

The road climbs abruptly and offers views of Horseshoe Park and its tightly meandering stream and moraine dam. There are good exposures of glacially polished and striated bedrock here, quite near the road. Both granite and metamorphic rocks can be seen at road's edge. Banding in the gneiss and schist is beautifully displayed in cliffs above the road—a striking feature inherited from layers of sandstone, shale, and perhaps volcanic rock far back in Precambrian time.

Watch for the scars of avalanches and rockslides, for rock-scoured potholes in the streambed, for glacial grooves and striae, and for hanging valleys

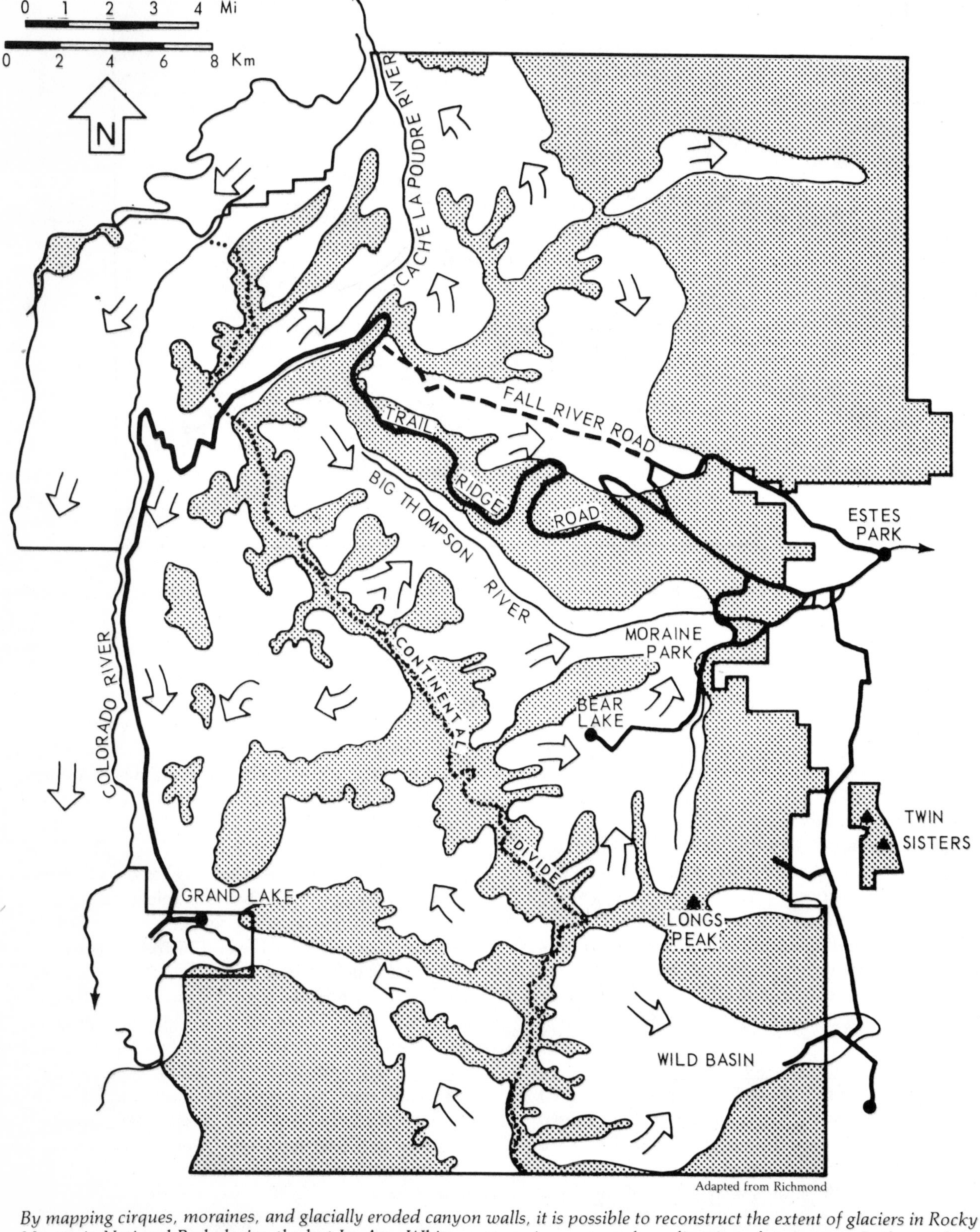

By mapping cirques, moraines, and glacially eroded canyon walls, it is possible to reconstruct the extent of glaciers in Rocky Mountain National Park during the last Ice Age. White areas are ice; arrows show direction of movement. In the northern part of the park, part of the Colorado River glacier flowed east across the Continental Divide.

shaped by small tributary glaciers that could not cut downward as rapidly as the large glacier of the main valley.

Near Fall River Pass, a cloverleaf cirque marks the head of the valley. The pass is 3,595 meters (11,796 feet) above sea level.

Glacier Gorge. Of all the trails in Rocky Mountain National Park, the one to Glacier Gorge, Mills Lake, and Jewel Lake cannot be too highly recommended. The trail is not difficult, and the reward is great.

The entire valley is a superb lesson in glacial erosion. At its lower end, the great ice river that carved it joined with glaciers from Loch Vale and Chaos Gorge to grind over Glacier Knobs, rounding and smoothing them but never wearing them down completely. What a rasping, groaning, cracking mass of ice it must have been, for these knobs lie right in the paths of the three glaciers. Below them the ice must have tumbled in an immense icefall of jagged blue-green wedges and then reformed to flow on down into Glacier Basin.

Once above Glacier Knobs one can see almost straight up the gorge. Its U-shaped profile is somewhat modified by joints that control the sloping west flank of Longs Peak and the ridge variously known as Music Mountain or Keyboard of the Winds. If you are lucky, and the wind is just right, you may hear its eerie music penetrating the quiet air within the gorge.

The lakes in this canyon occupy solid rock basins scooped by moving ice as it ground its way toward Glacier Knobs and Glacier Basin. Several small alpine glaciers combined at the head of the valley in cirques that can be seen from vantage points along the trail.

Hidden Valley. To an observer in Horseshoe Park, Hidden Valley is concealed by the lateral moraine of the large Fall River glacier. Marshy ground and small ponds near the road show that moraine material contains fine clay-sized particles of rock flour that prevent water from draining right through the otherwise coarse gravel.

Longs Peak (elevation 4,345 meters, or 14,256 feet). As the highest summit in Rocky Mountain National Park, Longs Peak carries raw marks of glaciation on every flank. Its vertical east face, the magnificent "Diamond," is the headwall of a cirque now occupied by Chasm Lake. A view of this face from Twin Sisters lookout reveals the glacier's path, its union with a smaller glacier from Mount Meeker's north slope, the U-shaped valley of the combined glaciers, and large lateral and terminal moraines forested with thick stands of pine. Water freezing in cracks and joints plays a role in maintaining the Diamond, cleaving the great facet along major joint planes and piling the rubble as talus at its base.

On the west side of the peak another precipitous rock face plunges nearly 1,000 meters (3,000 feet) to the lake-studded valley of Glacier Gorge. The shape of this face is also governed by joints—steeply slanting ones that may be due to expansion of the granite itself. The granite constantly spalls off, even today, along these steep planes. On the south, Longs Peak bears the cirques of several small glaciers that united and flowed together into the larger St. Vrain glacier, which drew most of its sustenance from cirques along the Continental Divide.

Some geologists believe that the flat summit of Longs Peak is a small remnant of the beveled, almost worldwide plain created by erosion at the end of Precambrian time. A similar surface atop Mount Moran in Grand Teton National Park bears a small cap of Cambrian rocks, and the horizontal Precambrian surface in the depths of Grand Canyon underlies Cambrian sandstone, too. But the Longs Peak surface may just as well have been worn flat as the Ancestral Rocky Mountains were planed away late in Paleozoic time, for at Black Canyon of the Gunnison and Colorado National Monuments, Triassic sedimentary rocks cover the beveled base of another island range of the Ancestral Rockies. Along the Wyoming border and at the mouth of Big Thompson Canyon (east of the park), coarse red Pennsylvanian sedimentary rocks lie on the planed surface.

Hikers who tackle Longs Peak trails, even if they are not bound for the top, will see that frost and ice still sculpture the land above timberline. Fields of jagged boulders, known as fellfields, patterns of frost-sorted rocks, and frost-heaved soil are common in the alpine tundra.

Moraine Park. Outlined by lateral and terminal moraines, this open valley is the site of a glacier-fed lake that gradually filled in with sand, silt, mud, and plant material. The Big Thompson River and other streams meander aimlessly, with almost no gradient, across its level floor.

Moraine Park lies just at the 2,400-meter (8,000-foot) level usually considered the lowest limit of glaciation in this part of the Rocky Mountains.

Specimen Mountain. Reddish volcanic rocks of Specimen Mountain tell of a volcano that was active in or near Rocky Mountain National Park about 27 million years ago, at the end of the Oligocene Epoch. Bighorn sheep are often seen on its ledges of volcanic breccia and obsidian. Though Specimen Mountain was once thought to be part of the volcano itself, recent research suggests that flows here came from volcanoes in the Never Summer Range to the west. Tuff from an ash flow appears above Iceberg Lake, and beds of whitish ash mark roadcuts near Poudre Lake.

Trail Ridge Road (U.S. 34). A treat for mountain-lovers and flatlanders alike, this highway is one of

Jack Rathbone photo

The towering Diamond, Longs Peak's magnificent east face, is carved in solid granite. Banded metamorphic rock appears in the foreground ridge.

National Park Service Photo

Geologists disagree as to the meaning of Longs Peak's flat top, the size of a city block. It may date back to Eocene, late Paleozoic, or possibly Precambrian time, or it may be simply a level in the efficacy of alpine weathering processes.

the highlights of the park. It climbs to 3,600 meters (12,000 feet) following an old Indian trail—a spectacular way to cross the mountains.

From the east the climb is gradual. The road swings up the granite ridge that separates Horseshoe Park and Fall River drainage from Moraine Park and the Big Thompson River. Looking down on either side of the ridge, you can see tree-covered lateral and terminal moraines outlining grassy, once lake-filled valleys. Notice the sinuous, meandering routes the rivers take across the low-gradient "parks."

Near timberline, trees are scattered and dwarfed by frosty blasts from the west. Everywhere are exposures of the massive pinkish granite that forms this part of the Front Range. Its principal minerals are quartz (glassy, clear grains), feldspar (opaque pinkish or very pale gray grains, usually with flat surfaces that catch the light), and black mica or biotite. Above the trees, in the tundra, are more rocks, and unimpeded views of the peaks and highlands of the Rockies.

Rolling upland surfaces on Flattop Mountain, Hallett Peak, and Trail Ridge itself are thought to have formed when the mountains were young and much lower in elevation, probably in Eocene time.

At Forest Canyon overlook, you can look down into a deep glacial gorge occupied now by the Big Thompson River. Before glaciation, Forest Canyon was probably as crooked as the present Big Thompson Canyon east of Estes Park. Glaciers steepened its walls and straightened its sides, truncating every spur.

From the overlook you can also see hanging valleys on the other side of Forest Canyon, each with little alpine lakes. The valley directly opposite is named for Ferdinand Hayden, a pioneer geologist who led a geologic and geographic survey of the western territories from 1867 to 1879. Nestled in cirques below the sharp ridge of the Continental Divide are a few living glaciers, not remnants of Pleistocene glaciers but new ones that developed only a few thousand years ago. Unless there is evidence of movement, an icefield or snowfield can't really be called a glacier. There has been some dispute about whether these are indeed true glaciers; since they have been melting back recently, they may no longer qualify.

Most of the rock you have been seeing near the road is granite. A short distance northwest of Forest Canyon overlook, there is a change to gneiss and

A fellfield of jagged, frost-broken boulders is high on the north slope of Longs Peak.

schist. Much of the upland surface is covered with jagged fragments of these rocks, shattered by frost action. (The climate here is equivalent to that at sea level north of the Arctic Circle.) Moisture from snow and rain seeps into tiny cracks in the rock and, when it freezes, pries the rock apart. Freezing and thawing, repeated winter after winter and often night after night, creates the stony surfaces called fellfields. Frost ultimately breaks these rock fragments down to sand, most of which blows away in winter gales. Frost and wind are the main agents of erosion at this altitude.

Freezing and thawing also cause patterned ground, heaving soil into continuous trails that look like mole tunnels, or moving rock fragments gradually into polygonal patterns. Rocks and soil on sloping surfaces are frost-lifted at right angles to the ground surface. When the frost melts they are lowered vertically. The net result is a downhill movement—soil and rocks together creep slowly down the slope, commonly coming to rest in stepped patterns like tiny terraces. Other terraces are created as sun-warmed, water-saturated soil slips downhill across permanently frozen soil underneath.

Clusters of shattered rock fragments upended by frost break through the tundra. Similar fragments stud the tundra surface near the old Ute Indian trail that gives Trail Ridge its name.

OTHER READING

Chronic, Halka. 1980. *Roadside Geology of Colorado.* Mountain Press, Missoula, Montana.

Chronic, John and Halka. 1972. *Prairie Peak and Plateau, a Guide to the Geology of Colorado.* Colorado Geological Survey Bulletin 32.

Curtis, B.F. (editor). 1975. *Cenozoic History of the Southern Rocky Mountains.* Geological Society of America Memoir 144.

Lee, Willis T. 1917. *The Geologic Story of the Rocky Mountain National Park, Colorado.* National Park Service.

Richmond, Gerald M. 1974. *Raising the Roof of the Rockies.* Rocky Mountain Nature Association.

Wegemen, C.H. 1961. *A Guide to the Geology of Rocky Mountain National Park.* U.S. Government Printing Office, Washington, D.C.

Theodore Roosevelt National Park

Established: 1978
Size: 285 square kilometers (110 square miles)
Elevation: 691 to 870 meters (2,266 to 2,853 feet)
Address: Medora, North Dakota 58645

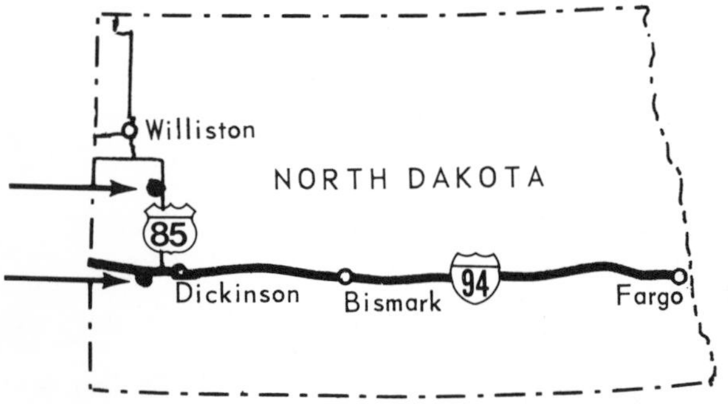

In poorly cemented siltstone with a large component of volcanic ash, rivulets cut deep channels between rounded, undulating, almost lifelike ridges.

STAR FEATURES

- Sculptured badlands carved in flat-lying, 60-million-year-old Tertiary strata by the Little Missouri River and its tributaries.
- Evidence of faraway mountain uplifts and volcanism that contributed to these sedimentary rocks.
- Samples of other geologic processes: wind erosion, slumping and landslides, collapse above burnt-out coal seams, and development of the Great Plains.
- Petrified logs and stumps, and seams of low-grade coal—clues to past climates and environments.
- An interpretive program of campfire talks, guided walks, visitor center exhibits, self-guide trails, and scenic drives with explanatory wayside displays.

SETTING THE STAGE

Described by Theodore Roosevelt as "barren, fantastic, and grimly picturesque," the rugged terrain of the Little Missouri Badlands provides us with pictures of the environment of western North America 60 million years ago. Flat-lying rock layers exposed here by the river's downcutting consist of fine, poorly cemented sandstone, usually tan or buff-colored, and of gray siltstone and shale mixed with, or alternating with, bentonite, a blue-gray mixture of clay minerals that form from volcanic ash. Bentonite absorbs water quite readily and swells to make a sticky, cohesive mass. When it dries again, it leaves a puffy, crumbly crust that succumbs easily to erosion by wind and rain. As pelting raindrops and sudden gusts sweep the loosened crust away, the layers beneath absorb water, swell, and later dry and erode in their turn. This multistage process is particularly effective in

The popcorn surface of a bentonite layer crumbles at the slightest touch and becomes easy prey for wind and rain. (Dime shows scale.)

arid or semiarid regions with sporadic but heavy rain, where surfaces unprotected by vegetation dry completely between one storm and the next. Bentonite's odd properties are in part responsible for the absence of vegetation, as plants are unable to gain footholds where the surface is periodically sloughed away.

In parts of the park, as at Caprock Coulee and near Oxbow Overlook in the North Unit, bentonite pulls another trick. There, a thick layer of it caps many ridges. With successive wettings, the outermost layer of the bentonite little by little creeps downslope as a thin, blue-gray, cohesive mat, almost jellylike, adhering to and making a new coating for the slope below.

The Little Missouri Badlands also contain low-

Under the right conditions, sheets of bentonite creep downslope, blanketing the layers below. Note the lack of vegetation on the bentonite mat.

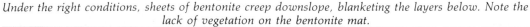

grade brown coal or lignite. You'll see its dark seams throughout the park, some no thicker than your finger, others as thick as 30 centimeters (1 foot). Like other coal, lignite forms from vegetable matter—leaves, stems, and other plant material—that accumulated in ancient swamps and marshes. Beneath the weight of overlying sediments, the plant materials compress first into peat, then into lignite. In regions of still greater overburden, or where mountain-building forces add new kinds of pressure, bituminous (soft) and anthracite (hard) coal form.

If they are ignited by lightning or by lightning-caused grass fires, seams of lignite may smolder underground for years. Heat from their burning alters overlying clay and shale layers, firing them like bricks in a kiln, turning them bright brick red or the softer salmon pink of terra cotta. Where joints and other cracks provide air passages, the fires become more intense, and a blast furnace effect melts and fuses some of the rock into dark slaglike masses that later resist erosion and stand up as irregular pedestals or walls. Watch for these features as you drive around the South Unit scenic loop. The reddened strata are locally called scoria, a misuse of a geologic term with another meaning. The correct term is clinker.

The Little Missouri River brings most of its water from areas south of the park, in the Black Hills and the region around Devils Tower. Flowing north from there, it turns abruptly eastward in the North Unit of this park and joins the Missouri near Twin Buttes, North Dakota. In both units of the park its tributaries show a dendritic (treelike) drainage pattern, with branching and rebranching of the tributaries, ending up with the narrow, deeply grooved furrows that flute the steepest slopes. In this land of scant rainfall (annual precipitation averages 35 centimeters [14 inches]), the tributaries are usually dry. During spring or summer downpours, though, rivulets born in branching furrows plunge into gulches and ravines. At such times, normally dry stream bottoms may be swept by flash floods.

In the North Unit particularly, large "cannonball" concretions weather from some of the rock layers

A pond occupies a depression caused by collapse over a burnt-out coal seam, near Coal Vein Trail in the South Unit.

Deeply carved rivulets, columnar jointing in siltstone heated by burning coal, and large sandstone cannonball concretions occur near Squaw Creek Trail in the North Unit.

and accumulate at the foot of slopes. Some are a meter in diameter and nearly spherical. These sandstone concretions formed when minerals that were dissolved in groundwater attached themselves, molecule by molecule, to a sometimes quite insignificant nucleus—a buried plant leaf, a mineral grain, a bit of bone or wood. Once started, the concretions continued to grow by continued deposition around the ever larger center. Their growth, therefore, is from the inside out, and they do still contain the grains of the original sandstone. Some are layered like onions; others are structureless. Concretions are fairly common, but ones as large and round as those in this park are rare. Their abundance, though, in the lowest formation of the Fort Union Group, a unit not exposed in the national park, led to its descriptive name: the Cannonball Formation.

GEOLOGIC HISTORY

Cenozoic Era. Sixty-five million years ago, as the Cenozoic Era opened, this region was emerging from a wide, shallow sea that extended across the continent from Alaska to the Gulf of Mexico. Here the emergence was slight, just enough to bring the land above the water, to create a broad, gently shelving plain similar to the country along the Gulf Coast today, surfaced with layers of dark gray, fossil-bearing shale.

Several hundred kilometers away to the west and southwest, in a band that stretched from Canada to Mexico, the upheaval was more dynamic. There, the long ranges of the Rocky Mountains were rising, immense corrugations in the earth's crust—folded, broken, and in places thrust over each other. At the same time, volcanoes erupted among the new-risen mountains, releasing towering clouds of volcanic ash that drifted eastward on prevailing winds and fell to earth hundreds, even thousands, of kilometers from their source.

Through the millions of years involved in the building of the Rockies, debris washed from them was carried by streams and rivers out onto the surrounding plain. Although the nearest Rocky Mountain ranges were 400 kilometers (250 miles) away, western North Dakota received its share of the debris. Transported by streams and rivers, dropped, picked up, reworked again and again, the finely ground rock material eventually came to rest (along with volcanic ash) as layered Paleocene sediments of the Fort Union Group, the rocks you see in Theodore Roosevelt National Park.

The group is now divided into three formations, from bottom to top (oldest to youngest) the Cannonball, Tongue River, and Sentinel Butte Formations. The Cannonball Formation is not exposed here, and the Tongue River appears only in the lowest parts of the South Unit near the river and in its tributary canyons. Elsewhere all the rocks in the park belong to the Sentinel Butte Formation. Varied in texture and to some degree in color, they tell us a good deal about the environment in which they were deposited. Repeated horizontal bands of silt and sand, for instance, record churning floodwaters and bring to mind the Mississippi, Ganges, or Yangtze floods that still break through man's puny dikes and levees to lay silt across the land. Cross-bedded sandstone occurring in lens-shaped outcrops defines channels of shifting streams. Blue-gray layers of bentonite remind us that volcanoes lay to windward, belching tremendous quantities of ash into the air. Layers of coal tell us of coastal swamps similar in nature to those of southeastern United States today — the Everglades in Florida and Okefenokee Swamp in Georgia, for instance. Petrified tree trunks tell us of deciduous woodlands and groves of cone-bearing trees. The climate then was wetter, and the shifting network of rivers may have resembled the vast web of the Amazon today.

Petrified stumps, their woody tissues replaced by silica, weather from the Sentinel Butte Formation. Dark lignite bands the hills.

Deposition here did not stop with the Sentinel Butte Formation. After the close of the Paleocene Epoch 54 million years ago, more layers of silt, sand, and volcanic ash were deposited. At times, too, erosion gained an upper hand, so that the rock sequence, though thick, is not complete. Even with periodic erosion, by the end of Miocene time (12 million years ago) a vast sedimentary wedge stretched eastward from the mountains, with thick layers of coarse sediments near the mountains and thinner layers of finer and finer ones as the distance from the mountains increased.

Renewed uplift in Pliocene time, though, changed the picture. This time, the uplift was a broad warp hundreds of kilometers wide, extending from Kansas to Utah and from Canada to New Mexico, an upwarp of such immense extent that the slope of its flanks was hardly discernible. Its eastern flank today is the surface of the Great Plains — seemingly level to the eye but actually inclined gently eastward all the way to the Mississippi Valley. Along the Rockies, at the center of the uplifted area, the land was elevated 2,000 meters (6,000 feet). But North Dakota, on the north slope of the uplift, rose no more than 600 meters (2,000 feet).

With their headwaters so strongly lifted, many streams showed renewed vigor and began to cut down through the layers of sediment they had so recently deposited, carving themselves broad, usually shallow valleys. Gradually, too, they removed the uppermost sedimentary layers from the shoulders of the mountains and stripped the post–Paleocene sand, silt, and mud from areas near the mountains. Some valleys then were cut down into the upper parts of the Paleocene strata. Among these was that of the ancestor of the Little Missouri River.

The ancestral river, as well as the ancestral Yellowstone River, drained northward at that time, toward Canada. Their confluence was farther west than it is now, near the town of Williston. Near the Canadian border they joined the ancestral Missouri, also northflowing, and the combined waters of the three rivers then flowed northeast to Hudson Bay.

Why did these rivers change course? How could they leave their own valleys and alter the whole direction of their drainage, surmounting the major divide that must have separated northeast and southeast drainage? For answers to these questions we must look at events that took place in very late Plio-

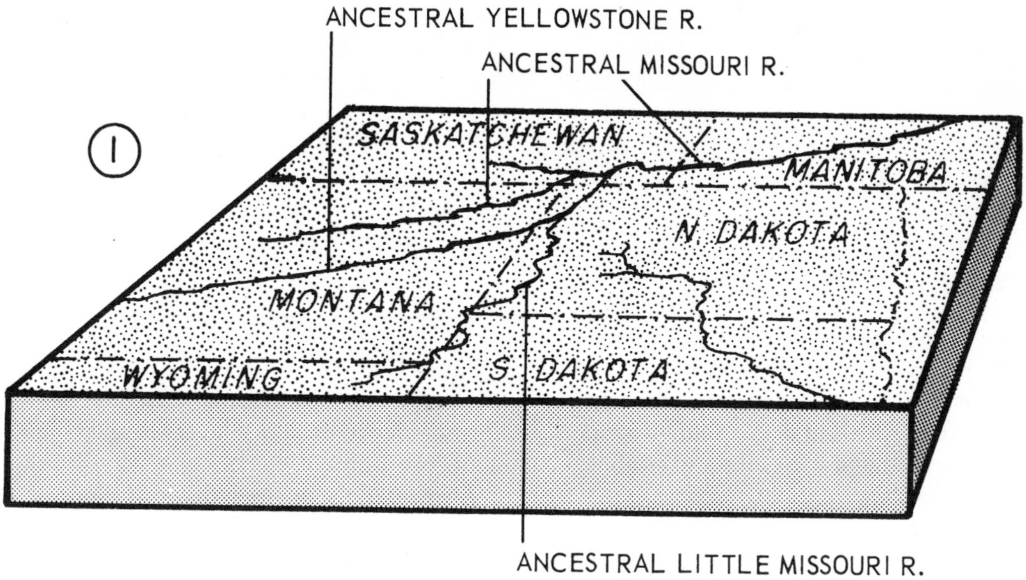

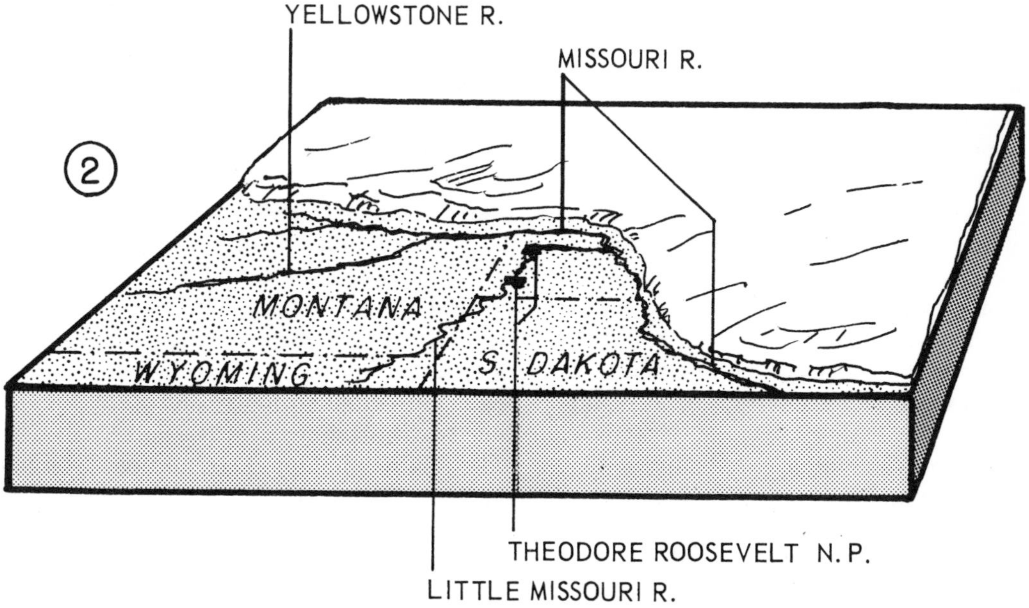

① In Pliocene time, 12 to 3 million years ago, the Little Missouri flowed into the Yellowstone River near Williston. Together they joined the Missouri River, which at that time flowed northeast to Hudson Bay.

② In Pleistocene time, advancing ice cut off the Hudson Bay route, forcing the Missouri and Yellowstone Rivers to turn east toward the Mississippi River. At its maximum extent, the ice dammed the Little Missouri, turning it eastward as well. Rapid downcutting by the ice-fed Missouri steepened the gradient of the Little Missouri, causing excavation of badlands along its course.

cene and early Pleistocene time, within just the last three or four million years.

• To start with, the ancestral Little Missouri did not then, as it does now, turn east at Oxbow Bend in what is now the North Unit of the national park, but flowed north to join the ancestral Yellowstone. Enlivened by Pliocene uplift, it had carved itself a wide, shallow valley not as deep as its present one.

• Another stream rejuvenated by the uplift, one with a southeasterly course feeding ultimately into the Mississippi drainage, cut headward toward the Little Missouri.

• Climate changes of the Pleistocene Epoch sent immense ice sheets across southern Canada and into our northern states. In North Dakota the southern lip of the ice lay along the route of the headward-eroding stream, barely reaching into the present North Unit of the national park. Glacial ice dammed the northward river route, impounding the Little Missouri.

• Fed by heavy rains that accompanied Ice Age climate changes, the lake overflowed into the headward-eroding stream, which in essence "captured" waters that before had drained northward.

• Working together, the two streams excavated a channel deeper than the Little Missouri's former north-flowing valley, draining the lake and establishing the Little Missouri on an easterly course.

• Faced with a similar ice barrier, the ancestral Missouri was also forced to abandon its northward route and to take up an eastward one, meeting its former tributary, the Little Missouri, 90 kilometers (60 miles) downstream from the old confluence.

• By the time the ice receded, these rivers had become well established in their present courses, in channels deep enough to discourage a return to northward drainage.

Since Pleistocene time, the Little Missouri has widened its floodplain; it now swings lazily from one side of the valley to the other. Final touches have been added to the scenery – detailed fluting of valley walls, erosion that leaves ledges of harder rock standing out from slopes of softer rock, wind-blasting that polishes the walls of Wind Canyon, collapse of regions underlain by burning coal, slumping and sliding that are important processes in widening the valley, and, above all, development of badland topography.

Badland formation came about gradually as the climate became drier and the vegetation less dense. The new confluence of the Little Missouri with the Missouri was lower in elevation than the old confluence with the Yellowstone. The river therefore flowed more swiftly and cut down through the soft Paleocene sediments of its former shallow valley floor. Their gradients steepened too, its tributaries carved deeper channels, incising the gullies and ravines that are so much a part of badlands. Initially, badland development was limited to the area nearest the mouth of the Little Missouri, where it entered the Missouri, for there the gradient was steepest. Gradually, though, as the Little Missouri channel deepened, badland erosion crept farther and farther upstream, until today the badlands extend south nearly to the South Dakota line.

Periodically, with vagaries in weather, the river overflowed its immediate inner channel and deposited sand and silt on its nearly horizontal floodplain. Remnants of old floodplains now form river terraces, notably the one on which Pleasant Valley Ranch and the nearby picnic area are located, in the South Unit. At present the Little Missouri appears to be in a stable, no-downcutting phase, but it is widening its immediate valley by undercutting its banks, thereby causing more slumps and landslides and more badland erosion.

BEHIND THE SCENES

North Unit. Badland strata and structures are well exposed in the North Unit. Only the Sentinel Butte Formation occurs here – layers of silty shale and fine sandstone in tones of gray and grayish brown.

At several places along the road there are excellent examples of tilted, wedge-shaped slump blocks which have rotated back toward the cliff from which they slid. The blocks are easily recognized because of their tilting strata, unusual in this layer-cake land. The same rock layers, untilted, are visible on the hills behind them.

Near Squaw Creek Campground, cannonball concretions lie scattered at the base of the cliff. Note in particular the sharp change in the angle of the canyon walls as they meet the nearly horizontal valley floor, the "moats" of clear ground at the base of each cliff, and the decorative fluting of the slopes. A nature trail leaflet points out other geologic features.

Caprock Coulee nature trail leads into a canyon where badland features are well developed and can be seen at close range. Petrified wood is abundant here; both logs and stumps litter many slopes. (Park designation protects the petrified wood, and collecting is not permitted.) Here and there, thin sheets of blue-gray bentonite drape the upper part of the hillsides. They come from a conspicuous layer known as the "Big Blue" bed, an easily recognized unit that stands out boldly as a cap to hills and ridges.

The river's present valley lies along the southernmost limit of Pleistocene ice. Boulders of granite and other igneous and metamorphic rock, quarried in Canada and transported southward by flowing ice, dot the grassy upland here. Since there are no similar ice-transported erratics south of the river, we know that the glacier never got that far.

From Oxbow Bend Overlook you can gaze down upon the Little Missouri's sharp change in direction. Now flowing eastward, it has abandoned its former north-flowing channel, which can still be recognized northwest of the overlook. Notice also the chaotic, hummocky slope below the overlook. Here a large landslide, instead of remaining in one piece like the rotating slump blocks described above, broke apart as it slid. The Little Missouri, meandering across its broad floodplain, occasionally cuts away the bases of

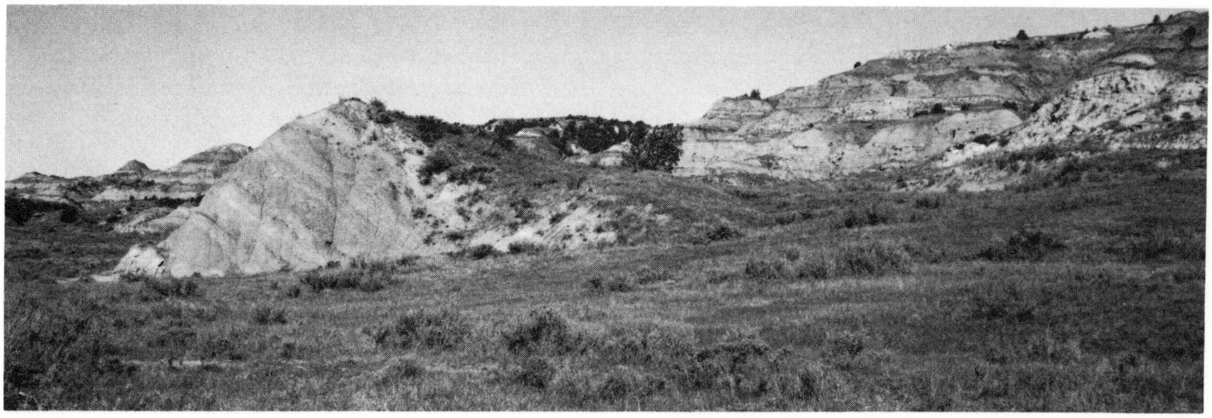

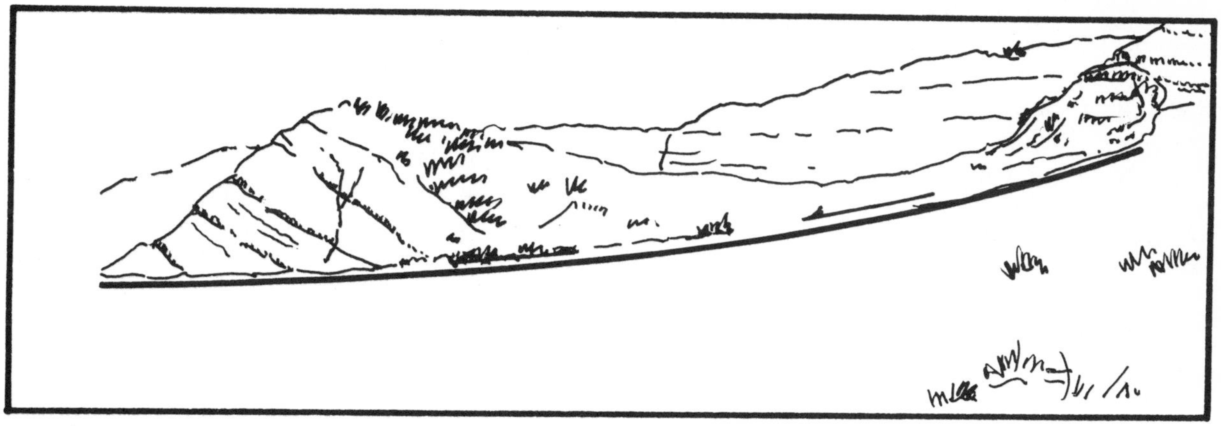

Retaining even its cap of vegetation, a block has slumped along a curving glide plane that tilts its strata back toward its parent hills.

Petrified kindling cascades down a hillside. Its cellular structure is so perfectly duplicated in silica that it splits like real wood.

the valley walls, undermining them and causing slumps and landslides. This process is an important one in valley widening.

Painted Canyon Overlook. From this viewpoint the suddenness of the change from Great Plains topography to Little Missouri Badlands topography can be well appreciated. Characteristically, the branching watercourses of badlands cut headward into the flat plains surface, eating their way back and enlarging little by little the badlands area at the expense of the plains.

Sedimentary rocks visible in the badlands belong to the Sentinel Butte Formation: gray and gray-brown clay and sand and silt layers derived from the rising Rocky Mountains about 60 million years ago. Some of the material no doubt came from the region just west of the Black Hills, near the headwaters of today's Little Missouri River.

You may be able to pick out thin black or red layers among the drab gray ones. The black is lignite or brown coal; red layers were colored by oxidation as coal seams burned underground. Blue-gray layers contain a large proportion of volcanic ash.

South Unit. Most slopes in the South Unit display the characteristic layer-cake sequence of fine, poorly consolidated sandstone, siltstone, and clay of the Sentinel Butte Formation, marked occasionally by reddish bands of baked shale or black seams of coal. Near the river the top of the Tongue River Formation occurs, looking much like the Sentinel Butte Formation.

The scenic loop drive goes through some of the badlands country and to the trailheads of several short nature trails. Watch for petrified logs and stumps, burnt-out coal seams marked by red clinker, cross-bedded sandstone deposited in former stream channels, and erosional features unique to badlands.

Coal Vein Trail leads to the site of the most recent coal vein fire in the park, a burn started by lightning in 1951. It smoldered until 1977. As the coal seam burned away, layered sediments above it collapsed, forming irregular depressions that now hold small ponds and marshes. Near the collapsed area you can see baked, reddened clinker as well as some of the slaglike material formed as fire raged in blast-furnace cracks. Fossil leaves—mere imprints now—can be found among the fragments of clinker.

The trail down Wind Canyon is interesting, too. Wind swooping across the wide expanse of the Little Missouri Valley funnels into this narrow ravine, cleaning away debris and keeping its walls smooth and polished by frequent sand blasting.

OTHER READING

Bluemie, John P., and Jacob, Arthur F. 1973. *Auto Tour Guide along the South Loop Road, Theodore Roosevelt National Memorial Park.* Theodore Roosevelt Nature and History Association, North Dakota Geological Survey Educational Series 4.

Laird, Wilson M. 1950. *The Geology of the South Unit, Theodore Roosevelt National Memorial Park.* North Dakota History, vol. 17, no. 4.

Schoch, Henry A. 1974. *Theodore Roosevelt, the Story Behind the Scenery.* KC Publications, Las Vegas, Nevada.

Timpanogos Cave National Monument

Established: 1922
Size: 1 square kilometer (0.4 square mile)
Elevation: 1,727 meters (5,665 feet) at visitor center; 2,051 meters (6,730 feet) at cave entrance
Address: RFD 2, American Fork, Utah 84003

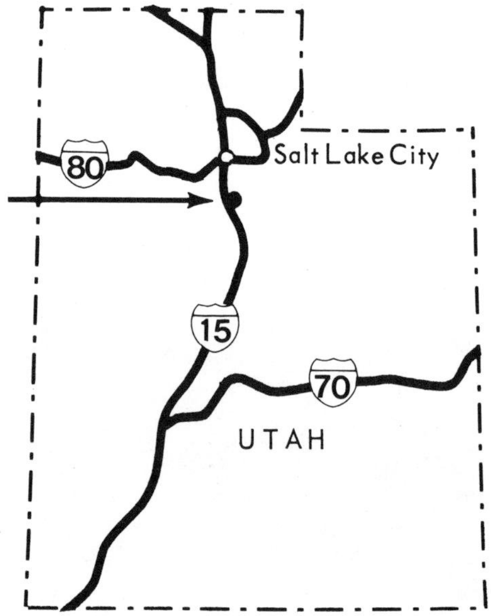

STAR FEATURES

• Three limestone caverns finely frescoed with helictites, stalactites, stalagmites, cave popcorn, and other dripstone and flowstone ornaments.

• Along the trail, a march upward through time from Precambrian rocks a billion years old to Mississippian rocks 330 million years old. Younger strata lie above the cave on the slopes of Mount Timpanogos.

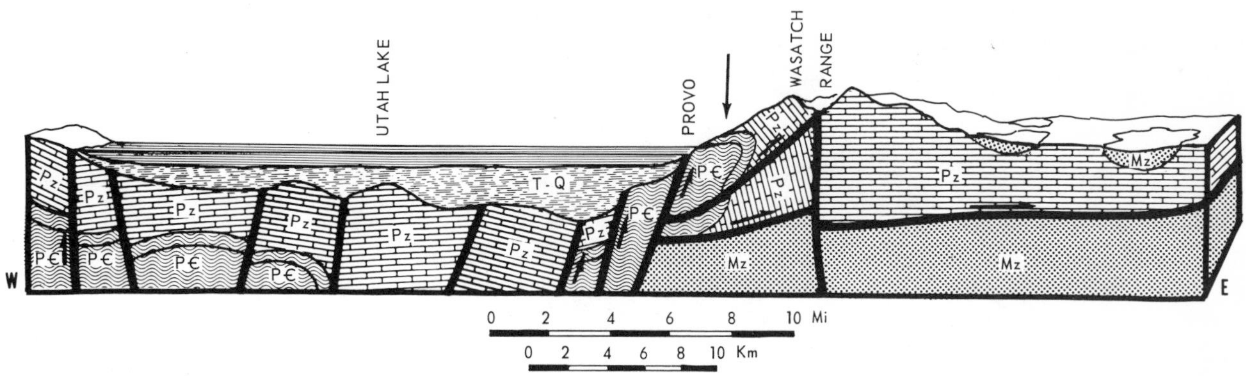

Complexly faulted and folded Paleozoic rocks of the Wasatch Range separate the Great Basin (left) from the uplands of eastern Utah. Timpanogos Cave is a few miles north of this section (below arrow).

• Visitor center, self-guided mountainside trail (along which the rock formations are labeled), and guided cave tours.

SETTING THE STAGE

Timpanogos Cave, Hansen Cave, and Middle Cave, now connected by man-made tunnels, lie near the west edge of the Wasatch Range in a geologically complicated area of intersecting faults and folds. These caves typify limestone caverns, having developed where groundwater, slightly acidified by absorption of carbon dioxide from air and soil, dissolved passages through cracked and faulted limestone. The massive layer in which the caves have formed is steeply tilted and is part of the southern flank of a large fault-edged anticline, cored with granite, that crosses the north-south trend of the Wasatch Range.

Solution of limestone caverns occurs most readily at and below the water table, where all the pore spaces, joints, and other openings in the rock are filled with water. Geologists feel sure that these caves formed at a time when the canyon of American Fork River was no deeper than the level of the present caves. There is evidence in the caves—stream-rounded pebbles of "foreign" rock—that the river or one of its tributaries once flowed through them.

As the river cut deeper, the water table dropped below cave level and solution ceased. But seeping groundwater derived from rain and melted snow still entered the cave, dripping from its ceilings, sheeting down its walls, and collecting in low spots as cave pools. As it percolated through overlying limestone layers, the water became saturated with calcium carbonate. In the caves it redeposited its calcium carbonate as calcite crusts and cave ornaments—stalactites, stalagmites, cave popcorn (globularites), draperies, and strange curling helictites.

A special word about helictites, for which this cave is famous. Their twisted curlicues seem at odds with the vertical patterns of stalactites, stalagmites, and draperies. They are thought to develop when thin layers of fine crystalline calcite coat cave surfaces in such a way as to seal the rock, so that water seeping into rock pore spaces cannot escape into the cave. Behind this thin dam, water accumulates and water pressure increases. Then, in places, the pressure pushes out tiny fragments of the calcite coating. Once the dam is breached, successive layers of newly formed crystals are pushed out at the same spots. Because the crystals may be wedge shaped, the growing helictites curve and curl, responding more to water pressure and crystal shape than to gravity.

Cave ornamentation is still going on here. Cave surfaces are wet and dripping, with every drop adding a tiny bit of calcite to the ornaments. Trickling water creates flowstone, solidly coating and rounding cave surfaces or sheeting into thin, translucent draperies. Around unruffled pools, lily-pad shelves grow outward. Fine needles of aragonite, another form of calcite, develop as frostwork. Tunnels joining the caves were completed in the 1930s, and half a century later show tiny bumps—incipient stalactites—where groundwater drips from their ceilings, a measure of the rate of growth.

An unusual feature of these caves is the variety of color in the ornaments—delicate tints of pink and yellow, green and tan. The colors are due to minute amounts of other minerals in the calcite. Iron and manganese oxides create buff and pink, lemon yellow is due to nickel, and green tones are a nickel-magnesium silicate. Don't confuse the green algae that grow near the electric lights with the green tint actually *in* the rocks!

The three caves lie in an almost straight line along a fault zone that cuts northeastward through the

NPS photo

The 2-ton "Heart" of Timpanogos Cave hangs from a ceiling intricately decorated with twisting helictites. The Heart is nearly 2 meters (6 feet) long.

NPS photo

Finger-like helictites, rare in most caves, are exceptionally abundant here. Hydrostatic pressure plays a role in their formation.

mountain. You'll see fault surfaces in the caves — a rare chance to look at a fault zone from the inside! Movement along the fault varies from about 30 meters (90 feet) in Hansen Cave to 40 meters (120 feet) in Timpanogos Cave.

GEOLOGIC HISTORY

Precambrian and Paleozoic Eras. Sedimentary rocks low in the walls of American Fork Canyon — the Tintic Quartzite, Ophir Shale, and Maxfield Limestone — are part of a great blanket that stretched from Arizona into Canada in late Precambrian time, about a billion years ago. Patterns of Precambrian deposition seem to have lasted into Paleozoic time. The equator then lay along the line of the present Wasatch Range, and for hundreds of millions of years the same line acted as a sort of hinge, with thick sedimentary strata characteristic of a deep-water basin deposited north of the equator (now west) and thin sedimentary layers accumulating in shallow seas to the south (now east). Then there is a gap — no record at all for the Ordovician, Devonian, and Silurian Periods. The region may well have been land, or

During the first part of the Paleozoic Era, the earth's equator ran almost along the line of the present Wasatch Mountain front. This was also the position of a hinge line, with seas deepening rapidly to the north (left).

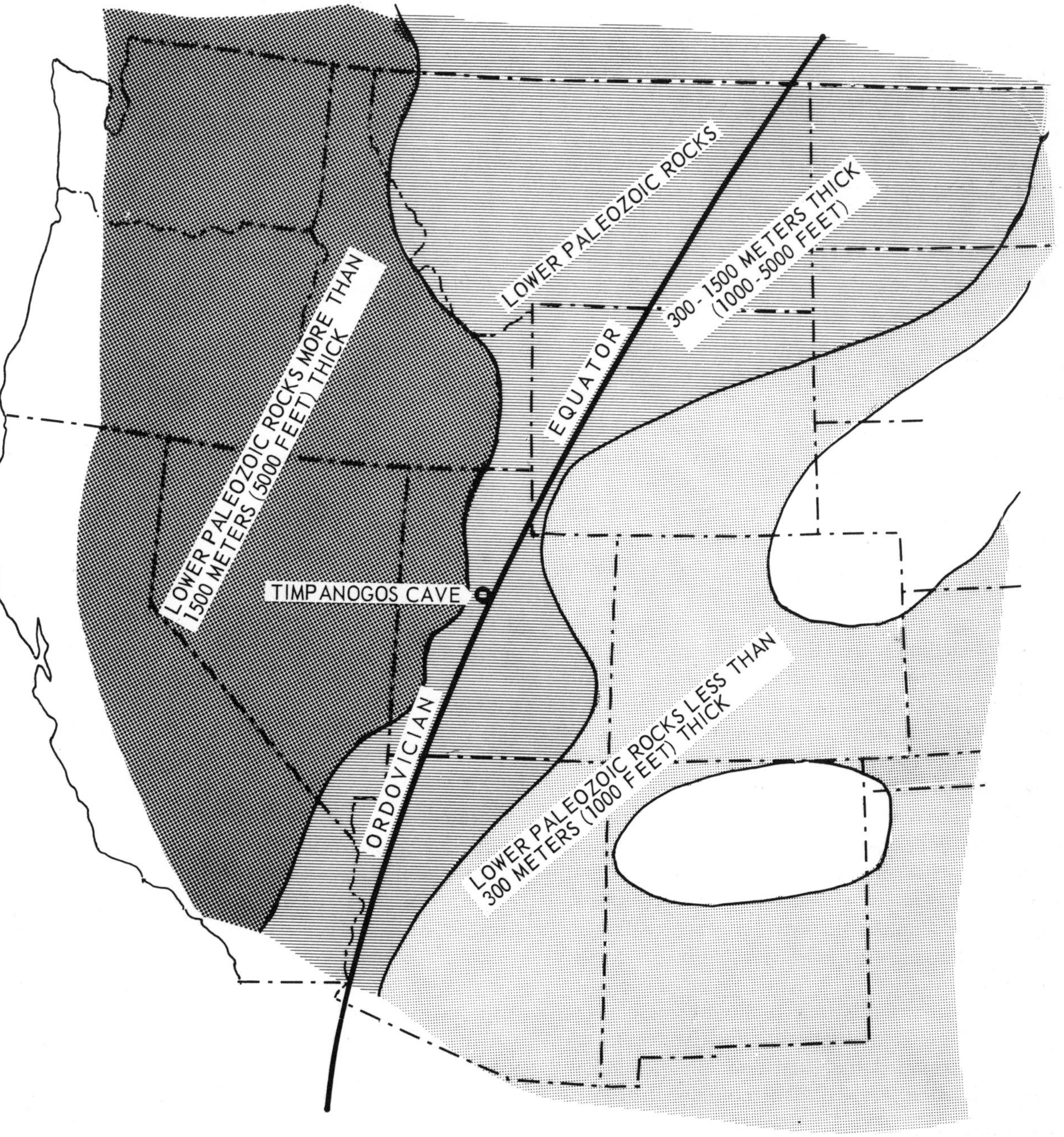

what sediments were deposited were later eroded away.

In Mississippian time, seas spread eastward again, and limestone layers formed from the accumulated shells of marine organisms—thousands of meters thick in northwest Utah, hundreds of meters thick along the line of the present Wasatch Range. The Deseret Limestone, in which Timpanogos and its sister caves lie, is one of several Mississippian limestone formations recognized here.

Rocks younger than Mississippian do not occur within the monument area. We know from surrounding areas that mountains rose both east and west of Utah in late Paleozoic time. Gradually, too, the continent was rotating and drifting north. By the beginning of Mesozoic time, Utah was well north of the equator and only about 30 degrees awry relative to the present position of the poles.

Mesozoic Era. Events of the Mesozoic Era involved uplift, erosion, and large-scale thrust faulting. A sheet of Precambrian and Paleozoic rocks slid perhaps 90 kilometers from west to east across younger rocks. Sedimentary strata outside the monument record a gradual change from shallow sea to delta and floodplain and then to sea again.

Cenozoic Era. By the end of Cretaceous time and through the Eocene Epoch, westward drift of the continent led to folding and faulting and uplift once more—uplift of the Rockies in Colorado and Wyoming, of the Wasatch and Uinta Ranges in Utah. Later, crustal stretching between the Wasatch Mountains and the Sierra Nevada resulted in the fault block mountains of western Utah, Nevada, California, and Arizona. Archlike uplift of the Wasatch-to-the-Rockies region finally elevated the mountain states, mountains and all, about 1,500 meters (5,000 feet)—an unprecedented uplift in the history of this region.

Pleistocene time—the last 3 million years—brought glaciation to the Wasatch Range as it did to other ranges of the Rockies and the northwest. American Fork Canyon, though never glaciated in its lower reaches, doubtless was influenced by the increases in snowmelt, icemelt, and precipitation that accompanied the Ice Ages. The abrupt face of the Wasatch Mountains and the steep, angular shape of the lower canyon indicate that this is a youthful mountain range, where lively streams have cut downward rather than swinging sideways. Steep rockslides on the north canyon wall are facilitated by the steeply sloping strata.

No discussion of this area would be complete without mentioning Lake Bonneville, the Pleistocene lake that once occupied the Utah and Great Salt Lake valleys. Terrace levels on the mountain front near Provo are old lake shorelines, and show that Lake Bonneville was far deeper and more extensive than its descendants. For most of its existence it was a freshwater lake; only after its level had dropped below its former northern outlet at the end of the Ice Ages did it gradually become salty.

OTHER READING

Hintze, L.F. 1973 *Geologic History of Utah.* Brigham Young University Geology Studies, vol. 20, part 3.

Perkins, R.F. 1955. *Structure and Stratigraphy of the Lower American Fork Canyon–Mahogany Mountain Area, Utah County, Utah.* Brigham Young University Research Studies, Geology Series, vol. 2, no. 1.

Wind Cave National Park

Established: 1903
Size: 114 square kilometers (44 square miles)
Elevation: 1,244 to 1,528 meters (4,084 to 5,013 feet)
Address: Hot Springs, South Dakota 57747

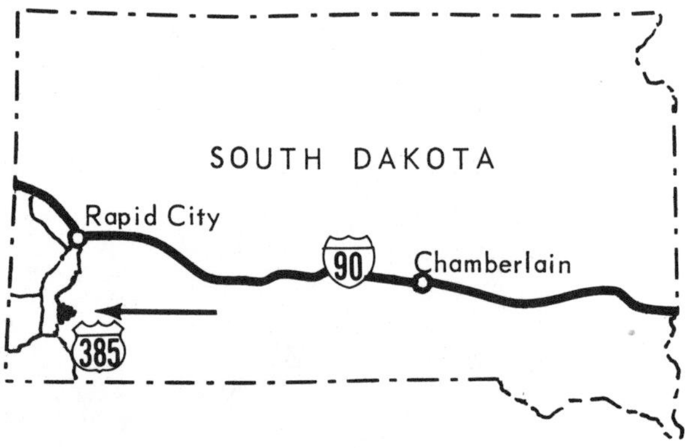

STAR FEATURES

• Intricate underground passages dissolved by groundwater, with unusual "boxwork" as the predominant ornamentation.

• The interesting Black Hills setting, where truncated edges of sedimentary rock layers encircle a dome-shaped uplift of granite and metamorphic rock.

• Visitor center exhibits, a self-guided nature trail, and evening talks emphasizing the history of the Black Hills region and Wind Cave. Easy walking tours in the cave, led by park naturalists, follow safe, hard-surfaced routes through 1.5 to 2 kilometers (1 to

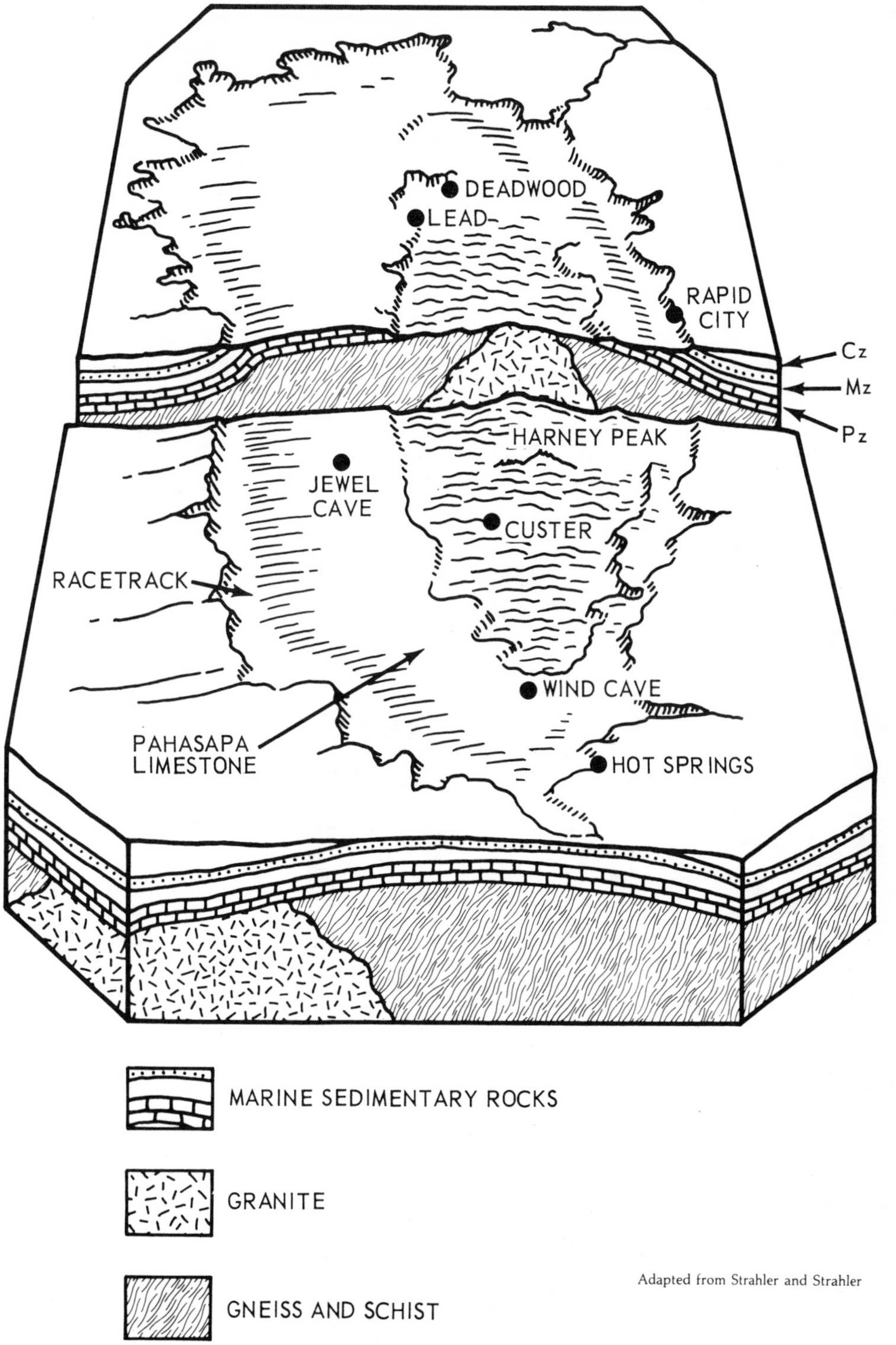

The elongate dome of the Black Hills, with its eroded summit, reveals the Paleozoic and Mesozoic history of this region. There are a number of other known caves in the Pahasapa Limestone ringing the central granite core of the range.

1.5 miles) of the extensive cave complex. Maps of the cave are available at the visitor center.

• For the hardy, spelunking tours into remote unlit and untrailed parts of the cave. Historic candlelight tours are also offered.

SETTING THE STAGE

In the Black Hills, a central highland of Precambrian crystalline rock a billion or more years old is surrounded by concentric rings of sedimentary rock. Among these, resistant sandstone and limestone layers stand up as ridges and define the oval shape of the range. Softer shale and siltstone form encircling furrows and the wide red valley known as the Racetrack.

One of the sedimentary layers is the Pahasapa Limestone, a Mississippian formation 100 to 200 meters (300 to 650 feet) thick and over 300 million years old. In the western Black Hills this massive limestone, dotted with fist-sized nodules of chert and flint, forms a broad, gently-sloping plateau. In the southern Black Hills it slopes southward, and here are found the many subterranean passages of Wind Cave and other caves. Below the Pahasapa Limestone are older sandstone and mudstone layers; above are orange-red soils, broken blocks of limestone, and around the margins of the Black Hills, younger sedimentary strata.

Wind Cave itself is a three-level complex of intricate, twisting, dividing and joining passages and low, narrow, contorted crawlways, not all of which have been fully explored. Painstaking underground mapping shows that many of the passageways—especially the large rooms and long, fairly straight corridors—run in a northeast-southwest direction, the direction of the most prominent set of joints (fractures) in rocks of this immediate area. Cross passages tend to run northwest-southeast, almost at right angles, along another joint set. Mapped portions of the cave occur within an area about 1,500 meters long by 900 meters wide (5,000 by 3,000 feet) and consist of 50 kilometers (30 miles) of passages. But the cave may with further exploration turn out to be much more extensive.

What caused Wind Cave? What hollowed its

Arthur N. Palmer photo

Wind Cave's branching crawlways and fluted surfaces result from solution by groundwater that widened cracks or joints in the Pahasapa Limestone.

rooms and corridors? Why is it not as highly decorated as some caves? Over many millions of years, groundwater seeping through tiny cracks and fissures in the Pahasapa Limestone excavated the underground caverns. Weak solutions of carbonic acid, formed as rainwater absorbs carbon dioxide from air and decaying vegetation, seep drop by tiny drop through rock joints—a slow process at first. But as the acidified water moves, it dissolves and washes away more and more calcium carbonate, the mineral of which limestone is made. Passages widen and the acidic water flows faster. Faster flow in turn speeds up the solution process, allowing still faster water movement.

Groundwater flow, and therefore solution of limestone, are also controlled by the position of rock layers. Groundwater tends to flow down the slope or dip of the limestone strata, following layers that are slightly more porous or more finely fractured or that have shaly or cherty impermeable layers below them. Here, where strata dip a few degrees to the south off the southern flank of the Black Hills, cave passages follow suit, also dipping southward. The deepest points in the cave are therefore at its southern end. Cave passages are at three "levels" defined by three soluble layers in the upper half of the Pahasapa Limestone. The upper level contains many small rooms and narrow passages, and sometimes it cuts into a layer of red soil and broken limestone fragments at the top of the Pahasapa Formation. Middle-level rooms are larger and corridors wider. Passages of the lowest zone are high, narrow corridors that include more types of cave deposits than do the levels above. Total vertical relief in the cave is about 170 meters (560 feet). Park Service tours drop down through all three levels, a vertical distance of about 100 meters (350 feet), and return to the surface by elevator. The cave may once have had more levels—higher ones now destroyed by erosion (fragments of cave deposits have been found on the present surface) and lower ones still filled with groundwater, below the level of the lakes in the deep southern parts of the present cave.

Wind Cave was almost certainly hollowed out at a time when the water table, the surface below which rock is completely saturated, was much higher than at present. At the time of its excavation, every crack and crevice of the Pahasapa Limestone was completely filled with water. After solution of the cavern, a process taking thousands, perhaps millions, of years, the interconnecting channels and corridors drained. No longer supported by water, some cavern walls and ceilings collapsed, leaving piles of rubbly "breakdown" on the passage floors. Most breakdown fell as the caverns drained. None has fallen since the cave was discovered in 1881. (You are safer here, where thick arched ceilings and massive walls have withstood the test of time, than you are in your own home.)

Oxidation of iron and other minerals present in small quantities in the limestone delicately tints walls and ceilings pink and orange. Black colors are from powdery oxidized manganese, a mineral that occurs in small quantity in the Pahasapa Limestone, and that was concentrated as the more soluble calcium carbonate dissolved away.

Rainfall seeping down from the surface, though in smaller quantity now than during the carving of the cave, continues to cause some changes. In rare instances it brings dissolved calcium carbonate into the cave, depositing it as ornamentation in the rooms and passages. Wind Cave, however, is not as highly ornamented as Carlsbad Caverns and many other caves. Except under surface streams and in the Lakes area at the south end of the cave, it is now dry, without the dripping water that builds stalactites, stalagmites, and travertine draperies. There is some fine frostwork, some cavities are lined with long calcite crystals known as dogtooth spar, and, especially in the

Calcite crystals known as dogtooth spar line small cavities in the Pahasapa Limestone. Crystals such as these were deposited before the cave drained.

Arthur N. Palmer photo

deepest parts of the cave, calcite helictites twist and curl with seeming disregard for the laws of gravity. The cave is renowned for its boxwork, an unusual type of ornamentation abundant in middle-level passages but less common in upper and lower levels. The boxwork had its origins at the time of the Black Hills uplift, about 60 million years ago, when many fine intersecting fractures were created in some parts of the Pahasapa Limestone. Percolating groundwater deposited tightly packed calcite crystals in these fractures. There are two schools of thought as to what happened next. Many geologists think that the original limestone was then selectively removed by solution as the cave was hollowed out, a viewpoint reinforced by the presence of delicate but unbroken boxwork on some of the breakdown. Others propose that the water level dropped and the cave dried out before the limestone matrix weathered and flaked away. In either case, only the fine intersecting fins of calcite are left, as if bricks were removed from a wall without disturbing the mortar. Fine calcite crystal frostwork edging some of the boxwork is thought to have developed during another period of submergence.

Wind Cave's wind, blowing through both natural and man-made entrances, results from changes in atmospheric pressure. The cave is large, but its entrances are small. When atmospheric pressure outside rises, air rushes through the small openings to equalize the pressure inside. Conversely, when outside pressure is low, air is drawn rapidly out of the cave. Wind may moan through the entrances at 70 kilometers (50 miles) per hour even on a calm day! Within the cave, wind currents in narrow corridors have led explorers into new passageways and extensive unexplored cavities, for where they blow there must be more cave beyond. Despite these winds, the temperature within the cave remains, winter and summer, close to 4°C (47°F), the year-round average temperature outside the cave.

Sedimentary rocks older and younger than the Pahasapa Formation are also present within the park. In the northern part of the park, some of the coarse-grained, billion-year-old granite of the Black Hills core rises as rugged hills that project above the general landscape. Even older mica schist into which this granite intruded can be seen in roadcuts. Between these ancient rocks and the cave are successive layers

The origin of Wind Cave's delicate boxwork relates to fine calcite-filled cracks in the limestone walls and ceilings.

Arthur N. Palmer photo

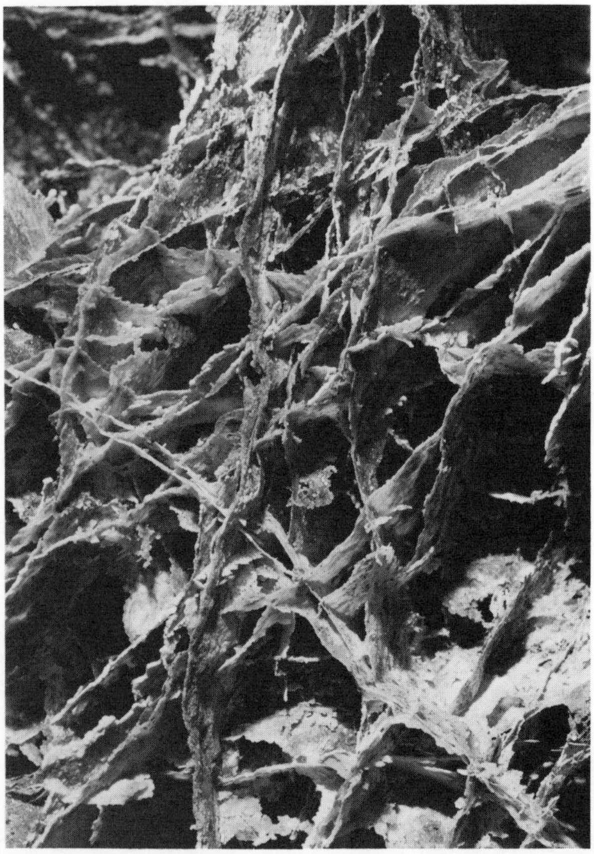

Cave popcorn is made up of tiny calcite crystals deposited when the cave was filled with water.

Arthur N. Palmer photo

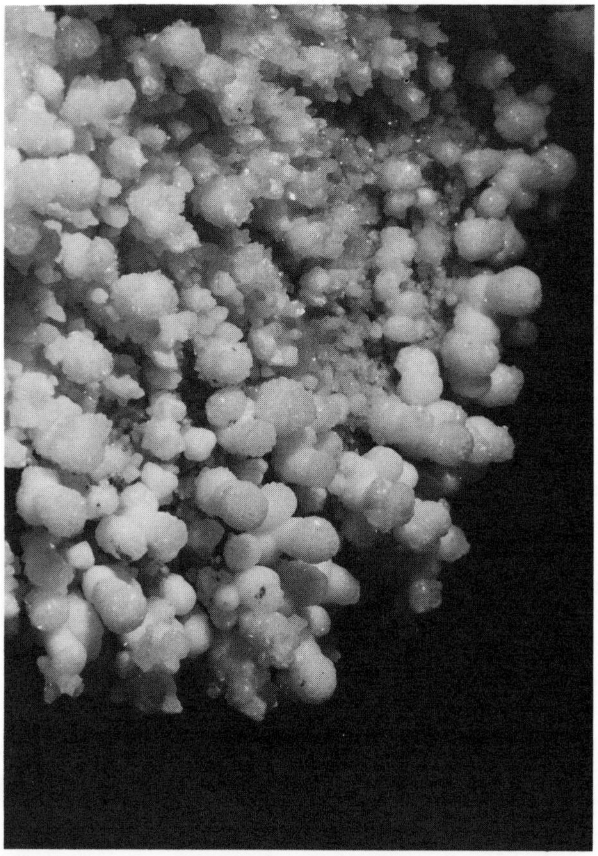

of Lower Paleozoic sedimentary rocks. In the southeast part of the park, red shales of Triassic age, the Spearfish Formation, mark the Racetrack valley that encircles the Black Hills. White blobs and veinlets in this formation are gypsum, often occurring as satiny selenite. Gypsum accumulates in a warm, dry climate where seawater is trapped in isolated basins and where salt and gypsum precipitate as it evaporates. Here the extremely soluble salt later dissolved away. The gypsum, carried in solution by groundwater, was deposited in fractures in the red siltstone of the Spearfish Formation.

GEOLOGIC HISTORY

Precambrian Era. The gneiss and schist that appear in the central core of the Black Hills show us that during part of Precambrian time thick sequences of sedimentary rock were deposited here, and later were deeply buried, intricately folded, and compressed. These metamorphic rocks were in turn intruded by molten magma that with long, slow cooling became the evenly grained granite of the central Black Hills, well exposed at Mount Rushmore National Memorial. Liquids distilled from the granite magma penetrated fissures in the solidifying mass and, as they cooled, formed pegmatite veins with unusually large tourmaline, rose quartz, mica, and feldspar crystals sought by mineral collectors.

During the last part of the Precambrian Era, this area (as well as most other parts of the continent) was eroded into a level plain.

Paleozoic Era. Through much of Paleozoic time the climate here was warm and tropical, for at that time this region was quite close to the equator. During much of the era the region was flooded by shallow seas. On the beveled surface of the Precambrian rocks, layer upon layer of marine sedimentary rocks accumulated: sandstone, shale, and limestone. Limy mud deposited during Mississippian time, 345 to 320 million years ago, eventually became compressed and hardened into the Pahasapa Limestone. This rock, fine and even-grained, was probably formed of the shells of millions—billions—of tiny one-celled marine organisms that lived and died in the warm, shallow sea. Larger shell-bearing animals such as clams, snails, brachiopods, and exotic relatives of today's sea urchins and starfish also contributed to the limy deposits. Brachiopod and mollusk shells can still be found in the Pahasapa Limestone, but details of smaller, more fragile shells were destroyed as the limy deposits turned into limestone. Chert nodules that project from the limestone (both on the surface and in the cave) formed from jellylike blobs of silica, probably in turn derived from organisms with silica shells or skeletons, such as one-celled diatoms and some sponges.

After the Pahasapa Formation was deposited, the flat sea floor rose for a time above sea level. The climate was still tropical, and in such a climate, limestone dissolves easily. Solution of the limestone formed caves and sinkholes and left on the surface a fine, silty, orange-red residue called laterite. Here and there, angular blocks of light gray limestone remained imbedded in this red soil. Many solution caverns collapsed, leaving numerous sinkholes and a rugged, irregular land surface. Laterite, with its imbedded limestone blocks, can be seen on the surface in the Wind Cave area today; watch for it in roadcuts and natural embankments. Look for it also in Wind Cave itself, for some old collapsed sinkholes and caverns formed in Mississippian time are intercepted by the present much younger cave, and the two generations of limestone solution occur together.

The Pahasapa Limestone was deposited around 330 million years ago in a quiet, fairly shallow Mississippian sea. Then for a time this region emerged from the sea. Weathering of the limestone surface produced solution pockets and small caves that can still be distinguished.

Arthur N. Palmer photo

Mesozoic and Cenozoic Eras. After resubmergence during the last part of the Paleozoic Era, this land rose again in Mesozoic time, so that it was above the sea in the time of the dinosaurs. It seems to have been part of a broad floodplain, delta, or coastal plain, with sandstone and siltstone, clay and conglomerate deposited on it—a region very like the Gulf Coast plain of the United States today. Then about 60 million years ago, after a brief new submergence, westward drift of the continent created mountain-building forces in the Rocky Mountain region. Precambrian rock here was pushed up into a dome-shaped uplift. Formerly flat-lying sedimentary layers were domed up too, and subjected to stretching and straining. Some bent, some broke. The massive Pahasapa Limestone fractured along thousands of minute breaks, tiny fractures which were ultimately to guide the solution of Wind Cave.

After uplift—a process that probably took millions of years—the slopes of the range were buried in a thick blanket of gravel derived partly from erosion of the Black Hills themselves and partly from the newly formed Rocky Mountains to the west. Only after a second pulse of uplift were these Tertiary gravels partly washed away. They still remain in surrounding areas as the Great Plains surface and can be seen in Theodore Roosevelt or Badlands National Parks.

Rainwater made acid by absorption of carbon dioxide from air and soil may have begun to penetrate and alter the fine cracks in the Pahasapa Limestone as early as 45 or 50 million years ago, in Eocene time, when the Pahasapa Limestone and the rest of the sedimentary rocks around the Black Hills were still deeply submerged under their gravel blanket. Over many hundreds of thousands of years, the slow, molecule-by-molecule excavation took place. It seems reasonable to believe that increased precipitation during the Ice Ages (that is, within the last three million years) contributed greatly to the process of hollowing out the caves. The Black Hills were never glaciated, but fluctuating groundwater levels, corresponding to fluctuations in rain and snowfall and to advances and retreats of the big continental glaciers, may have flooded and drained and reflooded the caves several times. Temperature changes related to glaciation doubtless influenced the temperature of water within the cave, for caves tend to take on the average surface temperature. Because temperature changes also alter the solubility of limestone, they may have controlled both solution and deposition in the cave.

When the last Ice Age drew to a close about 10,000 years ago, the Black Hills region looked very much as it does today. Stream erosion had swept away much of the Tertiary gravel blanket and had cut down through the mantle of older sediments to bare the Precambrian core of the range. Stream erosion of the Pahasapa Limestone at last intercepted, at a few points, the intricate hollowed passageways of Wind Cave, Jewel Cave, and other caverns in the Black Hills region, setting the stage for their discovery.

OTHER READING

Tyers, J.A. 1965. *The Significance of Wind Cave.* Wind Cave Natural History Association, Hot Springs, South Dakota.

Anonymous. 1977. *Geology of Caves.* U.S. Government Printing Office (pamphlet).

Yellowstone National Park

Established: 1872, the first national park
Size: 8,980 square kilometers (3,468 square miles)
Elevation: 1,620 to 3,462 meters (5,314 to 11,358 feet)
Address: Yellowstone National Park, Wyoming 82190

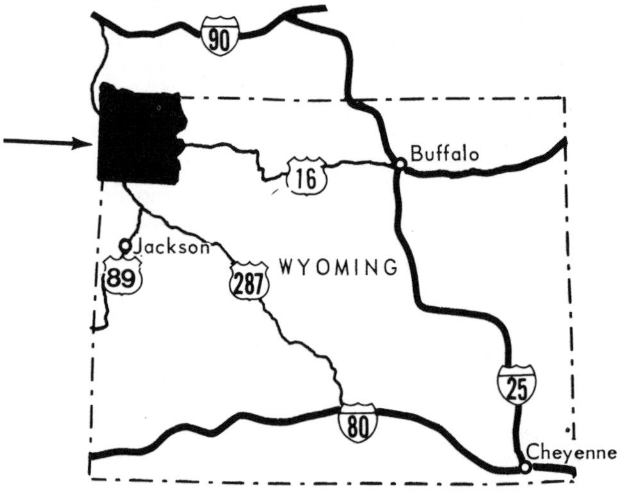

STAR FEATURES

• A plateau region born in the thunder of great volcanic eruptions, with young lava flows superimposed on the calderas of older volcanic explosions far more violent than any known in historic time.

• Volcanic rocks, including breccia, tuff, rhyolite, obsidian, and columnar basalt.

• Fossil forests buried in volcanic ash, with silicified trees that grew in a temperate or subtropical climate.

• A fascinating landscape produced by interaction of volcanism, ice, and water, with rivers, lakes, thundering falls, and the golden canyon that gives the Yellowstone River its name.

Castle Geyser erupts at about 9-hour intervals, throwing spray and steam 10 meters (30 feet) into the air. Its cone tops a large mound of siliceous sinter.

• Celebrated hydrothermal (hot water) features related to a now dormant volcanic region. Yellowstone contains thousands of hot springs and over 200 geysers, some of which erupt on predictable schedules.

• Many roads and trails that wind past the natural features. The interpretive program includes do-it-yourself trail guides, museum and roadside exhibits, and naturalist-guided tours of geologic interest.

See color pages for additional photographs.

SETTING THE STAGE

Yellowstone is first and foremost a geologic park. Most of it is a volcanic plateau 2,000 meters (6,000 feet) above sea level, with rolling, forested hills. Here and there are barren basins where boiling springs and geysers compete for attention with grotesque sinter and travertine deposits. Yellowstone Lake, near the center of the park, occupies a depression in the plateau, while the Absaroka and Gallatin Ranges, the Red Mountains, and Mount Washburn rise above it to elevations of 3,000 meters (10,000 feet) and more.

Yellowstone Lake is fed and drained by the Yellowstone River, a tributary of the Missouri and therefore part of the Mississippi River and Atlantic drainage. The Firehole and Madison Rivers in the west part of the park flow ultimately into the Missouri as well. However, the Continental Divide separating Atlantic and Pacific watersheds winds across southwest Yellowstone, and that corner of the park drains into the Snake River and ultimately to the Columbia and the Pacific.

Glaciation's distinctive fingerprints are in the cirques and U-shaped canyons of the Absaroka and Gallatin Ranges, in broad Hayden and Lamar Valleys, in glacial erratics, in scattered moraine deposits, and in water-laid deposits of lakes dammed by glacial ice.

Where the Yellowstone River crosses lava flows of the central plateau, it follows a wide valley underlain by volcanic rocks. Reaching an area of softer rock, it plunges over cascades and waterfalls into the celebrated Grand Canyon of the Yellowstone, a colorful gorge 37 kilometers (23 miles) long and 400 meters (1,200 feet) deep.

Careful mapping of rocks of the Yellowstone region reveals a remarkable volcanic history. Gigantic collapsed calderas, ringed with faults, cover nearly half of the park's area. The explosive eruptions that formed them, thought to have been many times greater than those that rocked Krakatoa in 1893, Thera in 1470 B.C., or Mount St. Helens in 1980, left a lasting imprint on the Yellowstone region. Mountains that now project above the volcanic plateau are fragments of the caldera rims.

The geyser basins as well as most of the hot springs and mud pots are concentrated in the former caldera area, although thin wraiths of steam rising above the forest show that steam vents and hot springs are widely scattered throughout the park.

What *are* hot springs and geyers? What makes them work? What geologic factors control their presence here?

The essential ingredients are heat, water, and subterranean channels through which water can flow.

The earth as a whole is a storehouse of heat, some of which has been there since our planet formed and some of which is produced internally by decay of radioactive elements. The earth's internal heat is great enough to melt rock, and in some particularly hot spots, molten rock (magma) accumulates in vast underground pools. From these it may flow to the surface as volcanic outpourings, or it may remain deep below the surface, slowly cooling by passing on its heat to the solid rocks that imprison it.

In the Yellowstone region, far more heat is given off at the surface than is emitted in nonvolcanic areas. We can guess from this, and from the abun-

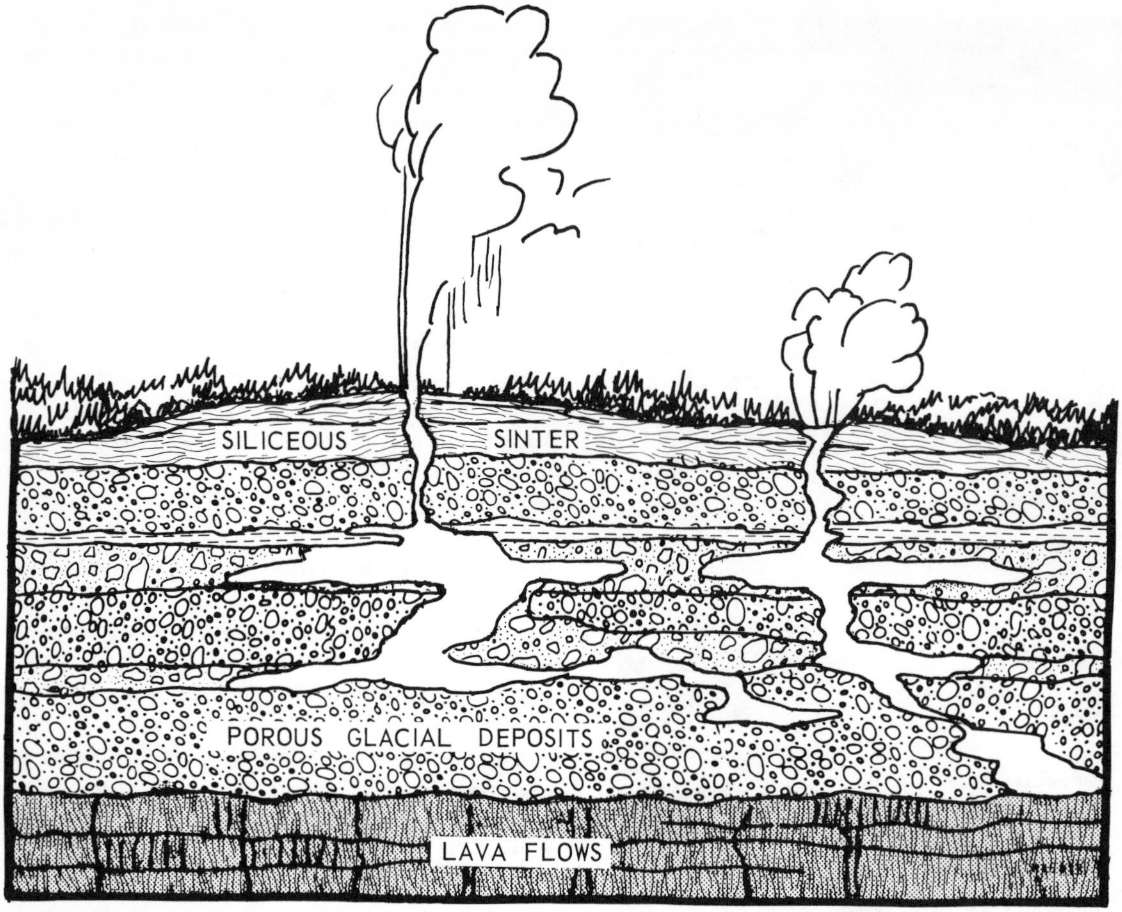

Whatever the configuration of the geyser conduit, a necessary feature is a constriction that inhibits the passage of large steam bubbles.

dance of volcanic rock, that not far below the surface huge magma reservoirs lie dormant. Seismic records and other measurements show that about 10 kilometers (6 miles) down, crustal rocks become so hot that they cannot break, yet can be deformed. Blanketed by thick layers of volcanic ash and lava flows, they are slowly—extremely slowly by human standards—giving off heat to the solid rocks around them.

Water necessary for geysers and hot springs comes from rain and snowmelt that sink into the ground or collect in the reservoir of Yellowstone Lake. Water percolating down faults and fractures that encircle the floor of the former calderas ultimately reaches rocks heated by the magma pool. These waters gradually enlarge every crevice through which they pass. The heated water, a far better solvent than cold water, opens up an intricate plumbing system. And as the water cools, it deposits some of its mineral burden, smoothing its channels, in places reducing their diameter, and in some cases closing them off completely.

So—here is what happens:

Water sinks into the ground. Following underground pathways along faults and fractures, it circulates down to 3,000 or 4,000 meters (10,000 to 14,000 feet) or more. When it comes in contact with rocks heated by the old magma reservoirs it, too, becomes hot. Since it must support the weight of all the column of water above it, it is under great pressure, and like water in a pressure cooker it can be superheated far above its surface boiling point. The hotter it gets, the less dense it is. So it rises toward the surface by convection, and colder, heavier water sinks to be heated in its turn—a fine example of convective circulation.

As it rises toward the surface, the superheated water is under less and less pressure because it is under less and less overlying water. At some stage there is not enough pressure to keep it from boiling, and boil it does. If pressure release is gradual, boiling is mild, as in most hot springs. However, if pressure is contained for a while and then released suddenly, boiling becomes violent. Water "flashes" into steam, vastly increasing in volume, and we get the special kind of hot spring known as a geyser.

At least 200 geysers occur in Yellowstone Park, more than in all other geyser regions put together. There are geysers in New Zealand, Iceland, Japan, Chile, Mexico, California, Tibet, and the Kamchatka Peninsula of USSR.

In a geyser's underground plumbing system, oddities of configuration must restrict upward flow of superheated water. A conduit may have a kink in it; there may be side channels or chambers; there may merely be a constriction in the main conduit, a bottleneck. Whatever the mechanism, the conduit is easily clogged by steam bubbles. (In many hot springs, you can see big steam bubbles floating surfaceward, expanding as pressure from overlying water decreases, then becoming smaller as their steam condenses in cooler near-surface waters.) Its upward flow restricted, the hot water gets hotter; pressures build up more and more. At last the cork pops out of the bottle – the steam bubbles break and gurgle rapidly up the conduit, forcing water in the upper part of the system to rise and overflow as the preliminary surge that signals the beginning of a geyser eruption.

Reduction in pressure results from this overflow and initiates a chain reaction deep down in the conduit, where only pressure kept the superheated water from turning into steam. Large amounts of water – including in some cases that from side chambers – flash suddenly into steam, expanding to hundreds of times their former volume. The tremendous quantity of steam rushes up through the geyser vent, carrying water with it and forming a tall white jet or clustered fountains of steam and spray. And of course for every bit sprayed out the pressure is further released, so more and more of the super-hot water turns to steam, prolonging the eruption.

A geyser display goes on for a few minutes, half an hour, or even longer. As it continues and as new cool water flows into lower parts of the conduit, heat and pressure are reduced. When the water reservoir is empty or the water is diluted below its boiling point, the eruption dies down; often some of the erupted water drains back into the vent opening. Then slowly the water supply is replenished and heated again, and the cycle is renewed.

Geysers – hot springs with a difference. Other variations on the hot springs theme are fumaroles, mud volcanoes, and mud pots. Fumaroles are vents through which only steam escapes; the supply of water is limited. Mud pots and mud volcanoes are hot springs that produce *some* water but not enough to flush away the claylike mud derived from surrounding rock. Many mud pots have so little water that they never overflow at all; as more mud is brought up, they get thicker and thicker, until they

Grotto Geyser's weird mound formed as tree trunks were covered with sinter. Grotto is in eruption about half the time, with eruptions 1 to 36 hours long.

John Chronic photo

take on the consistency and the playful doming and plopping of thick pea soup.

In most of Yellowstone's hot spring and geyser areas, underlying rock layers are rhyolite, a volcanic rock rich in silica minerals. These minerals are dissolved and transported by circulating hot waters. As silica-rich water cools at or near the surface, silica is precipitated as siliceous sinter (sometimes called geyserite), which forms the domes, grottoes, and terraces characterizing most of Yellowstone's thermal basins. At Mammoth Hot Springs in northern Yellowstone, however, hot water travels through channels dissolved in limestone and dolomite, and the hot spring water is charged with calcium bicarbonate. Where it surfaces and cools, calcium carbonate is deposited in beautiful travertine shelves and terraces.

GEOLOGIC HISTORY

Precambrian Era. Across the northern part of Yellowstone Park are ridges and knobs and rocky slopes of gneiss, Precambrian metamorphic rock. We know few details concerning the origin of this rock. It may have come into existence as sedimentary or volcanic layers deposited on the floor of an ancient sea. About 2.7 billion years ago it was compressed and recrystallized into metamorphic rock. As it is similar to rock underlying most of North America, we can assume it extends under much or all of Yellowstone.

Paleozoic and Mesozoic Eras. Starting about 600 million years ago, broad, shallow seas flooded this region repeatedly—at least a dozen times. Deposits of sand and silt, clay and limy mud were laid down in thick horizontal sheets, some of them in the sea and others near it on tide flats and river floodplains. Fossil shells in these sedimentary layers give us a record of marine conditions and spotlight stages in the development of life. They also serve as tools for identifying the age of the rocks. Devonian, Mississippian, Pennsylvanian, and Permian rocks appear in the far northeast and northwest corners of the park and in a few slender fault slices near the south boundary. They can be seen along the Gallatin River, near Pebble Creek Campground, or in the last few miles before the northeast entrance. Mesozoic rocks occur south of Heart Lake and near Mammoth. Cretaceous strata, for instance, make up the slopes of Mount Everts opposite Mammoth Hot Springs.

Late in Mesozoic time, about 75 million years ago, disturbances in the earth's crust flexed and warped the Paleozoic and Mesozoic sedimentary rocks, and eventually faulted them and slid them over one another, forming mountains. Precambrian metamorphic rocks were lifted and broken. Northern Yellowstone arched into a broad anticline and then pushed southeastward until its Precambrian core in some places lay over far younger Cretaceous strata. In southern Yellowstone, several small anticlines formed.

During and after all this activity, erosion stripped away the sedimentary layers of the highest parts of the anticlines and laid bare the Precambrian rocks below.

Cenozoic Era. The Cenozoic Era was a time of savage crisis in Yellowstone. About 50 million years ago, in Eocene time, volcanic eruptions began. Lava surged from volcanic vents and buried the pre-existing landscape, building up large, steep-sided stratovolcanoes. Layers of gloomy gray and dark red lava alternated with layers of lighter volcanic ash and dust and broken volcanic rock called breccia, to form rocks known today as the Absaroka Volcanic Series. Ultimately all the present national park area was covered by 1,000 meters (3,000 feet) or more of these rocks. Beds of fine ash sometimes buried and preserved thriving forests, and lava flows were sometimes mixed with stream and mudflow deposits made of volcanic material. Some intrusive rocks were formed at the same time, as magma unable to reach the surface cooled in volcanic conduits, squeezed between rock strata, or filled vertical fissures.

At the end of Eocene time volcanism diminished, though it did not abate completely. During the Oligocene and Miocene Epochs, the volcanic region was partly beveled and reshaped by erosion.

Then, in Pliocene time, the entire Rocky Mountain area was lifted by broad upward arching that raised the mountainous landscape nearly 2,000 meters (5,000 to 6,000 feet) above its previous level, an uplift largely responsible for its present elevation. What it was that caused this great upheaval we don't know, but its impact was to stretch and break apart the crust so that it was divided into large blocks, some of which rose while others fell. Exactly what the details were in the Yellowstone area we can't tell because the evidence was all but destroyed by later geologic events—some of the greatest cataclysms our world has known.

A little more than two million years ago, magma seems to have accumulated in an unusually vast, blisterlike magma chamber directly under what is now Yellowstone. Pushing upward, it stretched and began to rupture the upper part of the crust, the thick, irregular layers of Absaroka volcanic rock. Though highly charged with gas, it remained for a long time imprisoned by great pressures deep underground. Only a little escaped through a ring of fractures that developed above the magma chamber.

About two million years ago, more of the magma began to escape, suddenly lessening the pressure on the rest. The first—and most furious—geologic extravaganza was about to begin. The volcanic process

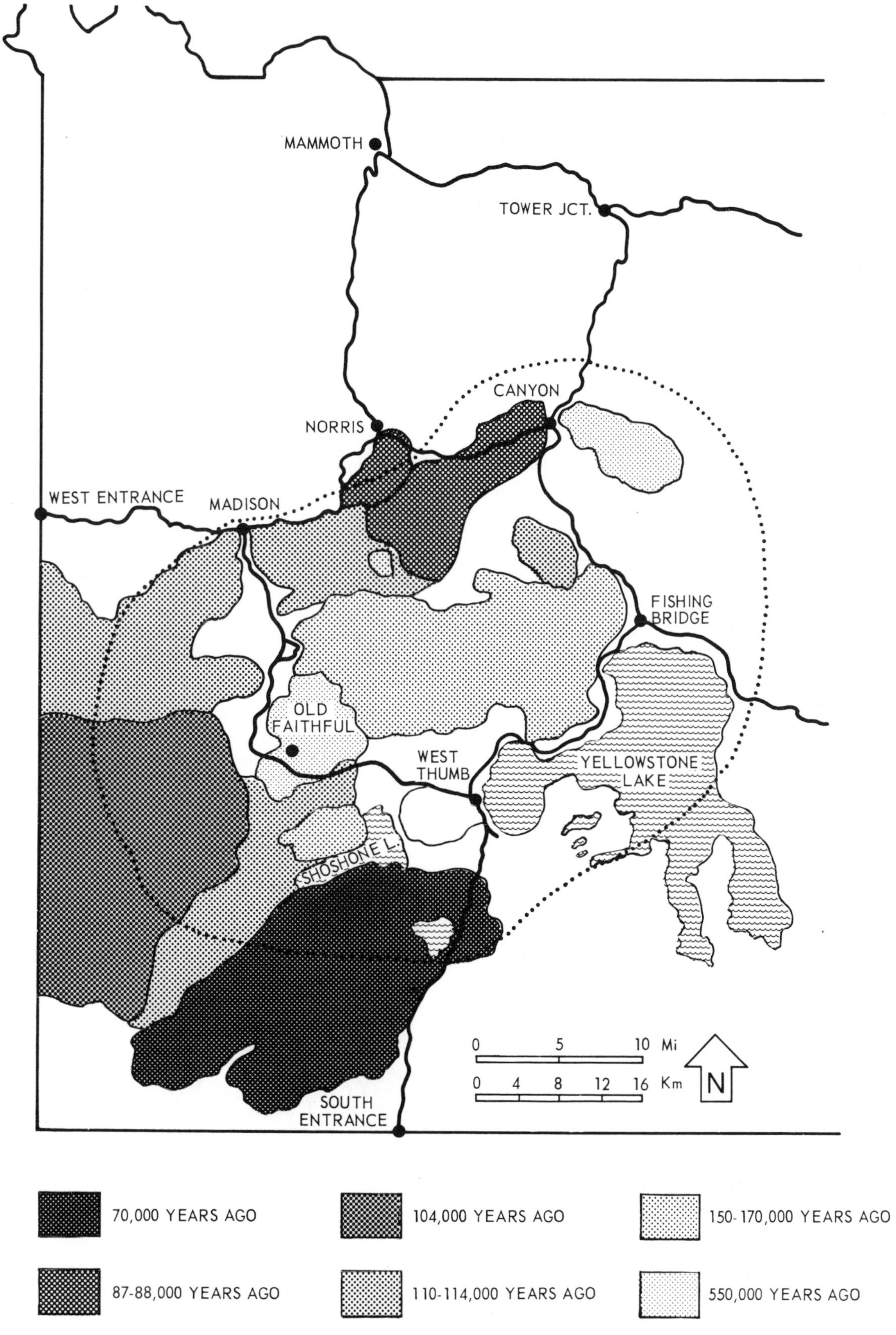

Thirty overlapping flows have been mapped and dated by the U.S. Geological Survey. Dots outline the Yellowstone caldera. Lightest flows are oldest; darkest are youngest. Only the largest are shown here.

from here on is surprisingly like a geyser eruption, when elimination of some of the overlying water lessens pressure and sets the stage for a full-scale geyser display. Like steam in a geyser, gases of the magma chamber expanded and burst upward through the vertical ring fractures in a titanic explosion, spewing hot volcanic rock and pumicelike froth and ash far and wide. In one indescribably savage moment, most of the Absaroka volcanoes were wiped out. Clouds of volcanic dust billowed into the sky, blotting out the sun and turning day into night. Propelled by the hurricane fury of expanding gas, ash flows in roiling clouds shot down the mountain slopes, still so hot when they fell that they welded themselves into rock. Thousands of tons of volcanic debris spread over the Yellowstone area as the Huckleberry Ridge Tuff, and drifted as far afield as Saskatchewan and Texas to lay a yellow blanket on the land. The mighty explosion has been likened to that of Krakatoa in 1883, but where Krakatoa demolished a 30-square-kilometer (12-square-mile) island, the Yellowstone eruption annihilated an area 100 times as large—a third or more of the present national park. More than 2,500 cubic kilometers (600 cubic miles) of debris were emitted!

When the explosion was over and the pressures exhausted, the roof of the immense magma chamber collapsed, dropping along the ring fracture zones and forming a giant caldera with its western tip reaching out of the park into Idaho. Little was left of the older rocks, the breccia and lava and ash layers that made up the Absaroka volcanoes.

But there was more to come. Around 1.2 million years ago, it happened again. Another eruption burst forth in the Idaho part of the old caldera, creating a newer, smaller caldera and distributing another layer of ash across Yellowstone—the Mesa Falls Tuff. Then more eruptions began in Yellowstone itself, lava that rose quietly as two new sets of ring fractures formed, defining a double-barreled magma chamber. About 600,000 years ago there was a renewal of violent activity. Then, as before, the contents of the magma chamber burst through to the surface to distribute the Lava Creek Tuff. This explosion culminated in collapse of the double magma chamber to create the Yellowstone caldera.

During the last 600,000 years, more lava flows have one by one obscured this caldera. Yellowstone Lake occupies part of it; fragments of its rims project above the horizontal plateau of central and southwest Yellowstone. At Obsidian Cliffs and along Firehole Canyon you can see some of the irregular, many-layered flows. Though most of them are a gray volcanic rock now known as Plateau Rhyolite, some are darker basalt.

Recently, geologists working in this area have suggested that Yellowstone lies over a "hot spot" in the earth's mantle and that, as the North American Plate slowly drifts southwest over the stationary hot spot, volcanism breaks out farther and farther to the northeast. If this is true, Yellowstone may be closely related to the Snake River Plain in Idaho. A succession of Yellowstones may have existed along this plain, only to be destroyed and covered by basalt

On the Snake River Plain, youthful basalt flows—the final product of eruptive cycles—may conceal the trail left by successive Yellowstone-like volcanic centers.

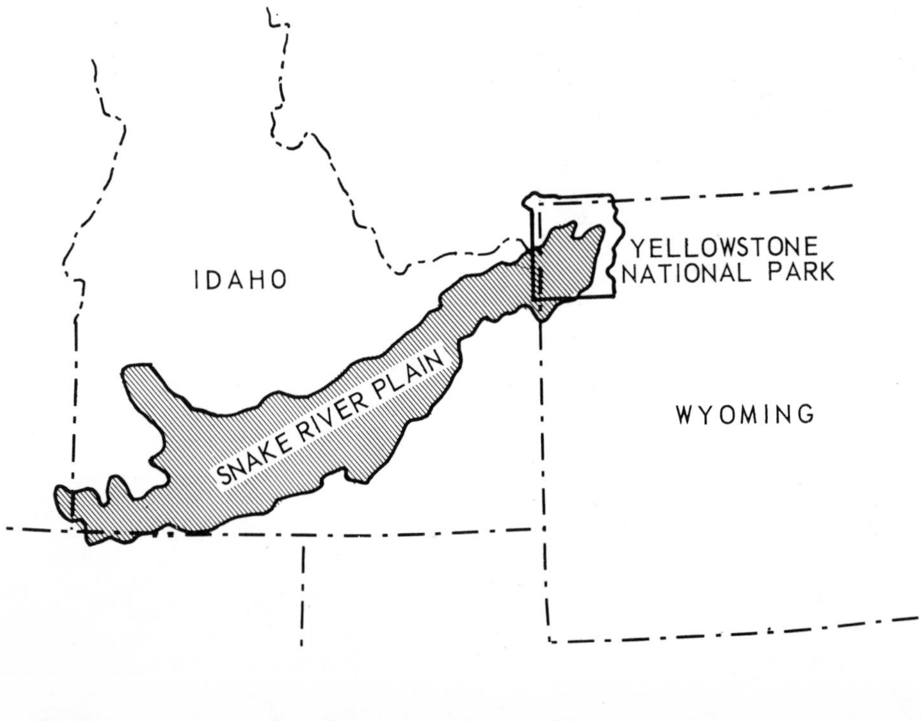

flows in the last stage of the eruptive cycle. By the same token, other Yellowstones may someday erupt northeast of the present one.

Before, during, and after eruptions of the Plateau Rhyolite, Yellowstone was the scene of Ice Age glaciation. Like several northwestern parks, it must often have seen the exciting interplay of fire and ice. Glacial erratics – boulders brought from nonvolcanic mountains farther north – are scattered near Canyon, in Hayden Valley not far upstream, and in the Lamar Valley near the Lamar–Yellowstone confluence. Both Hayden and Lamar Valleys contain moraines.

Two glacial advances have been recognized, the first climaxing perhaps 150,000 years ago,* the second between 30,000 and 13,000 years ago. During the first, known as the Bull Lake advance, sizeable glaciers flowed into Yellowstone from the Absaroka Range to the east and from the Beartooth and Gallatin Ranges to the north and northwest. Beartooth glaciers carried boulders of distinctive red Precambrian quartzite clear across the Yellowstone Plateau and the Continental Divide into Jackson Hole, so we have some measure of their extent. Retreating, they left similar erratics on the plateau surface and for a time dammed the Yellowstone River, creating a lake.

The second or Pinedale advance drew nourishment from interconnected ice caps in the Gallatin, Beartooth, and Absaroka Ranges and in high parts of the plateaus between. Again ice covered a large part of the park, ice that averaged 700 meters (2,000 feet) in thickness and that lay at least 1,000 meters thick over the present position of Yellowstone Lake. Discharging through the Yellowstone Valley and into Jackson Hole, Pinedale glaciers seem to have remained nearly full size for 15,000 years. Melting, "deglaciation," was rapid, yet for a time ice again dammed the Yellowstone, backing water up the length of the river's Grand Canyon.

Yellowstone is still an active region geologically, and hyperactive seismically. The Old Faithful Visitor Center records 1 to 100 small earthquake tremors daily. In August 1959 a major quake struck the western part of the park and adjacent parts of Montana and Idaho. Triggered 15 kilometers (10 miles) below the surface, the quake in turn triggered other events in the park. Rockslides were set loose along weathered, jointed canyon walls. Boulders as large as automobiles bounded down steep slopes. Trees toppled. Roads and buildings were damaged. Many geysers erupted simultaneously – whole basins in grand display. Long-dormant geysers not known to have erupted in historic time reawakened. Others changed their schedules, though Old Faithful's faithful timing was scarcely disturbed. Many long-term changes occurred in hot springs, too, changes in water level and temperature or in the cloudiness of the water. A few geysers ceased erupting altogether.

*Two sets of dates have been proposed for this advance. Maximum extent of the glaciers may have been 150,000 years ago, or there may have been a double maximum, with pulsations climaxing 115,000 and 90,000 years ago. Yellowstone glaciation is dated by measuring radioactive decay in lava flows that came in contact with ice or with glacier-dammed lakes.

BEHIND THE SCENES

Firehole River. Flowing along the ring of faults that seems to control the location of most of Yellowstone's geyser basins, the Firehole River channels through hot spring deposits and irregular layers of Plateau Rhyolite, both formed long after the explosion of the Yellowstone caldera. There are excellent exposures of these rocks along the river and highway. The Firehole River, to some extent warmed by water from the many geysers and hot springs that border it, does not freeze in winter.

Fossil Forests and Petrified Trees. There are several petrified forests in Yellowstone. One located up Specimen Creek in the northwest corner of the park and one on Specimen Ridge east of Tower can be reached by hiking. A branch road leads to a fossilized tree trunk west of Tower Junction. Many of the trees are still in their original upright positions.

Trees must be buried rapidly to be preserved as fossils. Here, burial was by ash falls and mudflows from Absaroka volcanoes about 50 million years ago. Seeping groundwater later dissolved silica from volcanic rock and slowly redeposited it in place of organic material in the tree trunks, preserving their fine details. You can count growth rings to determine the age of individual trees, and paleobotanists studying the trunks and well preserved leaves, nuts, cones, and needles have identified 100 species of trees and shrubs, mostly the types we might expect to find in low-elevation, mild-climate woodlands: fig, laurel, pine, sycamore, walnut, magnolia, oak, dogwood, redwood. When these trees grew, wide-scale uplift of this region had not yet occurred, and would not for millions of years. In some places, several buried forests lie one above another, suggesting that conditions leading to their preservation were repeated many times, with centuries between for soil development and growth of new forests.

Fountain Paint Pots and Lower Geyser Basin. This basin offers real variety in geyser gazing – lots of fumaroles, hot pools, mud pots, and assorted geysers. Excellent nature-trail leaflets tell how the springs and geysers work, as well as how they were changed by the 1959 earthquake.

Pearly linings of some springs, glimmering mounds

The Grand Canyon of the Yellowstone, a legacy of volcanism, hydrothermal activity, and erosion, exposes volcanic rock weakened by volcanic fumes and hot water.

surrounding them, barren grayish slopes, and long channels that carry off the water are all composed of siliceous sinter. Silica-charged water has been drawn by capillary action up the trunks of dead trees, drying into white "boots." Yellow and orange colors around the springs indicate the presence of algae able to live in the hot water.

As for mud in the paint pots, it is largely a clay mineral called kaolinite, also derived from volcanic rock. Its colors come from small quantities of yellow and red iron oxides.

Gallatin Range. Paleozoic and Mesozoic sedimentary rocks, now crumpled and torn, make up this range. There is Precambrian gneiss and schist at the south end. Antler Peak is part of a small intrusion. The Gallatins came into existence late in Mesozoic time as the northern part of Yellowstone pushed up into an anticline. They were raised again as a fault block in Pliocene time, and then partly engulfed by Plateau Rhyolite flows.

Golden Gate. Bright yellow lichens give this narrow defile its name. On the cliffs are layers of Huckleberry Tuff, ash from Yellowstone's first great eruption. Angular fragments of pumice and crystals of quartz and feldspar are scattered through the ash.

Bunsen Peak, east of Golden Gate, is a little igneous intrusion.

Grand Canyon of the Yellowstone. Sometime after the great caldera eruptions, the ancestral Yellowstone River eroded headward from its confluence with the Lamar and established a route through the volcanic debris that covered this region. Probably as a small tributary it eroded headward from the confluence, working its way in a broad arc around Mount Washburn. The rock through which it was cutting was soft and easily eroded—layers of Plateau Rhyolite leached by hot water and decomposed by volcanic fumes. Its route was occasionally shifted by new lava flows, and at least twice it was dammed by glacial ice.

Details of the architecture of the canyon are fully exposed. As you can see, the altered rock weathers readily into clay and sand, which slide or wash down the steep canyon walls to be swept away by the river. Notice the long rockslide paths, highly jointed cliffs, goblinlike hoodoos, and colorful patterns of altered rock. The yellows and browns and golds of the canyon walls come from iron minerals altered by sulfurous fumes; deep within the canyon, wisps of steam still rise from fumaroles and hot springs.

At the head of the canyon, the river thunders over the edges of resistant, unaltered rhyolite flows. The yellow canyon and Lower Falls present a view of exceptional grandeur, one that has justly been a favorite of geologists as well as photographers and artists.

At first glance this extraordinary canyon, V-shaped

in the extreme, shows little evidence of glacial erosion. However, nearby glacial deposits—erratics and moraines—tell us that glaciers were here. Patches of lake sediments high on the canyon walls tell us that the river was ice-dammed for a time. The present V-shaped profile is a product of further downcutting by the river and the softness of the altered volcanic rock, which is too weak to stand up in vertical cliffs.

Hayden Valley. Named after geologist Ferdinand V. Hayden, who led a scientific exploring party into this region in 1871, the open expanse of Hayden Valley displays many marks of glaciation. Pinedale glaciers flowing from the southern Absaroka Range across the depression of Yellowstone Lake left a rounded, smoothed landscape, glacial moraines, and scattered boulders not related to rocks beneath them. For a time a glacial dam raised the level of Yellowstone Lake until it invaded this area; whitish, thinly layered lake beds of fine sand, silt, and clay date from this period. The sinuous course of the Yellowstone River through Hayden Valley little forewarns of the "death-defying leap" it will take a short distance downstream.

Lamar Valley and Northeast Entrance. This beautiful valley also bears the imprint of glaciation. It has been straightened and widened by moving ice that flowed north and northwest from the central Absaroka Range. In many places it is crossed or bordered by moraines, some of them with little ponds in depressions left by melting cakes of ice. Scattered about are boulders of metamorphic rock, glacial erratics carried in by ice flowing from the north and northeast.

Glacial erratics carried into the Lamar Valley from high mountains to the north and northeast sheltered seedling trees, now grown to maturity.

Hills north and east of the Lamar-Yellowstone confluence are made of this coarse-grained gneiss, a Precambrian rock that weathers into rough, rounded boulders. Paleozoic sedimentary strata occur near Soda Creek as well as near Pebble Creek Campground and in the 10 kilometers (6 miles) nearest the northeast entrance. Some of the Paleozoic limestones contain abundant fossil shellfish, chiefly brachiopods and cephalopods. (National Park rules prohibit fossil collecting.)

The northeast entrance road crosses the Absaroka Range, where spectacular remnants of Absaroka volcanoes—formed of breccia, lava, and volcanic tuff—rise against the sky.

Lewis Falls. The Plateau Rhyolite, Yellowstone's most widespread rock unit, is made up of flows that range in age from 550,000 years to 60,000 years. The uppermost flows are of course the youngest. Lewis River cascades over the steep edge of a flow dated at 70,000 years and drops onto the surface of one probably 150,000 years old. Both these flows can be seen near the falls.

Mammoth Hot Springs. Part of the excitement of Yellowstone lies in the variety of its geologic features. At Mammoth we get away from geysers and waterfalls, volcanic rock and siliceous sinter—but not from hot springs. Here, heated, acidified groundwater flows through layers of Paleozoic and Mesozoic sedimentary rock. Instead of picking up silica as do hot waters elsewhere in Yellowstone, it dissolves limestone, which it carries in solution as calcium bicarbonate.

Coming to the surface, the water cools and calcium carbonate is precipitated as travertine. Because calcium carbonate is far more soluble than silica, growth of travertine deposits is more rapid than that of sinter deposits in the geyser basins. An estimated two tons of travertine are deposited every day! Some of the terraces at Mammoth grow so fast that changes are visible from month to month; walkways must now and then be rerouted. We can guess that the rising hot water has dissolved many an unknown limestone cavern in the hills around Mammoth.

On the other hand, many terraces at Mammoth are obviously "dead." Their travertine has lost its glistening, pearly luster and is turning gray and powdery. But new springs appear, and new terraces develop;

Travertine terraces lend graceful beauty to Mammoth Hot Springs. The springs deposit travertine at the outer edges of the terraces, where the hot water cools most rapidly.

the area as a whole is as active as ever.

The lower terraces are described in self-guide leaflets, and there are frequent and excellent naturalist-guided tours. Drive around the upper terraces or walk across them to see some of the old deposits. You may well see some of the newest. Among the upper terraces are interesting long, symmetrical ridges formed as hot water flowed from linear cracks and deposited travertine on either side. Isolated individual springs build up high, rounded mounds, of which the most famous is Liberty Cap.

If you examine the terraces closely you'll see that they are shaped like giant lily pads with turned-up edges. Where hot springs are active, each lily pad holds a pool. Most growth takes place right at the scalloped margin, where cooling is fastest and carbon dioxide comes out of solution most readily. Thin, flaky travertine "ice" sometimes forms on water surfaces, where it floats for a time before sinking and adding to the calcium carbonate at the bottom of the pool.

Colors are due to algae. When water is hotter than 75°C (167°F), no algae can grow and newly deposited travertine is snowy white. As the water trickles to lower terraces, orange and then yellowish algae grow on the travertine. Slender, flexible white or pink strands that wave like sea grass in the surging water of some of the hottest springs are produced by unusual bacteria able to survive even boiling water.

Midway Geyser Basin. This geyser basin contains several remarkable hot springs, including the park's largest and most colorful, elegant Grand Prismatic Spring. At the top of a great mound of siliceous sinter, its pool is 113 meters (370 feet) across. The striking color of the water – deep indigo blue near the center, then lighter blue, and finally pale apple green – is set off by orange and yellow algae inhabiting the cooler edges and overflow surfaces.

Nearby is Excelsior Geyser's awesome crater. Excelsior has not erupted since 1888. However, it regularly discharges 15,000 liters (4,000 gallons) per minute from its deep blue pool – far more than any other spring in the park. The hot overflow cascades down sinter slopes into the Firehole River, helping to keep it ice-free in winter.

When you are in this area, be sure to see lovely Turquoise and Indigo Hot Springs.

Mount Washburn. Mount Washburn is just a part of one of the Absaroka stratovolcanoes. Along the trail to the summit are coarsely layered volcanic rocks—gray breccia and fine volcanic ash. Notice the purple and gray blocks of lava imbedded in the breccia; some are a meter (a yard) across. Most of them are rounded and hazy edged as if glowing debris had fused with surrounding hot lava. Fragments in ash falls, on the other hand, are sharp and distinct as if they and the ash were cool when they fell. The layering of the breccia and ash, and dikes radiating from Washburn Hot Springs south of Mount Washburn, suggest that the center of the volcano was in that vicinity.

From the top of Mount Washburn, an easy hike, many faces of Yellowstone join in one mighty panorama. Here is the best view of the Yellowstone caldera. Far south across the shimmering expanse of Yellowstone Lake, the Red Mountains and Flat Mountain are parts of its southern rim. To the east rise the Absarokas, its eastern rim. You are standing on its northern edge. To the west, the rest of the Washburn Range and cliffs north of Madison Junction form other portions of the caldera rim.

The summit panorama includes the curved incision of the Grand Canyon of the Yellowstone, and from here you can see the nature of the rolling lava plateau through which it cuts. Southward are the grass-covered hills of Hayden Valley. To the northeast beyond Yellowstone Canyon is Specimen Ridge, site of layered fossil forests, and beyond that the Lamar Valley.

Mud Volcanoes. Surging, plopping mud volcanoes south of Canyon, nature's clowns, are some of the most amusing features in the park! Self-guide leaflets describe them well.

As in other Yellowstone hydrothermal regions, subterranean heat interacting with groundwater causes the mud volcanoes. They are undersupplied with water; there is just not enough of it to carry away the fine clay loosened and brought to the surface by the bubbling, surging springs. When thick mud splashes out and builds up a cone-shaped mound, a mud volcano is born.

The water in these springs is highly charged with gases—steam, carbon dioxide, and hydrogen sulfide among others. The hydrogen sulfide is most noticeable, with its rotten-egg odor. Gases bubbling up in the springs make them appear to be boiling, but the orange and brown algae could not survive if the water were really boiling.

Though the spring called the Dragon's Mouth appears to be discharging quantities of water, it really isn't. Look at its small overflow stream. Its wild surges resemble waves cast on a beach, and as with waves the same water is used again and again. Some unusual feature in this spring's underground plumbing must cause the savage, endless motion, made more ominous by bursts of steam.

Norris Geyser Basin. The hottest, most rapidly changing geyser basin in the park, Norris displays hot springs of many sizes and shapes, bubbling mud pots, steam vents, and geysers.

Though the 1959 earthquake broke some windows in the Norris museum and doubtless shook up the loosely consolidated gravel that underlies the hot spring deposits, earthquake-caused changes in activity were not as great here as in geyser basins farther south. Frequent shifts in activity seem to come about as sinter deposits block off old channels or rising hot water opens new passageways.

Trail leaflets are available at the museum, where exhibits explain again the theory behind the hot springs and geysers. Naturalist-conducted tours explore parts of Norris Geyser Basin as well as some outlying, seldom-visited thermal features.

Obsidian Cliff. A rhyolite lava flow here apparently cooled very rapidly, perhaps by flowing against glacial ice or into a glacier-dammed pond or lake. When lava cools so quickly, there is no time for crystals to form, and the whole mass solidifies as black volcanic glass, known as obsidian.

Across the road is a flat meadow and a beaver pond. Beavers are active geologic agents throughout the Rocky Mountains, building ponds that retard erosion but that fill in eventually with plant growth and silt.

Old Faithful and the Upper Geyser Basin. The greatest concentration of geysers in Yellowstone is in this basin; you can be sure of seeing several of them erupt if you stay here for even an hour. Predictions of some eruption times are posted in the visitor center, but most geysers don't work on precise schedules and seeing them perform is a matter of luck. Trail leaflets describe eruption patterns of the most prominent geysers, and naturalist-led tours are frequent.

If you can, watch an eruption all the way through, preferably not Old Faithful (though you'll want to see it perform, too) but one that you can safely stand close to or look down on. Notice how water rises slowly in the pool, gradually filling it. Then in sudden surges the pool overflows. Pressure is reduced on superheated water far below, and eruption is imminent. Suddenly the water begins to churn, and spray and steam rush upward as the spectacle begins. The eruption lasts for a few minutes or several hours, depending on the geyser, and ends as the supply of superheated water is exhausted. Then the pool is empty, and water from the eruption drains back into the vent.

Some geysers, like Sawmill and Grand, shoot water and steam in various directions from a central pool; these are known as fountain eruptions. Others, like Old Faithful and Beehive, erupt through a narrow nozzle, so water and steam shoot skyward in jet eruptions. Both types are most spectacular in winter, when cold air causes more steam to condense into visible clouds.

Tower Falls. Unable to cut down as rapidly as the powerful Yellowstone, Tower Creek plunges in a feather of foam over a cliff of coarse breccia formed during Absaroka volcanism. Weird, fingered pinnacles nearby, which give Tower Creek its name, are shaped in the same rocks. Tiny rivulets of rain water enlarge vertical cracks in a coarse ash flow, and then rain and wind ultimately sculpture the shapes you see.

Hills and valleys east and west of Tower Junction are dotted with erratic boulders of Precambrian gneiss brought here by glacial ice. Moraines are pocked with kettles where large blocks of ice melted. Many kettles are now occupied by small ponds.

West Thumb. The oval bay of the West Thumb of Yellowstone Lake is another caldera, smaller and younger than the great Yellowstone caldera but formed in the same manner, by rapid outpouring of volcanic gases and ash followed by collapse of the magma chamber roof. West Thumb came into existence between 200,000 and 125,000 years ago.

Thermal features at West Thumb include mud pots and lakeshore hot springs.

Yellowstone Falls. After flowing smoothly across layered rhyolite flows of Hayden Valley, the Yellowstone River plunges over two breathtaking waterfalls into its famous abyss, the gold and yellow Grand Canyon of the Yellowstone. Why here? The compact, resistant rhyolite flows, which came you will remember from fractures surrounding the Yellowstone caldera, have been leached and chemically weakened here by hot water rising through some of the same fractures. At the contact between hard, unaltered rhyolite and weak, altered rhyolite we find the Lower Falls. The Upper Falls mark an abrupt change between two unaltered lava flows, one more resistant than the other.

A trail leads to the brink of the Lower Falls, where glass-green water slides with a thunderous roar over the 94-meter (308-foot) precipice, vividly illustrating the relentless battle between volcanism and erosion that created the landforms of Yellowstone Park.

Yellowstone Lake. This lake, 2,357 meters (7,733 feet) above sea level, occupies a portion of the great caldera created 600,000 years ago. The west bay of the lake is a smaller, more recent caldera. Beneath the lake waters, the caldera floor is paved with rhyolite flows.

The lake itself covers about a third of the caldera. During Pinedale glaciation the lake depression was hidden beneath as much as 1,000 meters (3,000 feet) of ice. At a later time a glacial dam near Canyon raised the lake level so that all of Hayden Valley was filled with water.

The shores of the lake display typical lakeshore features, from small wave-cut cliffs to sandbars and beaches.

OTHER READING

Bauer, C.M. 1962. *Yellowstone: its Underworld—Geology and Historical Anecdotes of our Oldest National Park.* University of New Mexico Press, Albuquerque, New Mexico.

Crandall, Hugh. 1977. *Yellowstone, the Story Behind the Scenery.* KC Publications, Las Vegas, Nevada.

Fischer, W.A. 1960. *Earthquake! Yellowstone's Living Geology.* Yellowstone Nature Notes no. 33, Yellowstone National Park, Wyoming.

Rinehard, J.S. 1956. *A Guide to Geyser Gazing.* Hyperdynamics, Santa Fe, New Mexico.

Smith, Robert B., and Christiansen, Robert L. "Yellowstone Park as a Window on the Earth's Interior." *Scientific American,* vol. 242, no. 2, pp. 104-117.

The Yellowstone River plummets over Lower Falls where Plateau Rhyolite lavas are etched and chemically altered by thermal waters.

Glossary

aa (pronounced ah-ah) – a type of lava flow characterized by an extremely rough surface, with lava broken into irregular, clinkery fragments.

alluvial – deposited by rivers and streams.

alpine glacier – a glacier originating in mountains and flowing down valleys, also called a valley or mountain glacier.

ammonite – an extinct shell-forming mollusk related to the living chambered nautilus.

amphibolite – fine-grained, dark gray metamorphic rock containing abundant hornblende.

andesite – dark gray volcanic rock composed largely of feldspar, often having large feldspar crystals in a finer matrix.

angle of repose – the maximum slope at which loose material comes to rest.

anticline – a fold that is convex upward.

arête – a narrow rock ridge sculptured by glaciers.

ash – fine particles of pulverized rock blown from a volcanic vent.

badlands – rough, gullied topography in arid and semiarid regions, eroded by infrequent but heavy rains.

basalt – dark gray to black volcanic rock poor in silica and rich in iron and magnesium minerals.

bedrock – solid rock exposed at or near the surface.

bentonite – soft, porous, light-colored rock formed by decomposition of volcanic ash.

biotite – black mica.

bomb, volcanic – a fragment of molten or semi-molten rock thrown from a volcano.

boxwork – a network of intersecting blades in a cave deposit.

brachiopod – a marine shellfish having two bilaterally symmetrical shells.

breadcrust bomb – a volcanic bomb with a cracked outer surface resulting from internal expansion after the crust cooled.

breakdown – large blocks of rock material fallen from cave walls and ceilings.

breccia (rhymes with "betcha") – volcanic rock consisting of coarse, broken rock fragments imbedded in finer material such as volcanic ash.

calcite – a common rock-forming mineral ($CaCO_3$), the principal mineral in limestone, marble, chalk, and travertine.

calcium carbonate – $CaCO_3$, calcite.

caldera – a broad, basin-shaped volcanic depression formed by explosion or collapse of a magma chamber.

cave onyx – banded calcite formed in a cave.

cephalopod – a class of mollusks that includes squids, octopuses, chambered nautilus, and extinct shell-bearing ammonites.

chalcedony – a translucent form of quartz, somewhat waxy in appearance.

chert – hard, dense sedimentary rock usually in nodules in limestone.

cinder cone – a small, conical volcano built primarily of loose fragments of popcornlike volcanic material thrown from a volcanic vent.

cirque – a steep-walled, usually semicircular basin excavated by the head of a glacier.

columnar jointing – a polygonal joint pattern creating vertical columns in lava and volcanic ash, caused by shrinkage during cooling.

concretion – a hard, rounded rock mass caused by localized concentration of minerals in pore spaces of sedimentary or volcanic rock.

conduit – the feeder pipe of a volcano.

conglomerate – rock composed of rounded, water-worn fragments of older rock.

crater – the funnel-shaped hollow at or near the top of a volcano, from which volcanic material is ejected.

creep – slow downhill movement of soil and rock.

crevasse – a deep, near-vertical fissure in a glacier, caused by movement over an uneven surface.

cross-bedding – diagonal layering caused when sand or silt is deposited by wind or water currents.

dendritic drainage – a treelike pattern of branching streams.

desert pavement – a surface veneer of pebbles and stones left when finer sand and silt are blown away by wind.

desert varnish – a dark, shiny surface of iron and manganese oxides, found on exposed rock surfaces in desert regions.

diabase – a dark gray intrusive rock commonly found in dikes and sills, the intrusive equivalent of basalt.

differential erosion – erosion at different rates regulated by differences in resistance of various rock types.

dike – a sheetlike intrusion that cuts vertically or nearly vertically across other rock structures.

diorite – a medium-gray igneous rock, the intrusive equivalent of andesite.

dip – downward slope of a bedding plane caused by folding, faulting, and uplift.

dolomite – a sedimentary rock similar to limestone but containing a large proportion of calcium magnesium carbonate, $Ca\ Mg\ (CO_3)_2$, along with calcium carbonate.

dripstone – travertine deposited by dripping water, as in stalactites and stalagmites.

earth flow – downslope movement of a well defined mass of soil and weathered rock, usually as a result of saturation with water.

eolian – wind-caused.

epoch – a unit of geologic time, a subdivision of a period.

era – the largest unit of geologic time.

erratic – a boulder brought in by glaciers and of a different rock type than nearby bedrock.

exfoliation – a process in which thin concentric sheets of rock break away from a rock surface.

extrusive rock – rock formed of magma which reaches the surface and solidifies there (also called volcanic rock).

fault – a rock fracture along which displacement has occurred.

fault scarp – a steep slope or cliff formed by movement along a fault.

fault zone – a zone of numerous small fractures that go to make up a fault.

feldspar – a group of common light-colored, rock-forming minerals containing aluminum oxides and silica. Feldspars constitute 60% of the earth's crust.

fell field – an alpine area covered with rock fragments broken by frost wedging.

finger lake – a long, narrow lake in a glacier-excavated valley, commonly dammed by a moraine.

firn line – the highest level to which snow is melted off the surface of a glacier.

floodplain – relatively horizontal land adjacent to a river channel, with sand and gravel layers deposited by the river during floods.

flowstone – travertine deposited in caves by water trickling across cave walls or floor.

fold – a curve or bend in rock strata.

formation – a mappable unit of stratified rock.

fossil – remains or traces of a plant or animal preserved in rock; also long-preserved inorganic structures such as fossil ripple marks.

frost wedging – prying apart of rock by crystal expansion as water freezes repeatedly in rock crevices.

frostwork – a light, feathery calcite deposit found in caves, resembling frost crystals.

fumarole – a vent through which volcanic gases or vapors are emitted.

geyser – a hot spring that periodically erupts jets of hot water and steam.

glacier – a large mass of ice driven by its own weight to move slowly downslope or outward from a center.

globularite – a cave formation resembling popcorn.

gneiss – a banded metamorphic rock thought to form from granite (which it commonly resembles), sandstone, and other continental rocks.

graben – a down-dropped valley bounded by faults.

granite – a coarse-grained igneous intrusive rock composed of chunky crystals of quartz and feldspar peppered with dark biotite and hornblende.

groundwater – subsurface water, as distinct from rivers, streams, seas, and lakes.

group — a major unit of stratified rock, embracing several related formations.

gypsum — a common mineral, calcium sulfate ($CaSO_4 \cdot H_2O$), formed usually by evaporation of seawater.

hanging valley — a glacial valley whose mouth is high up on the wall of a larger glacial valley.

hardpan — a relatively hard layer of soil lying at or just below the surface.

hematite — a common iron oxide mineral (Fe_2O_3).

hogback — a long, narrow ridge with a sharp summit formed by the edge of tilted layers of resistant rock.

honeycomb weathering — weathering that creates numerous small, deep pits on a rock surface.

hoodoo — a bizarre rock figure created by weathering.

hornblende — a black or dark green mineral whose rodlike crystals are common in igneous rocks.

hot spring — a spring whose water temperature is higher than body temperature (37°C, or 98.6°F).

hydrothermal — hot-water.

icefall — part of a glacier deeply crevassed because of a steep drop in the valley floor beneath it.

ichthyosaur — an extinct group of swimming reptiles.

igneous rocks — rocks formed from molten magma.

incised meander — a stream meander retained as a river cuts down into underlying rocks; also called entrenched meander.

indurated — hardened by pressure, heat, and cementing of grains.

intertonguing — interlayering of sedimentary rock layers as they thin out among other layers.

intrusive rocks — igneous rocks created as molten magma intrudes pre-existing rocks and cools without reaching the surface.

joint — a rock fracture along which no significant movement has taken place.

kaolin — a group of common clay minerals derived from igneous rocks.

kettle — a steep-sided depression in a moraine or outwash plain, left when a detached block of glacial ice melts.

laccolith — a lenslike intrusion that spreads between rock layers, doming those above it.

lapilli — sand-sized and popcorn-sized fragments thrown from a volcano.

lateral moraine — a ridgelike mass of broken rock material deposited at the side of a glacier.

laterite — highly weathered, orange-red soil typical of tropical regions surfaced with limestone.

lava — molten magma that reaches the earth's surface, or the rock formed when it cools.

lichen — a plant community consisting of a fungus and an alga, appearing as flat circular crusts on rock surfaces.

lignite — brownish black coal intermediate between peat and soft or bituminous coal.

lime — a term commonly, though incorrectly, used for calcium carbonate.

limestone — a sedimentary rock consisting largely of calcium carbonate.

limonite — a yellow-brown iron oxide mineral ($2Fe_2O_3 \cdot 3H_2O$).

lithified — turned to stone.

magma — molten rock.

magma chamber — a reservoir of magma from which volcanic materials are derived, usually occurring only a few kilometers below the surface.

mantle — the zone between the earth's core and crust.

matterhorn — a glacier-sharpened peak, commonly with cirques on all sides.

meander — a sinuous curve in the course of a winding stream.

mesa — a fairly large flat-topped hill or mountain.

metamorphic rocks — rocks derived from pre-existing rocks as they are altered by heat, pressure, and other processes.

metasedimentary rocks — sedimentary rocks altered by heat, pressure, and other processes but still retaining sedimentary characters such as stratification, alternating rock types, or ripple marks.

mica — a group of complex silicate minerals characterized by closely spaced parallel layers that can be split apart.

mica schist — schist containing a large proportion of mica, which gives it a silvery, lustrous appearance.

minerals — naturally occurring inorganic substances with characteristic chemical compositions, prime components of rock.

moraine — rock debris deposited by a glacier.

mud pot — a type of hot spring containing an abundance of mud.

mud volcano — a mud pot that splashes or overflows enough to build a small volcano-shaped cone.

névé — beaded ice formed by recrystallization of snow.

normal fault — a fault in which the hanging (upper) wall moves downward relative to the footwall.

obsidian — black volcanic glass.

olivine — a green mineral common in deep-sea basalt and gabbro.

oreodont — an extinct group of sheeplike mammals.

outcrop — bedrock that appears at the surface.

outwash — stratified sand and gravel deposited by streams of meltwater draining the front of a glacier.

overthrust — a low-angle fault in which one part of the crust slides over another, placing older rock on top of younger; also used for the oversliding block.

oxbow lake — a lake formed in an abandoned meander.

pahoehoe(pronounced pa-HO-ay-HO-ay) — ropy, undulating lava, usually basalt.

pan — a shallow natural depression, usually with a flat floor, often with salt deposits.

pediment — a rock-floored erosion surface at the edge of a mountain area.

pegmatite — exceptionally coarse-grained igneous rock usually found as dikes or veins near the margins of large igneous intrusions.

period — a subdivision of geologic time shorter than an era, longer than an epoch.

petrified — turned to stone by gradual introduction of minerals.

phenocryst — a large, conspicuous crystal in a matrix of finely crystalline igneous rock.

piedmont glacier — a lobelike sheet of ice at the foot of a mountain range, formed by coalescing lower ends of several valley glaciers.

pillow lava — lava with a pile-of-pillows appearance, characteristic of underwater eruptions.

plagioclase — a group of feldspar minerals.

plate — a block of the earth's crust consisting of both oceanic and continental sections, separated from other blocks by mid-ocean ridges, trenches, and collision zones.

plateau — a flat-topped tableland more extensive than a mesa.

plate tectonics — a theory of the earth's crustal structure based on division of the crust into a small number of large, mobile plates.

porphyry — igneous rock that contains conspicuous large crystals (phenocrysts) in a fine-grained matrix.

pothole — a small, steep-walled, circular depression excavated by the grinding action of pebbles, cobbles, and sand swirled by running water.

pterosaur — an extinct flying reptile.

pumice — light-colored, frothy volcanic rock, often light enough to float on water.

pyroclastic — rock material fragmented by a volcanic explosion.

pyroxene — a dark, rock-forming silicate mineral group common in igneous rocks.

quartz — crystalline silica (SiO_2), a common rock-forming mineral.

quartzite — sandstone consisting chiefly of quartz grains welded so firmly that it breaks through rather than around the grains.

residual soil — soil that develops in place as rock disintegrates.

reverse fault — a fault in which the hanging wall moves upward relative to the footwall.

rhyolite — light gray volcanic rock with large quartz and feldspar crystals in a finer groundmass, the fine-grained extrusive equivalent of granite.

rift — a furrow or a valley formed by pulling apart of crustal material, frequently with a central block dropped down as in a graben.

ring fracture — one of a set of arcuate fractures surrounding a volcano, often associated with caldera formation.

rock flour — finely ground rock material pulverized by a glacier.

rock glacier — a mass of angular boulders and other rock material with enough interstitial ice to lubricate slow downhill movement.

rockslide — a landslide involving a large proportion of rock.

rose quartz — quartz colored pink by minute amounts of titanium.

saltation — bouncing transportation of sand by water or wind.

schist — crystalline metamorphic rock which splits easily along parallel planes, commonly formed from fine-grained sedimentary rock.

scoria – particularly bubbly volcanic rock, darker and heavier than pumice, and with larger bubble holes.

sea-floor spreading – movement of oceanic crust away from mid-ocean ridges by creation of new oceanic crust at the ridges.

sediment – fragmented rock material, as well as shells and other animal and plant material, deposited by wind, water, or ice.

sedimentary rock – rock made of fragments of earlier rock, animal shells, or chemicals precipitated from water, usually accumulated in discrete layers.

serpentine – silicate rock having a silky or greasy luster and a slightly soapy feel, found mostly in metamorphic rocks.

shale – fine-grained mudstone or claystone that splits easily along bedding planes.

shield volcano – a dome-shaped volcano formed by fluid lava.

silica – a hard, resistant mineral (SiO_2), which in its crystal form is quartz. It also occurs as opal, chalcedony, geyserite, and chert.

siliceous sinter – white, lightweight, porous silica deposited by hot springs and geysers.

sill – a flat igneous intrusion inserted between layers of stratified rock.

slate – fine-grained metamorphic rock that splits along planes that are *not* original bedding surfaces.

slump – a landslide in which rock and earth slide as a single mass along a curved slip surface.

soil creep – gradual downhill movement of soil and loose rock.

spatter cone – a small, steep-sided cone built by molten lava that spatters from a volcanic vent.

speleothem – cave ornament.

stalactite – a cylindrical or conical cave ornament hanging from a cave ceiling.

stalagmite – a cylindrical or columnar cave ornament projecting upward from the floor of a cave.

strata – layers of sedimentary (and sometimes volcanic) rocks.

stratified – layered.

stratigraphic – pertaining to rock strata.

stratovolcano – a volcano built of alternating layers of lava, breccia, and volcanic ash.

striae – scratches created on rock surfaces as glaciers grind rock against rock.

stromatolite – finely layered structures thought to represent fossil blue-green algae.

subduction – the downward plunge of one crustal plate below another, usually an oceanic plate under a continental one.

syncline – a fold that is convex downward.

talus – a mass of large rock fragments lying at the base of the cliff or steep slope from which they have broken.

tarn – a small, deep lake occupying an ice-gouged basin.

terminal moraine – an arc-shaped moraine that marks the farthest advance of a glacier.

thrust fault – a low-angle fault on which older rocks slide over younger ones.

titanothere – an extinct mammal resembling a rhinoceros.

travertine – hard, dense limestone deposited by lime-laden water of streams, warm springs, and caves.

trilobite – an extinct group of marine arthropods known only from Paleozoic rocks.

tuff – rock formed from volcanic ash.

unconformity—a major break in the rock record caused by non-deposition, structural deformation, and/or erosion.

valley fill – sand, gravel, and other rock material filling a valley.

varve – a very thin layer of sediment deposited in quiet lake water in one year's time.

vein – a thin, sheetlike intrusion into a crevice, often with associated mineral deposits.

vent – any opening through which volcanic material is ejected.

vesicle – a small hole formed by entrapment of a gas bubble in cooling lava.

viscous – thick, not flowing easily.

volcanic dome – a type of volcano characterized by very thick magma that piles into a rounded dome above a conduit.

volcanic neck – solidified lava that cooled within a volcanic conduit, generally more resistant than surrounding rock.

water table – the surface below which groundwater fills all available pore spaces in soil and rock.

welded tuff – rock formed of volcanic ash fused by its own heat, the heat of volcanic gases ejected with it, and the weight of overlying material.

Index

Page numbers in **boldface** indicate major discussions.
Page numbers preceded by a "C" refer to the color section.